REF
ML
3492
.E9
1987

Everyday culture

$65.

ML
3492
.E9
1987

Everyday culture

$65.00

DATE	BORROWER'S NAME	

Everyday Culture

Popular Music in Britain

Series Editors:	*Dave Harker and Richard Middleton*
Peter Bailey (ed.):	*Music Hall: The Business of Pleasure*
J S Bratton (ed.):	*Music Hall: Performance and Style*
Dave Harker:	*Fakesong: The Manufacture of British 'Folksong' 1700 to the present day*
Dave Laing:	*One Chord Wonders: Power and Meaning in Punk Rock*

Everyday Culture
Popular Song and the Vernacular Milieu

*Edited by Michael Pickering
and Tony Green*

Open University Press
Milton Keynes · Philadelphia

Open University Press
Open University Educational Enterprises Limited
12 Cofferidge Close
Stony Stratford
Milton Keynes MK11 1BY, England

and

242 Cherry Street
Philadelphia, PA 19106, USA

First Published 1987

British Library Cataloguing in Publication Date

Everyday culture popular song and the
vernacular milieu. — (Popular music in
Britain).
1. Folk-songs, English — Social aspects
I. Pickering, Michael   II. Green, Tony
III. Series
784.4′942   ML3650

ISBN 0–335–15289–9

Library of Congress Cataloging-in-Publication Data

Everyday culture.

(Popular music in Britain)
Bibliography: p.
Discography: p.
1. Popular music — Great Britain — History and
criticism. I. Pickering, Michael. II. Green, Tony,
1936–   . III. Series.
ML3492.E9 1988   784.5′00941   87–22094
ISBN 0–335–15289–9

Typeset by Marlborough Design, Oxford
Printed in Great Britain at the Alden Press

Contents

Preface

The subject of this book relates to but is not coextensive with what has been referred to, for just over a century, as 'folk' song. The invention of 'folk' song as category and tradition has over this stretch of time generated its own tradition of study. The approaches adopted here derive in part from that tradition, but also diverge from it and in part exist in contention with it. The old paradigm of 'folk culture' is slowly breaking up, even among professional folklorists, because of its lack of correspondence to actual cultural life as encountered by fieldworkers, and its lack of flexibility in response to historical change. There is no new paradigm to replace it, and it is questionable whether there will be or should be. We offer instead a focus on the use of popular song in everyday situations. The study of this diverse and shifting phenomena is in a provisional stage. There is as much disagreement as agreement among those addressing themselves to it on questions of theory, method and terminology. The essays in this volume reflect this. Yet all contributors would agree that a performing art should be studied as such. In practice this means that where it exists it should be studied *in* performance, and where it no longer exists, so that our only access is through the historical record, it should be studied *as* performance. It follows that the overall orientation is to the discipline of sociological and historical context. What this signals, most of all, is a fundamental refusal to see everyday culture outside of the social and historical contexts in which it exists or has existed. There is no one model and no one method which can be followed in the exercise of this discipline, and that is why this book was conceived from the start as drawing upon a range of academic practices.

The opening essay, jointly written by the volume editors, is not conceived as an orthodox introduction to the individual contributions – that task is undertaken in editorial prefaces to the case studies, which deal with various key issues in vernacular song study: popular historiography, repertory, parody, key songs, and the social organization of song performance. Rather it outlines the current theoretical situation in the study of vernacular popular song. Its intention is to introduce the debate, not close it. The purpose of the book as a whole is to encourage those interested in popular song within vernacular milieux to see this particular example of the everyday arts in terms of broader processes and structures. We also hope to indicate, for the benefit of the historian and social scientist interested in the culture of everyday life, ways forward in the use of popular song as a valid resource.

T. G. and M. P.

Notes on Contributors

Tony Green is Senior Lecturer in Drama at Bretton Hall College, and formerly Lecturer in Folk Life Studies in the Institute of Dialect and Folk Life Studies, University of Leeds. He is the co-editor (with John Widdowson) of *Language, Culture and Tradition*, Leeds and Sheffield 1981; he has published in the fields of popular song and verse, vernacular language and humour and popular theatre and spectacle; and was instrumental, with John Murray, in the making of the film *Soulcaking at Antrobus* (University of Leeds Television Service).

Michael Pickering is Senior Lecturer in Communication Studies at Sunderland Polytechnic. He is author of *Village Song and Culture* (Croom Helm, London & Canberra, 1982), which won the 1983 Katharine Briggs Memorial Award, as well as various other publications on popular song and music. He has also published in the areas of popular religion, working class writing, documentary and social investigation. He was co-organizer of the 1983 conference on Popular Culture in the North East, and is a member of the editorial board of the *Folk Music Journal*.

Sam Richards has since 1972 researched song and other aspects of vernacular culture, mainly in the Westcountry. His research has concentrated on farming communities, gypsies, children's lore, and covers song, speech and instrumental music. He is now Director of the Westcountry Folklore Centre, a project which has been made possible by funding from Southwest Arts. He is co-editor of the *English Folksinger*, a song anthology published by Collins, has prepared two LP discs of his own field recordings, and is co-director of Peoples Stage Tapes, a cassette producing company concentrating on field recordings and revival singers.

Ian Russell is a primary school head teacher and the editor of the *Folk Music Journal*. He has organized several conferences on folklore for the English Folk Dance and Song Society and for the Centre for English Cultural Tradition and

Language at the University of Sheffield, where his fieldwork recordings have been deposited. His doctorate from the Institute of Dialect and Folklife Studies at the University of Leeds was on vernacular singing and his research has been published in *Lore and Language, Folk Music Journal*, and the *Journal of American Folklore*.

John Smith is Senior Lecturer in Social Psychology at Sunderland Polytechnic. His previous publications have been concerned with the development of attitude theory from the ethogenic perspective in social psychology. He runs the Glebe Live Music Club in Sunderland and has published an album of his own songs entitled *Just for the Record* (1982).

1   *Towards a Cartography of the Vernacular Milieu*

MICHAEL PICKERING and TONY GREEN

One of the most significant facts about us may finally be that we all begin with the natural equipment to live a thousand lives but end in the end having lived only one.

Clifford Geertz

Vernacular culture in late capitalism

The threat of capitalist development in the modern world is the subsumption of all social life into the marketplace. This universalization of the market is, as Braverman has put it, 'one of the keys to all recent social history'. It is not only material and service needs which are threatened by this development; 'emotional patterns of life' also become increasingly 'channelled through the market' and 'relations between individuals and social groups' tend 'not to take place directly, as cooperative human encounters, but through the market as relations of purchase and sale'. The ascendancy of capitalist market relations is thus 'a process that involves economic and social changes on the one side, and profound changes in psychological and affective patterns on the other'.[1] Artistic products and cultural forms also become increasingly turned into a 'species of commodity ... marketable and interchangeable like an industrial product' to the extent that cultural process and market relations increasingly overlap.[2] 'Thus in capitalist societies we are witnessing on the one hand the promotion of culture by commerce and on the other the promotion of commerce by culture.'[3] As Richard Wightman Fox and T. J. Jackson Lears have put it: 'Although the dominant institutions of our culture have purported to be offering the consumer a fulfilling participation in the life of the community, they have to a large extent presented the empty prospect of taking part in the marketplace of personal exchange.'[4]

The penetration of capital into many areas of human need and relationship, the growth of a multinational culture industry, the massification of the means of communication, all these render highly problematic an interest in small-scale, localised forms of cultural performance. The 'kind of culture that has been developed *by* a people or by a majority of a people to express their own meanings and values, over a range from customs to works' is increasingly dominated by that 'different kind of culture that has been developed *for* a people … and embedded in them by a range of processes from repressive imposition to commercial saturation'.[5] The communications revolution of the modern period has greatly impinged on the making of people's own culture within the vernacular milieu,* and while the erosion of local attachments and loyalties has increased the potential for democratic participation in national political life, 'the growth of an informed citizenry has been profoundly thwarted by its assimilation to the imperatives of the mass market'.[6] Does this therefore mean that to pursue an interest in the role of popular song in vernacular cultures is to play a folk fiddle while Rome burns? Is not such an interest in the late twentieth century merely antiquarian and of minimal relevance to serious social and cultural enquiry?

Interest in amateur song performance is indeed retreatist and regressive when it is simply a blind reaction to capitalist development, when it involves a wilful refusal to acknowledge the use and aesthetic values of much commercially produced popular music, or when it is a sentimentalization of the songs of an idealized past. Such inclinations have dogged the study of vernacular song and music since the first discoveries of 'the people'. We make no grand claims. Our concern is to develop a better understanding of non-elite cultures, and we believe that the songs performed and attended to by members of subordinate groups and classes in the context of their everyday lives are a neglected source in the pursuit of that aim. We do not wish to decry the extensions of technical scope and capability, of song idiom and style, of modes of performance, of musical character, of audience pleasure and enjoyment, attendant on those forms which depend on electronic production and transmission. We appreciate these extensions as in many ways enriching our own cultural experience, and we have no stake in attempts to delegitimate the utilization of new forms of music technology in vernacular performances, as John Smith's essay in this volume makes clear. It is not our purpose to defend some embattled corner of sound or style as the sole locus of what is morally or aesthetically good, to employ any prescriptively defined category of song in order to establish certain forms and idioms as more culturally pure or more politically progressive than others. We therefore reject 'rockism' as much as 'folkism'. But equally we reject the charge that our object of study is of little or no interest. Our interest in amateur, locally performed popular song, and its role is everyday social life, arises out of the fact that, although eroded and marginalized by the industrialization of popular leisure and the commoditization of culture, the performance and reception of song in lived cultures is nevertheless significant. It remains, however modestly, alternative in motivation to the realization of profit, and alternative in

---

* The term *vernacular milieu* refers to the local environment and specific immediate contexts within which, as an integral part of their everyday life, people participate in non-mediated forms and processes of cultural life. By definition that cultural life is non-official, and while it is at times assimilated into the national culture, it is experientially felt and understood by its participants as quite distinct.

experience to mass market consumption. Indeed, its significance in many people's lives is precisely that it preserves an area of cultural activity and experience that is different to mass market consumption. It involves, in a divergent process, working on and with what is consumed, conserving older material that is of no current interest to the market, or creating new material that is likewise commercially unviable at the time of production. It is this engagement with, this appropriation and usage of, popular song in non-commoditized manifestations that we are interested in: how popular song is woven into the fabric of everyday social experience. It is this area of cultural life which constitutes our object of study.

Over half a century back, Gramsci pointed out that even though most songs are written 'neither by nor for the people', people nevertheless selectively and creatively adopt and adapt particular songs according to their own criteria of how they can serve their own 'way of thinking and feeling'.[7] Particular groupings seek out and take over products and artefacts, from both mediated and situated sources, which approximate to and can be used to inform their own sensibilities and social identities, their own understandings and social values. The ethnographic studies in this volume analyse the homological relations generated by this active though not necessarily conscious process. Some of the chapters focus on these relations in the context of individual biographies, though the individuals involved are situated within definite social groupings and class positions. Others concentrate more on the level of the group or community. It is important to state at the outset that in studying the homological relations between songs and groups, we should not assume that we can simply read off song content as an inscription of the social values, attitudes, norms and beliefs of particular groups. Indeed, song content may in part or in whole be discordant with the moral community, but of value precisely because it offers a symbolic, self-legitimating counterpart to that community. Songs, along with other kinds of artistic expression or product, often provide visits to 'other worlds' which interrupt the taken-for-granted pattern of everyday reality. These other worlds are alternative, symbolic 'realities' outside of that which remains paramount in ordinary social life. But while they are alternative to that life, they arise from within it, from its needs and deficiencies, and subsequently react in a dialectical process on the world of everyday reality. Songs constitute ways of handling the empirically experienced world, as do all imaginative acts and relationships, having either constructive or negative consequences for social action and interaction, and either supporting or challenging 'how things are', or how they are represented ideologically.

It is also important to emphasize that the homological relations between song and person, song and group, are never fixed for all time, so that when a particular song is handed down through successive generations, its symbolic meanings and cultural significance become modified and inflected by changed social circumstances and conditions, even though, at the same time, what has traditionally been made of it certainly affects how it can be made over within any given present. Michael Pickering's essay in this volume explicitly addresses the dialectic of tradition and change via the case study of a seventeenth-century ballad in late nineteenth-century performance, but we would argue more generally that the whole question of tradition and traditionality cannot be understood in isolation from the historical process. An item of tradition has no absolute meaning or value across time. What it signifies and stands for is as much a product of the process of engagement in particular periods and places as of its own inherent expressive properties and qualities, though this should not be taken to imply any neat or simple equation.

What is most distinctive of the kind of song studied in this volume is that its performance occurs in small groups and that it is rooted in shared, immediate, everyday experience. Within the group it can be said that 'all members know each other, are aware of their common membership, share the same values, have a certain structure of relationships which is stable over time, and interact to achieve some purpose'.[8] Members of such groups today are of course more articulated and orientated to other external social and cultural frameworks of reference than ever before, and this must not be forgotten. Conversely, the decline of the family and community in social life has augmented the value of their symbolic celebration. But in focusing on the relations of past and present songs and the social groups who have either created or more commonly adopted them, for a range of reasons and purposes, we are concerned with how these songs work as an integral part of the art and artistry of everyday life. This generally occurs in face-to-face forms of social interaction within the context of what Goffman has called 'focused gatherings'. For the participants this involves 'a single visual and cognitive focus of attention; a mutual and preferential openness to verbal communication; a heightened mutual relevance of acts; an eye-to-eye ecological huddle that maximises each participant's monitoring of [the others]'. Focused gatherings 'provide the communication base for a circular flow of feeling among the participants as well as corrective compensations for deviant acts'.[9] So far as the group's own dynamics are concerned, the cultural and aesthetic mode we are discussing differs from mass communication in the following major ways. It is generally two-way and participatory; it is usually confined to amateur performance, and where professionalism is involved it is generally at a low economic level; it is situation-specific and contextually local as a communicative event and process, and therefore its impact is only on those involved who at the time of the event and process bear a low relation to industrial and business structures; it involves little technological equipment and little division of labour; and as we have already indicated, it gives very low priority to the extraction of surplus value from the labour of its performance. That labour is unproductive in terms of market structures and relations, and thus holds a valid potentiality, at least, of subverting or reversing the alienation of the commodity form.

Everyday social life for the group and community is predominantly vernacular in orientation, and involves an intersubjectively constructed ordering of 'me'/'us' and 'them': subjects defined from within the complex of lived relationships of the group and community, though never of course in terms of any clear-cut or complete distinctions; ideology has for this reason been neatly termed the 'them' in 'us' by Willis.[10] This particularistic orientation has been most prevalent in working class life and culture, where the crucial spring is identification with one's own home, family, friends, fellow workers, locality, customs and institutions.[11] These subjective alliances and loyalties are of course readily courted into extended, abstract constructs such as country, nation and race precisely because the more immediate and concrete identifications of everyday life have been subject to a long process of ideological infiltration (eg. self-interest equated with national interest) and social change (eg. the loosening of community ties and indigenous patterns of mutual aid), and because such broader constructs are metaphorically experienced in terms of local and particular identifications. The disintegrative effects on the social basis of community life of the forces of mass production, centralized planning of housing patterns, geographical and social mobility, mass mediated forms of communication, the privatization of leisure and the rise of consumerism, are incontestable. But these social developments have not reduced the 'need for roots', for indigenous popular association and a sense of belonging. They can indeed be said to have magnified that need even as its denials have in the twentieth century been the prerequisite for virulent nationalisms, centralized bureaucratic structures and the supremacist power of the nation-state, all of them rejections of the intimate and local. The quest for community is thus as much a way of seeking sanctuary from the incessant disruptions in the modern experience of capitalist society as it is for seeking remedy for the 'hidden injuries of class' on the part of the structurally inferior.[12] 'Uprootedness uproots everything except the need for roots.'[13] The erosion of local distinctiveness is not then the same as its utter abrogation, and, as we hope to show, forces tending to the destruction of community can be said to exist in inverse proportion to the lived and symbolic reality of community identities and relations.

Methodological denials of the local

These social forces find their intellectual counterpart and reinforcement in schools of thought which are themselves ahistorical or so grossly historical as to posit universalist trends which deny or merely ignore the importance of local functions and interpretations. Cultural Evolutionism, particularly in its manifestation as survivalist Folk-Lore, is a classic example of the latter. Nominally historical, it ignored both the particularities of change over time and the possibility of positive and self-conscious action and choice by members of subordinate cultures (whether 'peasants' or 'savages'), and was quite unable to cope with the many syntheses that arise from the meeting of old and new, dominated and dominant, indigenous and exotic. Understandably, though regrettably, the reaction among a later generation of folklorists to its inadequate historicism and lack of explanatory force has led, as we shall see, to a rejection (or at least a neglect) of history as such. Methodologies based, ultimately, on the concept of human nature, such as behaviourism and psychoanalysis, have focused on the human being as, respectively, biological organism and individual personality, in a way that renders cultural analysis, as such, virtually redundant. Both have things to be said in their favour as accounts of human behaviour, but both suffer, again, from a totalizing tendency which ultimately denies that human beings individually *and* collectively, actively create meaning, and thus construct a springboard for action, out of circumstances which they have inherited or which subsequently impinge upon them. The way in which James Lyons, as an individual conscious of his class position and ethnic origin, made and subsequently used and glossed his repertory of songs and stories, illustrates exactly this.

The same problem arises with the various superorganically conceived analytical procedures commonly grouped under the heading of structuralism. Whether in the syntagmatic version derived from Russian Formalism,[14] or in the paradigmatic version most closely associated with Lévi-Strauss, structuralism is reductionist and deterministic in tendency: that is, it tends to reduce multiple form and meaning to a single, sub-textual entity. Again, it is not without its uses. Propp's morphology of Russian folk tales, technical and ostensibly abstract as it is, is a persuasive account of how story-tellers actually work in constructing their improvised performances upon a memorized framework. This is important, and its rather austere conceptualization has been importantly fleshed out, for a different but analogous genre, by A. B. Lord's seminal prosodic investigations of the epic.[15] But what does it *mean* to say that: 'All fairy tales are of one type in regard to their structure'?[16] Propp is scrupulously careful to maintain a formalist stance. But unless we believe that form and meaning have no mutual dependency, which is self-evidently absurd (were it so we would be unable to communicate at all), this observation must have semantic implications. It may be irrelevant to Propp's analysis whether the tsar gives an eagle to the hero or the princess gives Ivan a ring,[17] but presumably it was not irrelevant to the story-tellers who voiced these narrative formulations. To show how they do it is one thing; to show what they meant by doing it is quite another, and here Propp's method will not help us: we would need to ask them, if they were available, and just as importantly we would need to consider the circumstances out of which they were striving – through the medium of inherited linguistic and superlinguistic procedures – to make their own meanings. Likewise, Lévi-Strauss's celebrated analysis of the Oedipus myth, ingenious and intellectually stimulating as it is, in arriving at the conclusion that the myth is simultaneously about the friction between conflicting explanations of human existence and conflicting views on the proper definition of kinship, leaves us with the unanswered questions, for whom? when? where? For a French professional intellectual in the mid-twentieth century, evidently; but for a second-century BC Athenian historian and mythographer, or a fifth-century playwright, or a ninth-century epic poet, or for any of their audiences or readers? How can we know? And if it meant something different to them, *en masse* or variously, were they wrong? This is where such methodologies fall down. While the relationship between indigenous and scholarly understanding is always likely to be problematic, even where the scholar is discussing his or her own culture, there is a critical difference between approaches which attempt to assimilate indigenous understandings to their analytical procedures, and those which, however genially or gently, enough, reflects in the selection of its contents the growing ahistorical trend of the new folkloristics): 'In the thirties, the search for patterns was itself a pattern superimpose their own interpretations on whatever may be locally current. As Alan Dundes has neatly put in (in an influential textbook which, ironically of culture.'[19] He is right (not that it was confined to the thirties); and as soon as we start to historicize not only our data but our own practice, we are inevitably led back to the local and particular. If Lévi-Strauss could not have arrived at his analysis of Oedipus without the precedents of the *Gestalt* approach referred to by Dundes, then that analysis is, in some sense, a product of time and place. And what is true of Lévi-Strauss is true of Appollodorus, Sophocles and Homer, and of their peoples.

In reference if not in sense, cultural meaning is therefore local, and any methodology for describing it should begin with the defined locality. The obvious objection, 'How local is local?', is actually as meaningless as it is obvious. Both objectively and subjectively, the 'local' is infinitely variable. The spatial frames of reference of a desert nomad and a sedentary horticulturalist, of Sam Richards' traveller-gipsy and Ian Russell's Pennine shepherd, *are* different and are perceived by those people as different. Likewise the chronological frames of reference of pre-literate societies and societies with a long history of keeping written records, to which the literacy of their members gives them access, albeit selective and uneven. What is true of space and time is equally true of social groupings, of nationality, race, class and so on, and there is no need to labour the point further. The only requirement is that the student should define what is 'local' in particular cases, taking account of the subjective as well as the objective perspective.

As a starting-point, what can always be identified, because it is a function of human social life (and thus a genuine universal, as distinct from the questionable or specious universals referred to above) is the face-to-face interaction of the primary group, and the kind of locally varying performance which originates from it and is a vital part of its social and intellectual intercourse.

The object of such a strategy is that it militates against cultural abstraction, even if it cannot wholly prevent it. Faced with particular individuals and reference groups (preferably under their real names rather than pseudonyms), scholarly idealization, though not precluded, becomes more difficult. Conversely, studies concentrating on the local and particular can, of course, involve the equally grave dangers of anecdotalism and sentimentalization, even of escapism. To avoid these, it is necessary constantly to reincorporate such studies into a general framework of theory.

Lineaments of neighbourhood and community

The inevitable conflation of the lived reality with the ideology of community has long hampered the sociological study of local social life. While the term 'community' is almost as belaboured with unfortunate associations as the term 'folk', we need to give it some examination since it remains inseparable from our understanding of song performance in everyday non-commoditized cultural life. The tangle of difficulties surrounding the term can be said to stem basically from its 'high level of use' and 'low level of meaning'.[20] Furthermore, as Raymond Williams has pointed out, community 'can be the warmly persuasive word to describe an existing set of relationships, or the warmly persuasive word to describe an alternative set of relationships'.[21] The term is therefore extremely potent with semantic associations yet extremely elusive to attempts at definition, as Hillery's famous identification of ninety four definitions amply testifies.[22] Following Bell and Newby, we can classify most uses of the term as either empirical description or normative prescription.[23] But these two broad dimensions of use are neither separate nor separable, and it is simply not possible to arrive at any definitive, non-qualitative sense of the term. Here we would agree with Raymond Plant who states that Bell and Newby's implicit, and Hillery's explicit notion of the possibility of formulating just such a sense of the word, 'betrays a misunderstanding of the logic of the situation and an insensitivity to the extent to which the historical career of a concept structures our present understanding of it'.[24] We would not however go so far as Stacey, who has advocated avoidance of the term altogether, simply because of the absence of any viable alternative that could command widespread acceptance. We think the word is still worth fighting for.[25]

In his notes towards a theory of communities, Norbert Elias defines a community as 'a group of households situated in the same locality and linked to each other by functional interdependencies which are closer than interdependencies of the same kind with other groups of people within the wider social field to which a community belongs'.[26] The identification of interdependencies as key defining features of communities is one we welcome, though we do not want to confine our use of the term invariably to specific geographical areas: working class corresponding societies, Methodist circuits, journeymen's clubs and trade societies are historical examples of non-local, although more diffused, kinds of community interdependencies. In the modern world, the threads which are woven into local social interaction and relationships have, without doubt, become increasingly fewer because increasingly drawn into wider areas of orientation. Communities of interest are focused on a specific plane rather than a specific place, and through that focus on interaction and identity orientated to, in general, religious, cultural or political affiliations. Interest communities are also unlike place communities in that they can be either dispersed or relatively confined to particular localities. Yet both interest and place communities are manifestations of interdependencies and both provide situated sources of identity. In delineating either locally-based or group-based common means and ends, we must seek to scale the patterns of communication which are localized to specific places, or in some way interest-related, according to where they exist in a range from their manifestation as dominant to their manifestation as residual features of social and cultural life.[27]

Elias grades communities from those which are predominantly agrarian, existing within relatively undifferentiated societies with a tendency towards all-embracing interdependencies, to others in 'more differentiated and complex societies with a greater number of hierarchically ordered levels of integration'; here social functions are 'vested in higher level authorities' in a series of historical developments that characterize the emergence and formation of the state.[28] These distinctions do not imply an absence of conflict and a predominance of cooperation in less differentiated societies with a higher degree of internal interdependencies, as for example the vast literature on witchcraft accusations demonstrates. The idealized notion of harmonious organic communities of the past is a recurrent ideological ploy in the tradition of English social and cultural criticism which properly belongs to the dustbin of historiographical ideas. The central point arising out of these distinctions is rather, to put it in its simplest form, that 'communities become less differentiated as societies become more differentiated', and that this process is dialectical rather than unilinear in character.[29] The problem then becomes one of determining to what extent and in what ways any defined social area or grouping, in a complex social system, can still retain features of community organization and interdependent activities binding people together. In engaging with this problem we should, again, eschew the temptation to see social and cultural interdependencies as contributing to and constituting an integrated and harmonious whole. The attempt should be to gauge the relative dominance within particular locales and groupings of either the community or the society, though this should not be done by compiling a checklist of features of community and features of society against which one can, as it were, tick in relevant boxes down relevant colums and then simply count up the score to see which side wins.

There is today in the advanced societies generally a disjunction between people's public occupational roles, and their private leisure activities. This means that it is essentially in relation to non-occupational activities, and the interdependencies upon which those activities are reliant, that aspects of community life are still most in evidence, though there will always be certain exceptions, such as backyard industries, certain types of rural work, or the scrap recycling trade of travelling people. 'Common dependencies on educational, medical, religious, consumption and sociability needs can still be considerable and the response to social requirements of this type can still give a locality, an estate, a suburb, a village or a neighbourhood, to a greater or lesser extent the character of a community.'[30] Such aspects of community are residual in the sense that the majority of people's material and social needs today are dependent on extraneous sources of satisfaction or goal-achievement, and in a complex urbanized social system, community structures are less densely enmeshed in the whole pattern of social life. Though often residual, such interdependencies which are manifest in local or group contexts are, however, of considerable importance, *often in inverse proportion to their residuality*, and the networks of social relationships upon which they depend continue to be characteristic of community-oriented patterns of existence and attachment for those who move within them. One can therefore say that people are reliant upon the community or the society on a scale of more or less for the fulfilment of their everyday social and cultural needs. This more/less reliance can have various outcomes: for instance, frustration in one can lead to deliberate action to seek and create the conditions for fulfilment in either the one or the other, and examples of this in the two distinct but interrelated spheres would be community action on the one hand, and social reform effecting structural change on the other.

Community patterns of communication are not now necessarily confined to specific localities. Elizabeth Bott's words still hold true: 'In a small-scale relatively closed society, the local group and the kin group mediate between the family and the total society; in an urban industrialized society there is no single encapsulating group or institution that mediates between the family and the total society.'[31] Ignoring this and its many ramifications is perhaps the major weakness of the holistic view of communities as unitary combinations, and it is one of which we should beware in considering both the historical development of communities, and the manifestations of contemporary community life, in relation to changes in the total society. Though the folk-urban polarity should be rejected on the grounds of its artificial separation of traditional and modern, rural and urban, and its obscuration of class, gender, generational and ethnic stratifications, we must obviously recognize, historically and geographically, a morphological continuum (to adopt Frankenberg's phrase) between different types of community, and between community groups and networks and the 'national community'. Southall's continuum likewise identifies such key determining variables as low/high population density, diffuse/specific role definition, overt/latent role development, equality/inequality in role relationships, and durable/ephemeral social relationships.[32] Historically at least, working class groups have tended to manifest a greater reliance on informal communication networks; the development of such networks has been considerably more complex in working class communities than in areas or groupings associated with other social classes. Conversely, the middle and upper middle classes have tended to display a greater knowledge of, competence to use, and ability to take advantage of formal communications systems. Because such systems transcend local social contexts, this has had the effect of making the dominant class and its class fractions more nationally than locally oriented. Middle class 'community action' is in many ways a compensating mechanism for this effect, in that it is designed to encourage or create a sense of community or, to use the more emotive phrase, 'community spirit', within specific localities to which, very often, the instigators and prime movers of such action are relative newcomers.[33] Such 'action' is a superimposed, rationalized contrivance. Mutual aid, solidarity and fellowship in working class communities, although always a partial development, have by contrast been grounded historically in response to adverse material conditions of existence, and to structurally subordinate positions in the class society. The phenomenon may take two forms: the politically passive and self-protective stance, which Williams has termed the 'mutuality of the oppressed',[34] or a more positive, outward-looking and sometimes more belligerent definition of working class interests and the collective action required to promote or sustain them. Either way, there is a crucial distinction between community consciousness generated by common experiences of deprivation, and community consciousness generated from positions of privilege, in compensation for a discipline of individualist competitiveness and an autobiographical experience of social 'spiralism',[35] yet dependent on an absence of conditions of deprivation and an ability to escape those oppressive forces of social control symptomatic of relatively closed local social systems. The idea that human person and community are contradictory categories is historically a bourgeois one, though this does not of course mean that bourgeois social status is necessarily equivalent to complete absence of community orientation: 'the annulment of communal "alignment" guarantees nothing more than the cock-sure individualism of selfishness', and sensitivity to the logical end of individualism in its classical form has engendered in many a 'nostalgia for the lost community' and 'a desire to find their way back to it'.[36]

Vernacular cultural process: weaving the webs of significance

Most of the case studies in this volume relate to individuals and groups situated in common local areas, though Sam Richards' study shows how community bondings also exist among a group not confined to – indeed cut adrift from – any specific local area. A basic premise of the approach we are encouraging in this introductory essay is that situated contexts of performance must be understood not only in relation to their own immediate dynamics, but also in relation to the broader structural forces which shape the character and course of everyday social interaction. Such interaction in complex societies is in no sense confined to people's individual communities in any geographically limited sense. Indeed, Pahl has gone so far as to state that in modern industrial societies 'any attempt to tie particular patterns of social relationships to specific geographic milieux is a singularly fruitless exercise'.[37] This is a fair criticism of studies of community cultural life which treat it as socially autonomous; that said, it is incontrovertible that individuals do orientate themselves in a socio-spatial manner; in this sense they are community-conscious, and this consciousness may be geographically defined. It remains true that this community orientation should not be studied in isolation and without reference to the broader social structure in which it is set, and to which it relates in class-specific ways. We should thus focus on the dialectical interplay between national and local in terms of interdependence, orientation, organization, and distribution of power and resources.

In focusing on a distinctive interactive mode of cultural transmission and reception occurring between singer, audience and opus in community cultures, we are involved with the symbolic as well as the structural dimension of community. It is the former which is of primary importance in the study of vernacular milieux and cultures. What is central here is the idea of difference and distinction: the various identifications made through the medium of everyday practices which provide primary sources of identity are supported by their dialectical contrast with social others and with other cultures. As Cohen points out, 'people become aware of their culture when they stand at its boundaries'.[38] It is the intra-community perception and definition of these boundaries which count in the intimate sense of belonging: 'the elementary structures of belonging within the locality – family, neighbourhood, sect, friendship – mediate the experience of collectivity, of community. Belonging is the almost inexpressibly complex experience of culture'.[39] The boundaries of community and the sense of belonging within a community are thus culturally constructed and elaborated. The shared experience of community draws on the symbolic resources of the vernacular culture, and people develop a sense of belonging through the use of those resources in the process of individual meaning-construction within group contexts. The 'symbolic repertoire of a community aggregates the individualities and other differences found within the community and provides the means for their expression, interpretation and containment. It provides the range within which individuality is recognisable'. It unites people 'in their opposition, both to each other, and to those "outside". It thereby constitutes, and gives reality to, the community's boundaries'.[40]

Song assimilated into the structures of the vernacular forms an integral part of this symbolic repertoire. Vernacular culture constitutes a hotch-potch of resources for human usages and enjoyment, a mixed body of practices, expressions and artefacts whose significations are a product of the effort to create viable ways of life and coherent identities in relation to particular social conditions and circumstances. It is not so much the origin or uniqueness of such content which is important, though these factors should not be utterly discounted. Certain elements of culture may well be specifically local or regional, but they are usually borrowed from a range of different sources, and assimilated and sedimented within local groupings. What is much more significant is how the heterogeneous assemblage of chosen material is brought together to give identity and definition to individuals and groupings within specific positions in the social structure, and within specific geographical and occupational locations; how people weave the 'webs of significance' which constitute 'culture'.[41] It is the process of localization which is then under consideration: the process of 'making our own'. That which constitutes the social in this process is the field in which cultural forms are actively deployed, the set of relations and interdependencies through which people define themselves and each other, act and interact, in terms of the cultural resources available to them. It is in this sense that culture – and the vernacular as a distinctive cultural mode – is a concrete process of human interaction.

Cultural forms not only delimit social play but also 'the direction in which the play can go in order to change the rules of the game, when this becomes necessary'; they define the opportunities and possibilities for action, while 'human manoeuvre' in turn is 'always pressing against the inherent limitations of cultural forms'.[42] As Sidney Mintz points out: 'Without the dimension of human action, of choices made and pursued – of manoeuvre – culture could be thought to be a lifeless collection of habits, superstitions, and artefacts.'[43] This is of course precisely how 'folklore' was seen for so long. The categorizing preoccupations of folklife studies were the positivistic counterpart of the evolutionistic conception of cultural fossils surviving in the backwaters of modern civilization. Items of folklore so conceived could then be pinned down for display, presented as quaintly colourful relics, and later as the cold bones of formal types and motifs. In both these methodologies such items were utterly divorced from their usages in definite groups and communities as means by which people orient themselves within 'the ongoing course of experienced things'.[44] The symbolic associations of cultural forms are acquired and activated through their usages within given networks of social relations, where their role may be either affirmative or subversive, confirming or contesting existing patterns of social relationships and organization. We do not deny the validity of the study of the forms of culture. Our point is that the meanings of these forms pose questions which are social and historical in nature, not in terms of reflective or mimetic correspondences – ideas as the motor of social development, or economic-technological expansion as the fixed or absolute determinant of consciousness and culture – but in the sense of symbolic associations intersubjectively realized, and conditioned by the structure of power relations which characterize the social arenas in which such associations are constructed and reproduced.

Popular song in vernacular performance

In 1951, André Malraux made the statement: 'Folk art no longer exists because the "folk" no longer exists.'[45] For us the 'folk' have never existed. There have only ever been people who have been called the 'folk' by others existing socially and culturally outside of those groups so designated. The application of the term as a prefix to different aspects of vernacular popular culture inherits the indistinctness of sense and meaning involved in its use as an ascribed historical and anthropological category. It remains conceptually elusive. It is for this reason that it has been sufficiently malleable for use on both sides of the iron and bamboo curtains, in the East and in the West, and by both reactionary and progressive movements with quite opposed purposes and ends in view. Scholars, collectors and performers have debated endlessly about what is meant by 'folk' song and what is 'authentic folk song'. That debate has got nowhere because it has nowhere to go. The 'genuine folk song' is a figment of the conservative and radical imagination. What has to be recognized, at bottom, is that 'folk' song tradition is essentially an 'invented' cultural phenomenon. The term itself is prescriptive rather than descriptive; for the most part it identifies its object by excluding others from within its purified range, and then fabricating its alleged properties and character. It is not as though people never sang the songs we now identify, by long association, as 'folk'. But as Dave Harker has most recently shown, in a masterly account of 'folk' song mediation, these songs have from the start been selectively collected and presented, and then given definition by reference to prejudicial criteria.[46] Those criteria are not of popular origin, and the result has been a distortion of the historical evidence.

The 'folk' conception of orality has often suggested not only an absence of written literature but also of literacy. The existence of a print industry and broadside ballad trade from the mid-sixteenth century onwards did not leave popular singing traditions inviolate. Most of the songs and ballads noted in England by late Victorian and Edwardian collectors originated in broadsheet production and were commercially distributed by packmen and chaunters throughout the country. Though more research is urgently needed into the precise operations of this industry, there are some grounds for thinking that there may be a correlation between the areas most frequented by broadside traders and those found most productive by the collectors associated with the Folk-Song Society.[47] Recent research has also shown a much higher degree of literacy among working people throughout the nineteenth century than was previously thought to exist,[48] and where even only a few members of a community possessed the ability to read, in any period, then that would have represented an open channel through which print literature could have been absorbed into community cultures. The idea of the unlettered (and, until Korson and Lloyd, usually rustic[49]) worker as the key agent in popular song and singing traditions is therefore as misconceived as it is insulting: behind it lie all those derogatory and patronizing caricatures of chawbacons, clodhoppers and village Hodges. The interweaving of oral and literate forms began at least four centuries ago, with the commencement of broadsheet and chapbook printing in London,[50] though it may well go back further, via the manuscript song-book.[51] We cannot know, from the chance survival of a handful of examples, how widespread or important the manuscript song-book was, or how it was used; and of course what was true of London was not, until later, true of Carlisle, much less Kirby Lonsdale. But the fact is that we cannot, at any point in its recorded history, look at English popular song and claim that here we can identify a primitive, non-literate song culture. Sir Philip Sidney's blind crowder did not read; but we cannot be sure that his son or (less probably) his daughter did not read to him: his song, whether 'Chevy Chase' or 'Otterburn', was already in manuscript – including, significantly enough, the song-book of the minstrel Richard Sheale[52] – long before Sir Philip heard him sing, and it is only forty years later that one shows up on a ballad sheet.[53] In any case, what is called folklore is not exclusive to non-written media. And in the twentieth century recorded and broadcast media of communication have supplemented the previous non-oral sources of popular song available to amateur community performers.[54]

Recognizing the exaggeration of orality in the folk paradigm does not mean dismissal of the importance of oral transmission in the social communication of traditional symbolic forms. Similar caveats apply to the literate/oral distinction as to high/popular culture stratification and the community/society dichotomy: polarization produces oversimplification and distortion. When the culture of a social group or class is pervaded by print literature to a sufficiently high degree, then certain effects do become tendentially pronounced, such as the stability of expressive accounts over time, authorial individualism, privatized cognitive reflection, the idea of fixed, definitive texts, and possibly the expansion of vocabulary.[55] These effects are observable only in terms of degree, for members of even the most literate circles also transmit elements of culture in oral forms (eg. jokes, sayings, legends and superstitions). For popular vernacular cultures not so dependent on literate forms but which have nevertheless been deeply impregnated by them, some conception of orality clearly retains a heuristic value. This is particularly true in considering popular song, for such a cultural form in its performance is nothing if not oral, and whatever sense we have of traditionality, repetition by oral transmission is obviously a reasonable indication of song popularity within local cultural milieux or among distinct social groups. As one of us has previously suggested:

> It *may* be reasonable to infer that frequent reprinting means frequent singing, but it may also be true [historically] that broadsheets were functioning significantly as literature, among people who could ill afford books, rather than acting chiefly as a source of texts for singing. The large number of texts extant in printed form, compared with the rather small number of them that have ever been encountered by field-workers as *songs*, seems to suggest that this is so. Now if it is realistic to talk at all about 'working class culture', than I believe that we must mean the shared culture of the group, as manifested in public performance, not the poems that some working men and women read in private.[56]

Clearly there is always a danger of assuming or exaggerating repetition over time, and as Elbourne has pointed out, there are difficulties in distinguishing between the literary and musical functions of printed songs, particularly historically.[57] The existence of song in performance as well as in print does nevertheless show a conscious and wider degree of assimilation into the shared culture of the group. The native emphasis on the traditionality of certain songs *within* vernacular cultures remains the key factor, yet one which does not have the status of a shibboleth.

Orality and literacy then should be regarded as variable orientations rather than rigidly demarcating lines of cultural cleavage. This point applies also to distinctions between commercialized popular music and popular music in vernacular milieux, and between popular music generally and classical music: the differences between them should not be idealized and thus polarized, but seen in terms of a continuum, where overlap between categories of song and music is continually occurring. In the case of vernacular popular song, we can identify as guiding points certain recurrent characteristics. The performance of such song is often dramatistic, with certain ritualistic and functional consequences for the participants, in that it may prove mood-creating, group-defining or -binding, and norm-reinforcing. In contrast to the social and ideological category of classical music, it has not evolved a legislative set of intellectualized aesthetic criteria and the establishment of a body of exegetical critical literature, as in 'high' literary and musical culture.[58] The ongoing formation of a parallel body of conceptual and interpretative literature concerning song in vernacular cultures (along with other forms of local interaction) is an academic enterprise, but with the special feature of application in what is symptomatically termed 'revivalism'.

Historically, the unformalized aesthetics of vernacular song have by contrast been implicitly realized in the indigenous process of performance. Vocal and musical expertise in vernacular cultures has always been the result of conscious learning and practice; it has not sprung spontaneously into life. Its development in particular individuals ensues from imitation and adaptation, but this, unlike the reproduction of classical music, has not depended on educational establishments where skills and repertoires are formally taught and learned. The cultural transmission of songs, skills and styles in vernacular singing traditions has not, at least outside revivalist contexts of performance, been bracketed off from general social and cultural process in everyday life. Furthermore, such transmission has been facilitated by the closer integration between performers and audiences than is normally present in classical musical performance, or in commercialized popular music where the star syndrome prevails. Performers in vernacular milieux have also been more directly accountable to their listeners, in non-market terms, and their listeners more able to give immediate response in terms of evaluation and appreciation.[59] (The resilience of effective consumer power in the nineteenth-century music hall and popular concert hall should also be noted, as should more recent examples of reaction to lack of such power, as in the explosive youth rebellion in punk against business control, professionalism, artistic elitism and consumerism.[60]) The relatively closer integration of performer, audience and opus has been realized as well in the constituent features of vernacular performance, where monopoly of singing and music-making has been rare. The consequent exchange of roles between audience members and performers has usually served to reduce the differentiation between them. Such integration in vernacular performance has also been, in variable ways, reinforced by other connections – familial, amical, residential, experiential, political, and cultural (in the sense of shared codes and symbols) – which we have noted as the identifying cluster of usual but not imperative features of achieved (rather than ascribed) community life.

Certain old assumptions have been quite properly and generally discarded: eg. that, to be of value, a song must have longevity in vernacular cultural process; and that anonymity is a requisite feature of authorship and composition in local singing practice. It is time as well to move on from narrow conceptions of the term 'communal re-creation', as a central feature of popular transmission and tradition, which have remained prevalent in folkloristics and folksong scholarship: firstly, a concentration on the process of creativity and transmission in the abstract, on internal textual variation, and on the evolution of substantive elements of a tradition without reference to wider social forces and influences; secondly, an over-emphasis, as in the Finnish approach, on spatial and temporal diffusion as the result of geographical movement, and an under-emphasis on the localized evolution through time of particular traditions. A broader understanding of the process of 'communal re-creation' should amend these features by relating the working of the process to the structured occasions and situations of performance, to the cultural codes, conventions and frameworks through which meanings are made and understood within particular groups, and to the ways in which such meaning-construction is ideologically infiltrated and co-opted.

The politics of tradition

Any tradition develops an authenticating force and consensual power, and we need to examine in each specific case in what ways and to what ends these are put to use. The compulsive sense of tradition can of course wield a deadening influence, and the function of tradition-making can be to mystify social conflict and naturalize an unequal structure of power relations. The formation of an authoritative canon of folk song and ballad, its construction as tradition, has had precisely that ossifying effect, and in England has served precisely that political motive. But it will not suffice to leave it there. We need to distinguish between the retrogressive ideology of traditionalism, and uncontrived involvement in the active, indigenous usage of objects from the past for the sake of a progressively orientated social present. 'The contemporaneity of the tradition-receiver must be viewed ... as the vital site of tradition-making, a ground on which the so-called ideal object is not only received in active reception which *makes* relevant, makes *contemporary* ... active reception permits the persistence of the old but only on condition that the needs of the new are satisfied.'[61] The actual involvement in tradition shades into many intermediate positions; these opposed repressive and liberatory categories nevertheless seem useful to us analytically so long as we remember that in practice uneven, tacking movement constantly occurs between them.

The selective fashioning and shaping force of tradition can actively contribute to processes of class cultural incorporation and legitimation, and in this hegemonic sense other, more particularistic orientations to continuity with other significant pasts are deeply compromised. It is therefore essential, in considering these orientations, not to lose sight of this 'deliberately selective and connecting process which offers a historical and cultural ratification of a contemporary order'.[62] Yet because these public representations of English pastness and of 'our national heritage' are dominant, a concomitant danger for cultural criticism lies in turning attention away from the more localized and privatized forms of traditionality which, however indistinct in practice from dominant constructions, are not wholly identical with them. These other senses of pastness, while only partially achieved, are part of the structure of everyday life, and are sustained through a whole array of forms. Traditionality in ways of life that are at all settled serves as a basic source of collective identity and works through what Bourdieu calls the 'habitus' of particular groups and communities: 'a set of generalised schemes of thought, perception, appreciation and action'.[63] These provide the fundamental conceptions and frameworks through which people regard and respond to the social world, and through which they adapt to new situations and practices. In the case of the particular cultural medium and content we are studying here, the processual features of tradition-ality should be understood as giving 'an *emphasis* within a wide range of musical activities' rather than constituting 'a distinct *category* of music'.[64] What is drawn from and made of the material of the past at a national level works predomin-antly in favour of established, dominant interest groups. The moral stake which minority groups have in their other senses of pastness is by contrast usually hidden from wide public view and often actively repressed. There are of course ambiguous cases, such as the Orange Order in Northern Ireland, but whether silenced and marginalized, or marginal and vociferous, these other senses still exist as a mode and mechanism of group and community self-legitimation, often increasing in symbolic importance for those on the 'inside' because of the pressures bearing down upon them. And where minority interests are concerned, traditionality can give emphasis to behavioural models and moral values that may challenge the status quo and imposed practices at any particular time: radical historiography's concern to amplify their subdued voices would not otherwise be explicable. What is meant by traditionality and how it is formed is not something that can be explained only in terms of the colonization of people's past-present relations. Alasdair MacIntyre has written:

> Traditions, when vital, embody continuities of conflict. Indeed when a tradition becomes Burkean, it is always dying or dead ... A living tradition then is a historically extended, socially embodied argument, and an argument precisely in part about the goods which constitute that tradition ... an adequate sense of tradition manifests itself in a grasp of those future possibilities which the past has made available to the present. Living traditions, just because they continue a not-yet-completed narrative, confront a future whose determinate and determinable character, so far as it possesses any, derives from the past.[65]

American Folkloristics and the repression of history

But is traditionality a necessary feature of vernacular song, or an essential methodological concept in the study of it? The dominant recent trend in American folkloristics – which is, by weight of numbers as well as by conceptual adventurousness, among the more important schools of thought about popular culture, in the English-speaking world at least[66] – has tended to downgrade this once central concept. In reaction against the evolutionary (or devolutionary) premise that gave us ritual survivals, and the inadequate historicism that crystallized the Child ballad as a medieval genre, American folklorists have increasingly, and selectively, adopted one or other version of synchronic methodology, whether derived from functional social anthropology and its subsequent developments, from psychoanalysis, from structural linguistics, from Russian formalism, or from human geography.

At its most moderate, this tendency is merely a matter of emphasis, however assertively it may be phrased. Henry Glassie's wide-ranging and provocative essay in aspects of American material culture may state boldly that 'the student of folk culture should listen more closely to the cultural geographer than to the historian, for he must labor in the geographer's dimension',[67] but his own map of the routes of cultural diffusion, and his numerous comments on the relationships between Old and New World forms, show clearly enough that he is sensitive to the temporal as well as the spatial dimension. In essence, his focus on culture-areas is a matter of heuristic concentration, rather than exclusiveness, deriving in the first instance from his subject matter: physical objects occupy space rather than time, and when those objects have the relative and static permanence of buildings and the relatively slow rate of stylistic change characteristic of vernacular architecture, it is plausible to see them as indicative of contrastive regions.

However, Glassie's heuristic focus is less innocent than it might seem:

> In general, folk material exhibits major variation over space and minor variation through time, while the products of popular or academic culture exhibit minor variation over space and major variation through time. The natural divisions of folk material are, then, spatial, where the natural divisions of popular material are temporal; that is, a search for patterns in folk material yields regions, where a search for patterns in popular material yields periods.[68]

There are several problems here. First, and fundamentally, culture has no 'natural divisions'; its taxonomies are created from inside, by its members, or from outside, by students, but either way they are *created*, and reflect the intellectual and ethical predispositions of their authors rather than anything which is naturally the case. Plainly, Henry Glassie knows this; but the loose use of language serves, in practice though no doubt unintentionally, to obscure a conceptual difficulty.

Second, while it would be trivial to challenge a heuristic generalization on the grounds that 'major' and 'minor' are undefined – especially as the body of his essay is tacitly addressed to the problem, and obviously he is thinking in terms of a continuum – it is easy to adduce examples which Glassie would surely accept as folkloristic and which contradict his view. Monica Wilson's study of ritual change in southern Africa as a result of contact between an indigenous people and white settlers and missionaries clearly demonstrates major variation through time:

> The change is described in the area of largest interaction: the frontier between Nguni and whites. There the wedding cake, borrowed from Europe, becomes two, one for the groom and one for the bride, whose health and fertility is felt somehow to depend on the proper division and consumption of the cakes.[69]

This cannot be dismissed as acculturation. The Nguni have not simply permitted a European ritual to displace local practice. They have assimilated an aspect of it to their own system of values, adjusting it as necessary. Few cultures, if any, are hermetically sealed from contact with others, so the fact that this strange but satisfactory synthesis derives from the meeting of two very different civilizations is neither here nor there. Further, while it is hard to know for certain whether this example shows, in Glassie's terms, major or minor variation over space (in itself a reflection of the difficulty of actually applying such a schema), most observers would feel that space has much less to do with the question, given that the Nguni and the Europeans are living next door to each other in the same area, than the historical contact between two different social systems, one of which in practice dominates the other, so that its actions and symbols are seen as prestigious, though not so totally as to debar the subordinate people from a robust and creative exploitation of them for their own ends.

Many such examples could be drawn from the historical record of contact and interchange between natives and colonists, and such interchange is not all one-way. The Sioux borrowed the horse and the gun from the Europeans, and transformed their way of life in doing so.[70] The Indians of the Atlantic coast taught Europeans to smoke tobacco. But it is not necessary to go to exotic cases to challenge Glassie's generalization. Gerald Sider has shown that the celebration of Christmas in Newfoundland underwent major variation through time and only minor variation through space when, in the nineteenth century, the family fishery replaced the servant fishery as the basic mode of economic organization.[71]

Third, Glassie's methodological thesis rests on a major distinction between folk and popular which is itself deeply problematic. Among other things, while it may be true – and in certain respects demonstrably is true – that in its vernacular, non-market based manifestations, popular culture tends to have a slow rate of change, nevertheless it *does* change. Differential rates of change are a crucial object of cultural analysis, and it is impossible to accept a premise which excludes them from the theoretical framework.

This is not a claim for pre-eminence of the diachronic approach over other modes of analysis. Social anthropologists, faced with a lack or shallowness of written records appertaining to the peoples they study, have evolved a synchronic methodology concerned with the structures of social relationships and the functions of social acts. Geographers, basing their investigations on a network of (until recently) imperceptibly changing ecosystems, which must be studied in the field, take spatial comparisons and coeval events as their point of departure. Historians look at transformations through time, exploiting the rich documentation of literate cultures in order to do it. And so on. All of this is entirely reasonable, and in practice no scholar in any of these disciplines refuses to work in other dimensions (ultimately an impossibility, in any case) insofar as they may contribute to his or her main focus. And neither, in practice, does Henry Glassie. Yet that idea of a static, self-sufficient, grass-roots civilization remains central to his theoretical thinking, when arguably it is unnecessary to what, as a scholar, he actually does. It is doubtful if his rich discussion of the typology of rural and maritime material culture would be diminished by its not being referred to a general theory whose problems can only be escaped by assertion, and which is likely, in its connotations, to cloud issues of the actual colonization and re-colonization of the north American landmass by, in the first instance, European peoples and ideas, and, in the second, the home-grown products of the emergent Anglo-American hegemony.

It has been worth spending some time on Glassie's book because it illustrates so well the virtues, and the central fault, of the school of thought to which it belongs: a lively and well-informed sensitivity to questions of social ecology and the internal organization and interplay of local systems, coupled with an unwillingness to pose, at a theoretical level, the historical questions which empirically the work itself raises.

What Glassie has done on a regional scale, Alan Lomax has done on a global scale, and in a far more complex way, in the extraordinarily ambitious and challenging series of ethnomusicological studies which culminated in *Folk Song Style and Culture*. The basis of the enterprise is succinctly described by Lomax and a collaborator: 'from our ruling hypothesis, that song style reinforces and expresses the major abiding themes of culture, we set out to show that the patterning of similarities and dissimilarities among contemporary styles reproduces a faithful picture of world ethnohistory'.[72] In principle, any work which sets out to discover formal and substantive correlations between song as a social act and the society of which it is a part, and to demonstrate that 'esthetic style – the structural aspect of the beautiful – has a positive and dynamic relationship to the socially normative – the structural aspect of the good',[73] must be applauded as a constructive approach to artistic problems. And in practice the work offers stimulating generalization on, for example, the correlations between song styles, basic modes of subsistence, and sexual norms, even if, as more than one ethnomusicological reviewer has noted, its geographical conclusions concerning the division of the world into stylistic regions are self-evident where they are not questionable.[74]

What exactly, however, are 'abiding themes of culture'? And how are we to proceed when the culture we are studying tolerates (or does not tolerate, but cannot free itself from) 'themes' which are not merely different from but opposed to each other? Since this has certainly been the case, for a long time, in all the countries of the developed world, and is now very probably the case everywhere (there are very few isolated peoples left, and they get fewer every year as a result of genocide, accidental or calculated), the question is a reasonable one. May not a song style, in reinforcing and expressing one 'abiding theme' (democracy or sexual repression, for example), *ipso facto* subvert and reject another (autocracy or sexual liberation)? Lomax's formulation seems to imply that societies are ideally stable and conflict-free, which is to make the elementary error of confusing social and statistical norms. Finally, what precisely is this 'ethnohistory' that is somehow by definition different from 'history'? Perhaps it is just a technical branch of the discipline, like economic history or political history, devoted to the history of indigenous peoples. But if so, what would the ethnohistory of Britain or France be? Would it include the English and the French, or only the Welsh, the Highland Scots, the Bretons and the Basques? And if it would, what is it likely to tell us about the history of those two peoples, given that common ethnic indentity has stopped neither of them developing any number of internecine conflicts over which 'themes' should continue to 'abide'? Again, at bottom, we sense that the analysis stands upon an idealization: a stable, organic, self-regulating, and in principle unchanging community of common interest.

As one reviewer warily observed, the system must be 'verified or rejected at the level of analysis Lomax does not undertake – the gritty, detailed study of single music systems'.[75] At that level, questions arise very quickly indeed. Let us look, briefly, at what is said about Britain. The basic division which Lomax proposes is between two areas. One consists of Wales, the west and north of England, and the Hebrides (presumably the Highlands, which do not otherwise appear, are an accidental omission), in which an 'Old European' style exists.

This style is by characterized by a 'choral and cooperative' mode of deep, relaxed voices singing in blended unison, with polyphony (the simultaneous performance of different vocal and/or instrumental lines) a common feature. The other area, consisting of lowland Scotland and eastern and southern England, demonstrates the 'Modern European' style of harsh, solo voices with unblended unison or refrains, hypothetically derived from contact between the Old European style and the high-pitched, strident, solo mode of Eurasian musical culture.[76] It is very doubtful indeed that solo performance is any less common in the north and west of England than in the south and east, or, conversely, choral performance more common. Different modes of voice production are hardly noticeable enough, or consistent enough, to support geographical generalizations (in any case, recordings from the south and east, and from lowland Scotland, still hugely outnumber those from the other English-speaking areas), with the possible exception of the Highlands and Islands, which, we must grant, have supported a wholly different, albeit receding, culture to the present day. And, since the proposition is apparently that, at some stage, the south and east of England, along with lowland Scotland, abandoned a relaxed, deep-voiced, choral mode in favour of a tense, high-voiced, solo mode, where is the evidence, recorded or documentary, that this was the case?[77] And where is the evidence to show why the north of England, sandwiched between the two and in continuous cultural contact with both, did not? We may grant that popular polyphony is noteworthy in south Wales and south Yorkshire[78]; but this is to do with non-conformity and new traditions of worship, not to mention local choral societies, rather than with 'ethnohistory'. Of course we need, ultimately, to know why non-conformist hymnody and choral training apparently permeated the social life of those regions more thoroughly than that of others, but that is a question answerable only by detailed local and comparative research, not via a global schema; and in the meantime we may remind ourselves that popular polyphony is not unknown in the south.[79]

Thus far, in this discussion of American new folkloristics, we have considered cases where, methodologically, a socio-geographic focus has been given pre-eminence over an historical one while, at the same time, the thinking is underpinned by a generalized historicity eerily reminiscent of cultural evolutionism. That is one main trend. In another, linked to it, history disappears altogether.

The development of this position during the 1960s and early 1970s is easily traced by anyone who cares to read the *Journal of American Folklore,* particularly for the period 1968 to 1971. The concentration is on the text in its immediate context of performance, with an increasing tendency to see the object of study as the performance itself[80] as a 'complex communicative event'.[81] This is a very necessary shift of emphasis. The contentions of pioneers such as Phillips Barry and Herbert Halpert, that all oral tradition should be seen as a social process, not as a random collection of artefacts, and that vernacular understandings of cultural facts were essential to scholarly enquiry,[82] were taken up and incorporated into a methodology which laid emphasis on verbal play and rhetoric, on role-play and status relationships, on the individual aims and social functions of performance, and on the means and purposes of particular communications, within the dynamics of a complex social interaction.[83] The result was a number of studies of great ethnographic richness and analytical subtlety, such as Abrahams' account of urban black oral traditions[84] and Edward Ives' work on song-making in New England and maritime Canada[85] – researched and published, notably, during the conduct of the methodological debate in the learned journals: clear evidence of a healthy interplay between scholarly theory and practice.

Such was the explanatory force of this synchronic methodology for the microscopic examination of highly localized cultural events, and so vigorous the interplay between new field-procedures and novel analytic questions, that ultimately the object of study itself fell under question; and the shibboleth of folklore studies, the concept of tradition, was finally stripped of all meaning in 1971. Dan Ben-Amos's 'Toward a Definition of Folklore in Context'[86] argues rigorously, and rightly, that 'there is no dichotomy between processes and products. The telling is the tale; therefore the narrator, his story, and his audience are all related to each other as components of a single continuum, which is the communicative event'. He invokes the indigenous interpretation of such events to show that traditionality, far from being essential to them, is contingent upon genre and situation ('in past-oriented cultures, the sanction of tradition may be instrumental to the introduction of new ideas' whereas 'the lore of children derives its efficacy from its supposed newness'), and that, either way, tradition is 'an analytical construct... a scholarly and not a cultural fact'. Finally, and less rigorously, he asserts that 'Folklore ... is an artistic action'. On the basis of these propositions, he calculates that 'folklore is artistic communication in small groups'. We can safely leave it to students of magic and medicine to decide whether wart-cures either are art or are not folklore, a case which Ben-Amos does not pause to consider. Our concern here is to note two features of this definition.

The first of these we have been pursuing throughout this discussion. 'Tradition' is of course an analytical construct – so for that matter is Ben-Amos's definition, and that is in itself no reason to bar anything from further consideration. Everything exists in time, and every identification, vernacular or scholarly, of a 'tradition' – in art, in politics, in religion – constitutes a recognition of relationships over time, and of relationships which act, or have acted, as a relative constraint on behaviour at the historical juncture where the identification is situated. At the extreme, the wholesale acceptance or total rejection of such constraints would constitute respectively a thoroughly conservative or a thoroughly radical culture, which would necessarily affect crucially the nature of artistic communication, in small groups or big ones. To this extent, Ben-Amos's theoretical construct is ridiculous: it could not be put into practice. The voicing of it is merely the *reductio ad absurdum* of a useful scholarly tradition of synchronic study, vis-à-vis which Ben-Amos has adopted the position of extreme conservatism.

The second feature links Ben-Amos with Henry Glassie. What purports to be a 'definition of folklore' is actually a description of his preferred object of study: 'artistic communication in small groups'. It is easy and desirable enough to study that from any number of points of view, but there is no need to invoke the idea of 'folklore' at all in order to do it. Apparently by accident, Ben-Amos has deconstructed his discipline. It remains true, as we trust we have made clear, that the study of vernacular performance now requires a knowledge of the synchronic ethnographic studies of American folklorists – as even some social anthropologists, traditionally hostile to folklorists, recognize.[87] If we prefer to reinstate historical considerations, it is because we see society as by definition in a continuous state of change and struggle for change, and therefore view with suspicion any methodology which *ultimately* ignores or denies that (whatever it may reasonably and provisionally do for particular and local heuristic purposes). But the central concept of the rhetorical statement from a particular social position, and under the presure of particular social constraints, may readily be incorporated into an historical methodology, and, unsurprisingly, there have been occasional pleas for this among American folklorists too.[83]

Idealization of the world we have lost

We must return to stress the fact that vernacular social groups are never uniform and their members rarely co-equal. One of the ways in which the folk paradigm has worked ideologically – in the sense of promoting misrecognition and mystifications – has been in its concealment and displacement of class and patriarchal relations. The role which vernacular singing traditions may have in fostering and creating a sense of community does not occur in isolation from those unequal social relations; indeed, it is often contingent upon them and the tensions and conflicts they engender. Whether as a legacy of the folk paradigm, of sociological organicism or of anthropological functionalism, or as a consequence of the reductionist application of structuralist methodology, notions of homogeneity among vernacular social groups or communities, of unified world views and of cognitive poverty or simplicity continue to creep back into the discourse of folkloristics. Vernacular popular groupings are invariably hierarchically ranked and distinguished internally by relative positions of advantage. Song texts themselves work upon this reality. For instance, in an illuminating contextualist study of English popular songs concerning gender relations and roles, Vic Gammon has shown that these have worked historically to conserve and reproduce, for the most part, the patriarchal structure of early modern and modern society. The uncritical celebration of 'traditional' songs risks the continued reproduction of attitudes and ideas about appropriate gender roles which women today rightly find repressive.[89] In a similarly exemplificatory essay, Dave Harker has shown how a celebrated group of songs in the industrial North East existed as a symptom of intra-generational and class rivalry among Tyneside youth groups during the early nineteenth century.[90] The songs 'ritually pilloried' one kind of worker – the collier lad – in the interests of a petty bourgeois stratum of tradesmen and clerks, thus working to reinforce an endemic feature of class consciousness in capitalist society: deference to those above one's own position in the hierarchy of class relations, and hostility to those below.

We have emphasized that consideration of the structural context is axiomatic to our approach to the study of the vernacular milieu, and that by the same token transformations in the structural context need to be understood in relation to responses from within vernacular milieux, whether in the form of actual retaliation or in the symbolic affirmations of community and tradition. In this latter respect we would agree with Anthony Cohen when he says that 'the greater the pressure on communities to modify their structural forms to comply more with those elsewhere, the more are they inclined to reassert their boundaries *symbolically* by imbuing these modified forms with meaning and significance which belies their appearance'. Community therefore, 'whether local or ethnic, or in whatever form, need not ... be seen as an anachronism in urban-industrial society. Rather, it should be regarded as one of the modalities of behaviour available within such societies'.[91] Quite so: yet, as we have indicated, the assumption of a 'lost community' associated with traditional society, and a desire somehow to regain it in contemporary social life, runs very deep in Western thought and culture. What this assumption presupposes is that historically there is a fundamental cleavage between traditional and modern societies, and in the work (or subsequent application of it) of Maine, Tönnies, Durkheim, Weber and the Chicago school of sociology, this assumption gave rise to a series of conceptual polarities:

> Status and contract, *Gemeinschaft* and *Gesellschaft*, mechanical and organic solidarity, informal and formal groups, primary and secondary groups, culture and civilisation, traditional and bureaucratic authority, sacral and secular associations, military and industrial society, status group and class – all these pairs of concepts represent as many attempts to grasp the structural change of the institutional framework of a traditional society on the way to becoming a modern one.[92]

These opposed categories are germane to the same historical process, and represent different ways of trying to encapsulate the fundamentally antagonistic dimensions of the modern experience. While they have been and remain of undoubted value in the analysis of social change, the danger of these opposed categories is that they can set up an either/or dichotomy between two types of society. It was precisely such a dichotomy which informed the nineteenth century development of ideas about 'folk' culture. Such culture was that of the small rural community, a culture that had irrevocably passed and left only tantalizing survivals, and its opposite was the rampantly commercial culture of the industrial town, synonymous with moral degeneration and a decline in artistic standards, feeding off the malaise of uprootedness, anomie and fragmented social bonding.[93] The idealization of community was therefore fundamental to the idea of 'folk'.

As we have seen, this idealization was dependent on the erroneous notions that rural social relationships of the past were less complex and more equal than those of contemporary urban society, and that processed (urban) culture inevitably corrupts lived (rural) culture. At the same time such idealization was made in a backward-looking reaction to the adverse social consequences attendant on the development and consolidation of industrial capitalism, and to perceived aesthetic decadence in the realm of high culture. It was part of a bourgeois taking-of-cultural-stock that provided a mythic base for the establishment of a conservative, pseudo-feudalist sense of Englishness. England in the late nineteenth century was a world of collapsing values, a decaying world impeded by the fear of developing new values appropriate to a new world that appeared 'powerless to be born'. The attempt to locate and tap an essential racial/rural stratum of national character and culture was a major response to this crisis. The quest was for a more stable and self-confident past capable of reconstruction, and as a result it is from this period that many ancient English customs and traditions derive.[94] The triumphant proclamation of the virtues of Progress switched to an accent on social nostalgia. The cultivation of economic dynamism was compromised by a celebration of moral stability as it had been of yore, in the ' "collective, unalienated folk society", rooted in time and space, bound together by tradition and by stable, local ties, and symbolised by the village'. The 'traditional village community was seen as the cell from which English society had been built up, remaining, through its decline, the "fly-wheel" of national life', the 'repository of the moral character of the nation'.[95] The image of country life and rustic values became remade in compensation for the ravages of industrialism and the anarchic forces of capital accumulation and reproduction.

The ideology of ruralism and 'the folk' was not of course confined to the anti-urban crowd sentimentality of Tory nostalgia. It had its radical utopian dimensions as well. The rural folk community offered a vision of 'fraternity, the devolution of power, emotional involvement, participatory democracy'.[96] There were numerous and varied manifestations of folk celebrationism: the genteel antiquarian collection of country lore, the growth of the rural novel and country writing extolling sturdy 'peasant' virtues and 'haunts of ancient peace', pastoralist painting and photography, parochial and regional histories, paternalist village Arcadianism and the bourgeois reformation of 'immemorial' customs and rituals, preservationism, Gothicism (pre-1870), cottage-style gardening, the Arts and Crafts inititaive, and Morris's communist prefigurations. The construction of a national 'folk' song tradition was part and parcel of this heterogeneous ruralist movement, and it found adherents right across the political spectrum.[97] What has to be stressed is that the attachment to the past, and to a South of England paradigm of the countryside, 'had different meanings and uses because various individuals and groups interpreted the meaning of tradition and the demands of modernity in very different ways indeed'.[98]

It is easy to note with hindsight the inconsistencies involved in its conservative advocacy. The effort to utilize 'folk' culture in rejuvenating and reforming contemporary life sat uneasily with the social Darwinism of the day and the evolutionist conception of cultural development. The view of rural labourers as illiterate, ignorant, dim-witted and dirt-ridden was coextensive with their portrayal as 'peasants', associated with simplicity, innocence, purity, goodness and attachment to the soil. Genteel versions of traditionalism served both as a source of fond regret and a yardstick for backwardness, unenlightenment and folly. What such antinomies amounted to was a conception of 'the folk' and 'folk culture' as the Other of bourgeois society and culture, delivering, in positive and negative modes, an ideological articulation of social conscience and ruling class rationale. This articulation had its parallels in representations of the urban proletariat and in the iconography of blacks.[99] Such constructions provided similar antitheses to the dominant culture, in senses both benign and malign: degenerate and brutish images on the one hand, sentimentalized objects of social pity and philanthopy on the other. While the oscillation between these kinds of twinned contrarieties displayed an identical movement, there were of course radical differences in the ways these particular conceptions were put to use. In the case of 'folk' and its antinomies, conservative understandings were rooted in a mystical apprehension of the 'soul' of the English race, and as such could be variously utilized in the causes of class conciliation, cultural reformation and nationalist mobilization.

The assemblage of an English folk song tradition occurred as part of a conscious manufacture (though by no means uniformly conceived) of a national musical culture, and involved a concerted effort to remould the popular in the image of the dominant culture. What was then presented was a travesty of the actual musical culture of the people, and this was then relayed back, through its extractions and abstractions, as the 'real' song culture of the English, part of the 'genuine folk tradition' that was in danger of becoming buried beneath the sham popular culture of the town with its music halls, beer-houses, race-meetings, football, and sensationalist popular press. What was being celebrated was a hegemonic reconstruction of the song culture of everyday life.[100]

The development of the folk construct and of traditionalist values during the second half of the nineteenth century occurred initially as an undertow of the bourgeois critique of custom and tradition, and then grew subsequently into a counterflow of cultural reconstructionism. A way of life was sentimentally extolled from positions of privilege and comfort that had been gained through the erosion and marginalization of that way of life. Regret was expressed for a perceived social stability of the past destroyed by the process of modernization whose choicest fruits had fallen into bourgeois hands. The unleashing of productive forces based on an instrumentalist means-end logic and competitive individualism had been dependent on the critique of custom and tradition as the main frameworks for action and legitimation. Against the threat of mass democracy, the subsequent transformation of conceptions of tradition and traditionality was then an attempt to resuscitate, in a changed social formation and for the benefit of a newly ascendant dominant class, the institutional structures by which power in pre-industrial England had been transmuted into legitimate authority.

Looking ahead to the past

Yet this celebration of an invented popular tradition cannot simply be dismissed in those terms. We need to understand its development not only as a crucial process of mediation and struggle: what was also being expressed was a discontent with modernity, the feeling that economic growth and social change had been made at the expense of old ties, loyalties and values, that the present was divorced from the past, community relations had become fragmented, release from traditional bonds had produced loneliness, rootlessness and anomie rather than freedom, and the sense of belonging to a natural and cosmic order had been sacrificed at the altar of scientific rationality. The world had lost its enchantment. The fascination with 'folklore', with traditionalized song, was rooted in these feelings of dislocation and alienation.

The whole idea of a traditional society, of the need for a sense of continuity and a settled way of life, only arises and makes sense in relation to its antithesis: the experience of modernity's frenetic rhythm and relentless pace, its incessant demand for innovation and its denunciation of any resistance to techno-social change as Luddite. Constant transformation of the means of production, and hence of all productive and social relationships, is, as Marx first diagnosed, axiomatic to capitalist formations:

> Constant revolutionising of production, uninterrupted disturbance of all social conditions, everlasting uncertainty and agitation, distinguish the bourgeois epoch from all earlier ones. All fixed, fast-frozen relationships with their train of venerable ideas and opinions, are swept away, all new-formed ones become antiquated before they can ossify. All that is solid melts into air, all that is holy is profaned, and men are at last forced to face with sober senses the real conditions of their lives and their relations with their kind.[101]

Marx's prophetic assertion that the scales will inevitably fall from people's eyes as a result of immersion in the whirlpool of modern life is debatable, but his conception of the dynamism of capitalist economic and social development has never been excelled. It is the contradictory nature of such development which is crucial:

> In our days everything seems pregnant with its contrary. Machinery, gifted with the wonderful power of shortening and fructifying human labour, we behold starving and overworking it. The new-fangled sources of wealth, by some weird spell, are turned into sources of want. The victories of art seem bought by the loss of character. At the same pace that mankind masters nature, man seems to become enslaved to other men or to his own infamy. Even the pure light of science seems unable to shine but on the dark background of ignorance. All our invention and progress seem to result in endowing material forces with intellectual life, and stultifying human life into a material force.[102]

It is in this brilliant evocation of the experience of modernity that we gain a sense of the dialectical movements and shifts that are involved. We do not get the utter displacement of certain aspects of that experience entirely to the past, which are then idealized as the opposite pole to other aspects of the experience, confined to the present and at the heart of our malaise. These different aspects, the conceptual polarities of classical sociology, do not signify historical incompatibilities but enduring conflicting social tendencies. The weight and force of such tendencies is never equivalent at any one time, but the ascendant existence of one does not imply the utter abrogation of the other; rather, they develop in a movement of constantly varying relationship with each other. The basic conceptual distinction devised by Habermas in his work on modern culture – between 'rational-purposive action' and 'communicative action' – has also been criticized for excessive polarization: the two do not easily separate out in empirical terms.

> Rather than concrete acts being instances of rational-purposive behaviour *or* communicative behaviour, both types of behaviour may be mixed together in any specific act or event. The distinction between rational-purposive action and communicative action may be useful, not as a classificatory device, but as an analytic distinction highlighting different *dimensions* of behaviour.[103]

The danger lies in flattening out and rendering static the uneven relations between such contrary dimensions of action and experience for the sake of a preconceived thesis. All too often we are confronted with analytical perspectives which adopt a once-and-for-all outlook of *either* cultural pessimism *or* cultural optimism – either a bleak Marcusian view of one-dimensionality or a blithe McLuhanesque view of a post-Gutenberg galaxy – each closing the other out and prohibiting any conceptual transaction.

The success of any critical cultural movement or theory depends on keeping the contradictory forces manifest in modern life simultaneously in view, rather than cleaving to one or other polarized position, for the experience of modernity is both emancipatory and destructive: it consists of both these tendencies at the same time, pushing and pulling against one another and creating a constant sense of disturbance, conflict, jarring ambivalence. The uncritical or idealized celebration of community and of vernacular cultures on the left – in Merrie Englandism, post-war 'folk' revivalism or sixties counterculture – have singularly failed in this regard. Such celebration as reaction to the costs of modernity 'leads to a logic of local defence against the outside world, rather than a challenge to the workings of that world'. The 'emotional logic of community, beginning as a resistance to the evils of modern capitalism, winds up as a bizarre kind of depoliticised withdrawal; the system remains intact, but maybe we can get it to leave our piece of turf untouched'.[104] The inadequacies of certain community-orientated initiatives and projects, such as the sentimentally anarchistic commune movement, feminist community activism,[105] community crime-control[106] and – in the case of the popular arts – community art and the bunker mentality manifest in the folk club 'community of the already converted',[107] have become all to obvious: under the current restructuring of capital no piece of cherished turf is sacrosanct. The quest for community can simply become yet another way of dreaming of flowerbeds of ease in the middle of a burning field.

It remains true, as Octavio Paz has put it, that modernity is 'cut off from the past and continually hurtling forward at such a dizzy pace that it cannot take root, that it merely survives from one day to the next: it is unable to return to its beginnings and thus recover its powers of renewal'.[108] The fact that an espousal of what has become conceptually ossified as 'folk' song is often a sentimentalist reaction to this traumatic experience of historical process should not have as its necessary corollary the denial of any exploration of what, how, when, where and why ordinary people sing for themselves among themselves, outside of the context of a culture of mass distribution and consumption, with its ideology of stardom and success. Contrariwise, that exploration should not be fuelled by a blanket condemnation of modernism, or mass culture. Modernization has brought both rewards and penalties, relief and regret: the liberation from morally claustrophobic local groupings and the loss of community; the breakdown of social inhibitions on solitude in popular life and the privatization of that life; the exhilaration of new urban forms of cultural experience and the mental anguish of anonymity in the metropolis; the growth of cultural imperialism and the internationalization of cultural life; the widening of intellectual horizons and the loss of, indeed the impossibility of, moral certainty; the 'desire to be rooted in a stable and coherent personal and social past', and the 'insatiable desire for growth – not merely for economic growth but for growth in experience, in pleasure, in knowledge, in sensibility – growth that destroys both the physical and social landscapes of the past, and our emotional links with those lost worlds'[109] We need to retain a sense of these contradictory forces in developing a proper conceptualization of song as vernacular communication, as a form of cultural process alternative to the production of cultural commodities, because pleasure in and identification with that form corresponds to real – if not realized – needs in the experience of modern life: the need for achieved community, for social and geographical roots, and a sense of non-vicarious participation in cultural practice and cultural tradition.

The postwar 'Folksong' revival

The attraction of songs of the past or songs connoting pastness remains lodged in the reassuring psychological and affective balm they continue to offer for the anxieties that accrue from the constant disruption of what has seemed stable and durable. Even though this turbulent motion has been experienced for generations, each generation feels anew the ever-onward march of change and destruction. The devaluation of forms of co-presence upon which song in vernacular cultures centrally pivots imparts to them a new symbolic significance. Group identification with particular songs from the past provides ballast to memory as it rides the waves of incessantly changing chart-busters and new star sensations, though this only becomes marked with the onset of age or the conscious affiliation to what are regarded as non-commercial forms of song and music on the part of socially disenchanted groups. The durable *needs* the ephemeral, and ephemerality in popular culture has long brought its own rewards: the danger of cleavage to one or the other perpetuates the duality of conservative elitism and romantic populism. The pleasures and satisfactions derived from the immediate consumption of commercially processed popular music are different to those derived from the reproduction of material from the past in lived cultures, and are in many ways defined by that difference. But the point is not to elevate one above the other in the name of a dogmatically asserted 'authenticity', in either glorification of or repulsion from the turmoil of modernity.[110] What is sought in songs of past times we have never personally known is a sense of identity in relation to difference with what has gone before. Continuity is established with those who produced these songs in ways of life long disappeared, and this produces a way of assimilating the transformations that have endlessly ensued. What is provided may be a source of compensatory meaning for our own feelings of loss, violation and anxiety about our place in the historical process, but what is also involved is a way of negotiating that process through a counter process of traditionalization, which so often serves to make a deficient 'now' unequal to a sanctified 'then'. While these identifications may be partially or wholly delusory, the feelings that generate them are not. Songs of past times assimilated into vernacular cultures and then performed or attended to within succeeding periods bestow 'an aesthetic correlative', fulfilling a social function in 'focusing the emotional conceptions of a particular culture' in any particular present.[111] What is then also important is how this aesthetic correlative is deployed politically. In relation to a whole body of song of past times, the two 'folk song' revivals provide object lessons in the different ways this can happen.

The paradoxical quality, or even double-think, identified here as characteristic of the 'Folk-Lore' movement in the later decades of the nineteenth and earlier decades of the twentieth centuries finds its counterpart in the postwar, second revival. Partly, of course, this is because the second revival unavoidably had its intellectual roots in the first, and specifically in the documents which the first had beqeathed: (i) the collections, both manuscript and printed (as a generalization, it was a little while before postwar folksong enthusiasts began to *listen* systematically to the recordings of country singers and musicians made by Grainger and later by the BBC – they were not easily available until the initiatives of Caedmon, Topic and Leader in the 1960s and 1970s – and when they did, it was often, initially, with a sense of shock at the alien-sounding styles, so different from the sound-ideal of folk-clubs and the studio-recordings of professional revivalists); (ii) the learned articles, notably in the *Journal of the Folk-Song Society* and its successor, and the monographs of Sharp and the ballad-scholars. But there is more to it than this, for the second revival did not take on wholesale the ideological and institutional baggage left behind by the first. Some, indeed, was curtly, not to say with drunken ribaldry, thrown overboard. Out went expurgated texts, and in came the bawdy and erotic *ad infinitum* and sometimes *ad nauseum* (James Reeves' partly useful, partly crack-brained anthologies played a special part here[112]). In came 'industrial songs' under the influence of Lloyd and MacColl.[113] Out, in general, went both the actuality and the ethos of parlours, pianos and floral prints. In, crucially, came the folk song club, characteristically located in the convenient assembly-room of a public house, where performers and enthusiasts could congregate informally in a setting which had the various advantages of being agreeable in itself (to all but teetotallers), open to the public, usually free to the club (most licensees were happy to see their turnover increase by anything from a couple of dozen to a couple of hundred drinkers weekly), and a direct link with the historical performance-context of the songs and tunes themselves.

Institutionally, the folk club may reasonably be regarded as progressive. It was cheap (sometimes free) to get into. It was broadly egalitarian (there were status distinctions within it, as John Smith's essay shows, but, as institutions go, it was among the more free and easy and comradely). Usually it was cooperative in organization, and largely non-profit making (profits made on a 'singers' night', i.e. a meeting without a booked guest artist, or by raising the price for charismatic performers such as MacColl and Seeger, were likely to be ploughed back into the club, to cover less financially successful bookings). The professionalism (quite often part-time) of the booked artists took the form of self-employment within a loosely-linked network of break-even collectives staffed by volunteers. Strangers, newcomers, and inexperienced performers were usually welcome, and offered a spot, even at the cost of the regular local floor-singers, and the response to their performance was likely to be tolerant if not generous. Young performers were encouraged to gain confidence and expertise in front of an audience. Further, folk clubs concentrated within themselves a great deal of creative energy. This was manifest in performance itself, in the need to extend the personal repertory to accommodate overlapping with other people and avoid the boredom of too-regular repetition, and in the creation of new songs and tunes. Ewan MacColl could no doubt have coped as a songwriter without the folk club, but it provided an important – perhaps, initially, essential – stimulus and support for the likes of Leon Rosselson, Ian Campbell and Johnny Handle – and here we are talking only of well-known names, not of the unknown number of singer-songwriters whose work was important locally. Creative energy was further manifest in the dissemination of songs, tunes, information, ideas and debate through the large number of little magazines associated with or sold in the clubs. These ranged from the internationally distributed *Sing Out* (published in New York) and *Sing* (published in London), through regionally-based but more widely distributed titles such as the Liverpool-edited and published *Spin*, to the (largely) local-market publications of the regional branches of the English Folk Dance and Song Society (e.g. the West Riding's *Tykes' News*) or university folksong societies (e.g. Oxford's *Heritage* and Leeds' *Abe's Folk Music*). Finally, the folk club movement incorporated a powerful radical strain, both consciously defined and, to a degree, managed by politically active artists such as Lloyd, MacColl and Campbell (or, from a different political tradition, the Quaker publisher and songwriter Sidney Carter), and relatively unconscious, in the attendance and support of large numbers of young people of left-wing sympathies.

Institutionally, then, the folk club had the potential to provide a basis for the development of socialist artistic practice, particularly through what might be termed its cabaretic function. Itinerant professional and semi-professional makers and performers could be drawn together with local amateurs, intellectuals as well as worker-performers and poets such as the late Jack Elliott and Ed Booth, of Birtley, Co. Durham, on a basis of relatively informal and free exchange of artistic ideas within a framework which was oppositional both generally (the structure of the institution itself ran counter to the prevailing trend of twentieth-century cultural life) and particularly (in its embracing and providing a forum for particular political movements of a popular front kind, such as the Campaign for Nuclear Disarmament in the 1960s).

Sadly, its artistic and ultimately its ideological base was something quite different. Here, the modified subscription to the old 'folk' paradigm (its modifications notwithstanding) contributed only to sterile debates about authenticity, in everything from substance to style, leading, at worst, to a purist version of cultural nationalism more reactionary than anything Cecil Sharp and his colleagues could have dreamed of. One might think it bad enough that the piano was scorned as a bourgeois imposition upon authentic folk music. It was, after all, a favourite working class instrument for informal sing-songs and dancing, and the pub assembly-rooms which housed folk-clubs usually had one. But worse still it became, in some quarters, heretical to accompany 'English' songs on non-English instruments such as the guitar and banjo – both of them in great supply because of the skiffle movement in which many folk club performers had served their apprenticeship – or even to accompany them at all. An analogous idea which gained great currency during the mid-to-late 1960s was that performers should sing only songs or versions of songs from their nation or even region of origin. As a matter of taste, this may have had a desirable effect in diminishing the number of performances in an assumed Lallans or Appalachian accent. But its correspondence to the actual workings of the tradition which the clubs purported to be reviving (even in its mostly heavily mediated and idealized form) is obviously nil. And, could the principle ever have been carried through to its logical conclusion, performance of any kind would have been virtually ruled out. How long before the undeniable gender dichotomy in British vernacular performance practice was invoked to prevent a man singing songs his mother taught him? Extreme, obviously, and absurd, and it could not be put into practice, or not fully. But pressure was, intermittently and selectively, brought to bear upon the playing of exotic instruments and the singing of exotic songs; and that such self-evidently ludicrous, authoritarian, and ultimately self-defeating ideas should have been current at all in a liberally organized institution brings into sharp relief the internal tension of the movement, and its consequent inadequacy as a basis for artistic progress. This was compounded by the fact that, because of its essential commitment to the first revival's notion of folk tradition, the second revival could cope with proletarian culture, rural as well as urban, only by the device of idealization, both positive and negative. The miner, the sailor, the farmworker, were working class heroes, inheritors of a rich and vigorous and strongly rooted expressive and political tradition: they were also the defeated victims of acculturation, no longer able even to distinguish between the gems of the 'folk' song tradition and the gew-gaws of Tin Pan Alley.

It may be an over-simplification to say that the second revival was a progressive institution housing a reactionary ideology, but that remains to be shown.[114]

John Smith's essay discusses one club which has attempted to come to terms with this dilemma by modifying its conception of what it is appropriate to sing, and how, while retaining the basic institutional format. Its inclusion here, with a set of essays otherwise concerned with subjects more familiar to readers of the literature of vernacular song (historical settings, both rural and urban; the singing traditions of travellers, of north country farmers, of agricultural labourers) is intended to signal a shift of emphasis in what may broadly be termed the contextualist approach to vernacular culture. This is an approach which locates meaning in relationships within actual social situations.[115] The methodological focus on artistic performance in small groups, within a defined social framework (whether *in the first instance* historical or anthropological) remains the same whether the concern is with the relatively old-fashioned performance context of a shepherds' meet in a moorland pub, or the relatively new institution of an urban folk club which has restyled itself as a 'live music club'. That there are sociological differences between them is self-evident, and a reading of Smith's essay and Ian Russell's provides some elucidation of these. It is not our intention to sweep them under the carpet, for such distinctions are crucial. However, the recognition of similarities, as well as differences, undermines the exclusive notions of 'tradition' and 'revival', of the 'authentic' and the 'inauthentic', which have hitherto bedevilled the study of popular culture, not least in the influential science of folkloristics. An exclusive definition of 'tradition' would rule out the central subject matter of Russell's essay (popular parody) just as much as of Smith's.

Envoie

This volume contributes via the study of one particular medium to the exploration of the dynamics of vernacular cultures and traditions. The power and importance of popular song and music lie in the inability of its commercial production to control how it is consumed and how meanings are made out of it in the course of everyday life. Vernacular cultures have not been wholly subsumed into mass commodity culture, despite – in some respects because of – the threat of a universalization of the marketplace. The two react against each other, colliding into and at certain points galvanizing each other in a continual process of tension and contradiction. As Christopher Lasch has put it, contemporary cultural criticism should not only attend to mass culture and the tradition of debate about it; it should also examine 'the persistence of allegedly outmoded forms of particularism ... that have not only proved resistant to the melting pot but continue to provide people with the psychological and spiritual resources essential for democratic citizenship and for a truly cosmopolitan outlook, as opposed to the deracinated, disoriented outlook that is so often confused, nowadays, with intellectual liberation'.[116] Anyone who is concerned with ideas and action directed towards the emergence of a truly alternative society to that obtaining under a capitalist economy ignores these persistences at their peril.

Notes

1 Braverman 1974: ch.13.
2 Adorno and Horkheimer 1979: 158.
3 Mierge 1979: 310.
4 Fox and Lears 1983: xii.
5 Williams 1975b: 128.
6 Chaney and Pickering 1986: 36.
7 Gramsci 1985: 195.
8 McQuail 1983: 35.
9 Goffman 1961: 18.
10 Willis 1977: 169. Cf Hoggart 1969: ch. 3. The distinction between 'them' and 'us' is never total: there is always something of 'them' in 'us' and this makes for internal division in any subordinate group describing itself as 'us'.
11 Chaplin 1972: 101.
12 Sennett and Cobb 1977.
13 Lasch 1981: 22.
14 Propp 1968.
15 Lord 1960.
16 Propp 1968: 23.
17 Propp 1968: 19–20.
18 Levi-Strauss 1965.
19 Dundes 1965: 207.
20 Mann, cited in Plant 1974: 14.
21 Williams 1976: 66.
22 Hillery 1955.
23 Bell and Newby 1975: 21.
24 Plant 1974: 28.
25 Stacey 1974: 13–26. Terms take their meanings not from any immutable relationship with objective reality, but from their use in discourse. It may sometimes be necessary to abandon them because, in a given context, they are irretrievably misleading. Here, we need some word to set against the large-scale structural abstraction of 'society', and 'community' is the best we have.
26 Elias 1974: xix.
27 It should perhaps be noted that 'although a group may be a community, a community can be a unit comprising several groups, or can be a stratum. The community is therefore not necessarily characterized by the "face-to-face" relationship; all we can say is that the community relationship is necessarily valid in "face-to-face" formulations as well'. Heller 1984: 35.
28 Elias 1974: xx-xxii.
29 Elias 1974: xxxii-xxxiii.
30 Elias 1974: xxviii. Elias adds (xxvii) that insofar as women have been and continue to be more involved in the personal and local sphere, then they are likely to be 'more closely bounded by community ties'.
31 Bott 1957: 100.
32 Frankenberg 1973: 248–52.

33   See Pahl 1968a.
34   See Williams 1975a: 131.
35   Watson 1964.
36   Heller 1984: 39.
37   Pahl 1968b: 293.
38   Cohen A. 1982: 13.
39   Cohen A. 1982: 16.
40   Cohen A. 1985: 21.
41   Geertz 1975: 5.
42   Wolf, cited in Whitten and Szwed 1970: 10.
43   Whitten and Szwed 1970: 10.
44   Dewey, cited in Geertz 1975: 45.
45   Malraux 1951: 487.
46   Harker 1985b.
47   Thomson 1975.
48   See Pickering 1982: 180 for references. Stephens 1986 appeared too late for assimilation into our argument.
49   Korson 1938 and 1943; Lloyd 1952; for earlier work on industrial traditions in Germany, see bibliography to Heilfurth 1954.
50   Rollins 1924.
51   Robbins 1952; Greene 1962.
52   Wright 1860.
53   Child nos. 161 and 162; Rollins 1924: no. 285.
54   Ferris 1970: 87–98; Glassie 1970; McCormack 1969; Oliver 1984; Pegg 1984; Pickering 1986a; Wilgus 1968.
55   Ong 1982.
56   Green 1971.
57   Elbourne 1975: 15.
58   cf Ostendorf 1982: 26–28 on Afro-American popular culture.
59   cf Anderson's 'Law of Self-Correction', Anderson 1923: 397–403; Glassie 1970: 41.
60   See Bailey 1986, Bratton 1986, Laing 1985.
61   Lentricchia 1983: 141.
62   Williams 1977: 116.
63   Bourdieu and Passeron 1977: 40.
64   Elbourne 1980: 114.
65   MacIntyre 1982: 222–3.
66   Dorson 1972: 1–50.
67   Glassie 1971: 33–4.
68   Glassie 1971: 33.
69   Wilson 1972: 188.
70   Utley 1963.
71   Sider 1976.
72   Lomax 1976: 75.
73   Lomax 1967: 216.
74   See Nettl 1970: 438–41.
75   Merriam 1969: 387.
76   Lomax 1959: 935–7.
77   The detailed work is yet to be done on the popular singing styles of Britain which would answer these questions, and confirm or assuage these doubts. But that is the

point: Lomax's grand generalizations and our reservations rest on the same evidence.

78　See Russell 1970, 1973, and Russell and Leader 1974.

79　Copper 1971.

80　Hymes 1962 was a formative influence.

81　Georges 1969: 317.

82　Halpert 1939, brief and modest as it is, remains one of the best contributions to the humanistic ethnography of singing traditions. Barry's insights are scattered and fragmented: the best summary is in Wilgus 1959.

83　See especially Abrahams 1968 and 1972.

84　Abrahams 1963.

85　Ives 1964 and 1971.

86　Ben-Amos 1972.

87　See Finnegan 1977.

88　Joyner 1975; Límon 1983.

89　Gammon 1982.

90　Harker 1985a.

91　Cohen A. 1985; 44, 117.

92　Habermas 1971: 91.

93　For reasons of space, it is not possible here to situate ideas about cultural and artistic decline more fully within the variety and complexity of contemporary debate on cultural standards. Lowenthal and Lawson 1963 provides a useful survey of this debate.

94　See Hobsbawm and Ranger.

95　Weiner 1981: 42, 51, 56. Note the criticism of 'the fatal flaw' in Weiner's book, in Wright 1985: 128. See also Dellheim 1985.

96　Cohen S. 1985: 119.

97　This movement belongs of course to a wider cultural tradition and context, to which Williams 1961 remains the best introduction; but see also Heyck 1982: ch. 7.

98　Dellheim 1985: 235.

99　See Keating 1971, and Pickering 1986d.

100　'Dominant groups can revitalise a hegemonic culture by incorporating what they imagine to be the instinctual vitality of the lower orders ... No top-down model of domination can explain the complex growth, dissolution, or transformation of hegemonic cultures.' Jackson Lears 1985: 587.

101　From *The Communist Manifesto* as in the translation by Berman 1983: 95.

102　Cited in Berman 1983: 20.

103　Wuthnow *et al.*1984: 236.

104　Sennett 1977: 295–6.

105　Chamberlain 1986.

106　Cohen S. 1985: ch. 4.

107　Rosselson 1979: 50.

108　Cited in Berman 1983: 35.

109　Berman 1983: 35.

110　For elaboration see Pickering 1986c.

111　Buchan 1968: 40.

112　Reeves 1958 and 1960.

113　Both via their performance practice, and as a result of Lloyd 1952 and MacColl n.d. and 1954.

114 This is not, obviously, intended as a full and final account of the second revival, the history of which is yet to be written. Our observations are made largely on our experience as participants in it, which includes performance (professional and amateur), club organization, and journalism, as well as audience-participation. The only book so far devoted to it, Woods 1979, is a brief introduction to a lot of personalities (mostly performers) and some places, and has some information on finance, but is otherwise of little worth. We have couched our remarks in the past tense not because the second revival is dead, but because its hey-day is past (the number of clubs has diminished during the 1980s) and because our close involvement in it is not up to date.

115 For elaboration see Pickering 1986d.

116 Lasch 1981: 89.

2 The Past as a Source of Aspiration: Popular Song and Social Change

MICHAEL PICKERING

Haveth ynowe and seythe Hoo.

John Ball

A leading consideration in cultural analysis is the interplay between continuity and change, both actually, at the level of social relationships, and symbolically, through the representation of those relationships in works of art. This is not confined to the field of popular culture: the question of classic status within élite literature, or, more generally the relationship between a literary work's moment of creation and its potentially infinite number of subsequent moments of reception, often over very long periods of time and through many changing social contexts and shifts of consciousness, are crucial problems in literary history as conventionally understood. However, the problem is particularly acute in a field of study where the notion of 'tradition' has for so long been a central heuristic concept.

Michael Pickering's essay focuses on a dialogic ballad extant from the seventeenth century, which seems to have achieved something close to classic status in the late nineteenth century, among the dwindling group of small farmers and the growing number of agricultural wage-labourers in the south midlands. The analysis is a challenge to the oft-criticized but still powerful notion of popular tradition as an unambiguously conservative process of serial repetition. A song-text may well be so established as to be relatively invariant – probably through frequent reprinting in cheap format – yet we cannot assume that its reception by singers, listeners (and indeed readers) is likewise invariant. A ballad which, at its moment of production, has a simple symmetry of message in attributing its dialogue to two equally identifiable contemporary social types, has become asymmetrical two centuries later through the virtual disappearance of one of them in the region under discussion, under the pressure of the capitalist reorganization of agriculture. Thus, though its form, looked at outside historical context, be ostensibly the same, its meanings – which, as with any work of art, can only be defined as its relationships to the known world – must have undergone a shift; and it is to this shift that the essay is addressed. In practice, the small farmers and farm-labourers of Oxfordshire appropriated the ballad as an element in their diverse, and not always coherent, critique of a world that was changing at others' behest and in others' interests.

The essay shows clearly that there is no simple and absolute demarcation between conservative and radical functions in popular culture. The 'retrospective idealisation' of a vanished world (just as common, as the opening essay of this book has shown, among twentieth-century scholars as among nineteenth-century labourers) carries with it the danger of blocking constructive movement into the future. But it may also, under the more urgently pressing circumstances of the immediate present, help construct and maintain a defiant self-respect in the face of a dominant class's contempt, which is in itself a vital element in the effort to create new and better ways of thinking and being.

In 1873, just prior to the formation of the National Agricultural Labourers' Union, an unemployed North Oxfordshire farmworker wrote a letter to his local newspaper. He was, he said, out of work 'to suit the farmer's pleasure'. He complained bitterly of 'those who have plenty'. The rich and leisured members of society had simply no need to think about the misery of forced unemployment for an impoverished worker and his family. We have, he concluded, 'been a downtrodden class of men that all other classes are depending on for their bread, and yet we have not been treated with respect'[1]

This chapter is concerned essentially with one question: why was a seventeenth century ballad sung in rural working class groups in the late nineteenth century? The ballad in question was known as 'The Husbandman and the Servantman'. It takes the form of a dialogue between a husbandman farmer and a servant to the gentry and aristocracy. Its concern is with the relative merits of their respective callings and life-styles. The servant attempts to persuade the husbandman to abandon work on the land in preference to the more comfortable and refined situation he believes he enjoys in the world of his social superiors. The farmer rejects the blandishments offered him in favour of his simple, homely pleasures, and the sense of his own contentment and social worth. These are measured against the servant's pleasures, their propensity to produce happiness, and the usefulness to society of a servant's work. The husbandman's case is clinched, in the end, by the servantman's recognition that it is the men of the land 'that all other classes are depending on for their bread'. The two protagonists conclude, jointly, with a demand for the kind of respect which that anonymous witness of 1873 saw as being denied to those who produced the nation's food. The ballad was widely known and sung throughout the region in which he lived.

The question of why this ballad was sung by English villagers during the late nineteenth century raises a difficult problem in cultural analysis and theory: the problem of why art outlives its origins. The issue is usually raised in connection with the artefacts and mentefacts of 'high' culture, but that only indicates the enduring bias of cultural critics and analysts, of both the left and right, towards an elitist literary canon. The problem is just as pertinent in the realm of the vernacular popular arts, for we can see there as well the active, intentional selection of certain elements of past artistic production as the constituent parts of a cultural traditon that shape and give continuity to the present. How then do we conceive the relationship between a song manifestly of the past, and response to that song in a subsequent and radically changed social formation?

The goddess Fame, as Marx says, could not emerge in a society that produces Printing House Square, or the hero Achilles after the invention of powder and shot. 'Greek art presupposes the existence of Greek mythology, i.e., that nature

The Husbandman and the Servantman

Well met! Well met my friend, all on the highway riding,
How peaceful and lowly you stand.
Come tell it unto me, what callin' you may be,
Pray, are you not some servantman?

Oh no my brother dear, what makes you to enquire
Of any such thing at my hand?
I have a thing to show, that anyone may know,
I am a downright husbandman.

I have a thing to show, that anyone may know,
I am a downright husbandman.

If a husbandman you be, pray tell it unto me,
And quickly out of hand.
For in a little space, I will help you to a place
Where you may be a servantman.

As for your diligence, I'll return you many thanks
But require no such thing at your 'and.
With me ploughin' and me team, therefore then I do mean
For to keep myself a husbandman.

Well, but Sir! Why, we do eat such delicate meat
Pig and ca-a-pon we do feed upon.
On luxuries we dine, we drink sugar in our wine,
That's the diet for a servantman.

As for your pig and ca-a-pon, give me some good fat ba-a-con
And some butter and some cheese now and then.
There's always brawn and souse, all in a farmer's house,
That's the diet for a husbandman.

There's always brawn and souse, all in a farmer's house,
That's the diet for a husbandman.

Well, but Sir! Why we do wear clothes costly rich and raa-er,
Our coats are daubed with gold lace upon.
Our shirts are white as milk and our stockings are of silk,
That's the clothing for a servantman.

As for your rich and rares, give me the clothes I wears,
And the bushes for to trample upon.
Give me a good great-coat, and in my purse a groat,
That's the clothing for a husbandman.

Give me a good great-coat, and in my purse a groat,
That's the clothing for a husbandman.

Well, but Sir! What a fine thing it is to ride out with the King,
Lord, Duke – or any suchlike man.
For to 'ave the 'orn to blow, see the 'ounds all in a row,
That's the pleasure for a servantman!

Well, but Sir! It would be bad, if there was none of us to be had,
The gentry to wait upon.
Neither Lord nor Duke nor King, nor any suchlike thing
Could do without the servantman.

Well, but Sir, it would be wuss, if there were none like us,
For to plough and to sow the land.
Neither Lord nor Duke nor King, nor any suchlike thing
Could not do without the husbandman.

Neither Lord nor Duke nor King, nor any suchlike thing
Could not do without the husbandman.

Well, but Sir! I must confess, and allow you your request,
Whatever man's station is upon.
Though ours is not so painful, yet yours it is so gainful,
I wish I was a husbandman!

So now good people all, I pray both great and small,
Let us pray for the king of the land.
And let us all forever, use our best endeavour
For to defend the husbandman.

And let us all forever, use our best endeavour
For to defend the husbandman.

and even the forms of society itself are worked up in the popular imagination in an unconsciously artistic fashion. This is its material'. Similarly, the ways in which within any historically located culture human behaviour and social relations are understood in the popular imagination, along with various received semiotic codes and conventions, constitute the discursive and technical material variously drawn upon by popular song in production, performance and reception. Recognition of the specificities of artistic texts and the peculiarities of aesthetic experience therefore needs to be balanced by working towards an understanding of how art is articulated to the structure of particular forms of social development, and of how it partakes the texture of particular modes of social consciousness, though of course challenge to the widely noted tendency of 'bourgeois' aesthetics towards the hypostatization of historically specific cultural characteristics into universal or transhistorical artistic qualities should not lead to the antithetical error of sociological reductionism. This latter error had dogged efforts to develop a materialist explanation of the question of why art of the past either retains or regains an active resonance in periods successive to its sociogenesis. We should therefore avoid the assumption that the text-context relation is characterized by a once-and-once only circularity of significance and circumstance, for if that were true then any sense of either cultural continuity or change would disintegrate. But accepting this does not mean that we need to espouse a position of anti-historicism in order to tackle the problem with which this essay is concerned. Popular song is usually an ephemeral cultural product, but where it has been taken up in vernacular cultures and when it has continued to have value to succeeding generations, the difficulty lies in understanding why it has come to afford a recurrent and extended aesthetic enjoyment, why it has remained culturally and perhaps politically significant, what reasons we can adduce for its remaining active in everyday culture as an element from the past felt to speak validly to the present. Marx's sketchy resolution of this difficulty with respect to Greek art is at best unsatisfactory, as various Marxist commentators have acknowledged. It may be that Marx himself acknowledged its inadequacy, for its location in what is now generally referred to as the Introduction to the Critique of Political Economy was not originally published, but replaced by another introductory piece known as the Preface. He did at least approach the issue as a historical problem, despite the inadequacy of his historical analysis of Classical Athens, and the throwback to Hegelian aesthetics in his references to the 'eternal charm' of Greek art and the 'unattainable model' which he claimed it to represent.[2]

To speak of a cultural text creating 'a moment of humanity'[3] that is recognized, and continues to be valued after the historical period of its production, does not mean that we have perforce to fall back upon the romantic notion of an essential, unchanging human nature to which that text speaks, voicing eternal verities beyond the specificities of concrete social conditions and relations that are necessarily regarded as external, without influence upon an inner self or soul. The related (but not identical) primitivist ideas of a 'folk' soul, of 'organic communities', of the cultural homogeneity and autocthonous artistic spontaneity of the peasantry, and of a kind of innate rustic simplicity of mind, have long bedevilled both folkloristics and people's history. Though understandable as intellectual reactions to the experience of modernity, their effect has only been distortive when deployed in historical cultural analysis. The durable value of the ballad with which we are concerned, within vernacular cultural tradition, cannot of course be detached from certain intrinsic qualities of text and tune, as recognized by succeeding generations. We need to acknowledge, as well, that we cannot reduce the question of meanings and effects to the history of a text's reception, that the 'text is not an empty space, filled with meaning from outside itself, and that 'readings do not spring unilaterally out of the subjectivities (or the ideologies) of readers'.[4] The abiding appeal of this song should be understood as neither constant and fixed, nor open to an infinite range of interpretations, but as being founded upon acts of appreciation and judgement that occurred within definite social relations. What was true of the first, early modern production of the ballad, that it was time-conditioned, applied also to succeeding processes of reproduction and reception within which (and only within which) it had a communal cultural existence. Reproduction and reception were subject to specific historical and situational conditions and, in consequence, the meanings and significance of the ballad, within different periods, would have been inflected by given historical circumstances and accented by the nature of particular performances and particular contexts of performance. A text, in other words, has an identity that is realized relationally.

Though it is possible to exaggerate the degree to which the celebration of a song of tradition was intentional and conscious, ordinary people in the nineteenth century did not mechanically reproduce songs from the past. The insulting notion of such passivity was, however, integral to the evolutionist and survivalist paradigm of Victorian and Edwardian folklore studies. To see a ballad such as this as a fossilized remnant from a previous age rules out any active participation in the process of negotiating and modifying tradition over time by those groups in which the text circulated. The singing activities of those ahistorically described as 'the folk' did not function as long-range pipelines to a distant past. To regard them as operating in that kind of way prohibits any explanation of why this text and not others manifested an enduring use value for working class people in the Victorian countryside. In order to develop such an explanation, we need to understand that response to songs of the past involves a dialectical relationship between contemporary consciousness, conditioned by specific circumstances and processes, and the historical representation and detail supplied by the song texts in question. The situation is dialectical in the sense that 'the identity of a thing and its relationship in time with other things are opposites which belong to and define one another'.[5] What is fundamentally important in this relationship is the difference between manifestations of aspects of past consciousness and circumstances, and the way people think, feel and interrelate in a given present. It is for this reason that the identity of a text is realized in relation to (though not at the total command of) the different responses made to it. It is because people and society change that songs may prove to have lasting value and outlive their origins, not because the nature of people or society is invariant. A sense of continuity is dependent upon a sense of contrast and difference, of irremediable breaks with the past, in an interactive process linking the two senses in a complex response in the present. That kind of response can of course be made in a range of different ways, as for example in association with a sentimentalist conservatism or as in the articulation of radical hope, but what is always in some way involved is the work of historical imagination, making the process of reception active, although of course in varying degrees, and enhancing the sympathy (or other response) that is dependent on the realization of difference, so that 'our delight in comparisons, in distance, in dissimilarity' is, as Brecht put it, 'at the same time a delight in what is close and proper to ourselves'.[6] In other words, we partly confront our own period 'in the distance provided by a sense of the otherness of a past time'.[7]

By the time of the historical period on which this chapter focuses, the ballad of 'The Husbandman and the Servantman' was roughly two centuries old. It was included in a rare black-letter collection of songs of 1686 called *The Loyal Garland*.[8] Another broadside version of the ballad has been dated c.1665, and though its wording differs in certain points, it is substantially the same text, with the same 'message'. It is possible that the 1686 text reprinted by the Percy Society was published at an earlier date, for the copy of *The Loyal Garland* possessed by its nineteenth-century editor, Halliwell-Phillips, was a fifth edition.[9] This edition contained certain additions, and these may have included 'The Husbandman and the Servantman'. The likelihood of its having appeared in print before 1686 is supported by the broadside scholar J. W. Ebsworth with regard to the version dated 1665, and by the fact that the woodcut accompanying this version had been previously used in Civil War tracts of 1641.[10] (It is true of course that woodcuts were often used on broadsides with little regard for their appropriatness, but this one is quite specific in detail and could not be applied very widely without appearing totally inapposite.) Subsequent broadside versions of the ballad have survived, often as a result of their having been reprinted in eighteenth and nineteenth century song collections, but it would seem also that the ballad was well established in local, orally transmitted song traditions of the nineteenth century. One possible indication of this is in fact the various broadside reprints, which may in some cases have been taken from oral sources.[11] But the song has also been noted by collectors from living informants in the south and midlands during the nineteenth and twentieth centuries.[12] It is however, and for obvious reasons, impossible to gauge with any accuracy the longevity of the ballad within particular song and singing traditions. It would be surprising if it had not entered at least some song repertoires and traditions through later reprints, rather than continuing in an unbroken line of oral transmission for two centuries or so. But this is not the problem at issue here. What is significant, as far as I am concerned, is not so much when or where the ballad entered oral tradition, but rather its very existence within particular song traditions during the Victorian period.

The song tradition of this period which I have studied most closely was that found in Adderbury, North Oxfordshire, and contained in the Blunt manuscript collection.[13] As I have shown elsewhere, the compilation of this collection was guided very much by the methodological notions of the first 'folk' song revival, and considerably misrepresents the full amateur musical culture of the place.[14] The version of the text and tune of 'The Husbandman and the Servantman' cited above was noted from Blunt's main informant in the village, William 'Binx' Walton (1836–1919; see photograph).[15] Binx commonly sang the ballad with his brother John (1832–1921), each taking one of the two parts.[16] John 'Happy Jack' Walton was in fact one of the most notable singers among the labouring class in Adderbury, but as his taste was more inclined towards Victorian parlour ballads and concert hall pieces, rather than the kind of material out of which a 'folk' tradition of popular song was ideologically constructed, Blunt had no truck with him as a collector. It was because Binx had a much greater preference for the songs associated with oral tradition that Blunt collected 'The Husbandman and the Servantman' from him. She also noted that it was sung in the village by her next major informant, Sam Newman (1863–1943; see photograph), a versatile and accomplished singer, born in Downton, Wiltshire, but spending most of his life in Adderbury.[17] Going by the meager evidence available, the ballad seems to have been widely known and sung throughout the south midlands region. According to Alfred Williams, the song was 'the favourite of the rustics' in the upper Thames valley, especially at harvest homes, and it seems likewise to have been much loved and often sung throughout Oxfordshire, at public gatherings and get-togethers.[18] At an annual Sibford Gower benefit club dinner in 1881, for instance, a version of the ballad was reported as having been 'capitally sung, and received with rapturous applause by an appreciative audience'.[19] This kind of popularity seems to have been long-lived. Dixon, for example, spoke in 1846 of its having been long used at country merrymakings.[20] Though the evidence is unavoidably sparse, it would seem that the ballad lost little of its appeal during the nineteenth century, at least in the south midlands countryside, and may arguably be described as a key song among the rural labouring class of the time and region.

In exploring the possible reasons for this continued popularity and appeal throughout the nineteenth century, I shall concentrate on developing an understanding of the ballad's identity and significance within the vernacular cultural tradition of Adderbury, and in the social and historical context of the lives of Blunt's informants and their everyday auditors. At a more general level though, my concern will be with the dialectical relationship between popular

William 'Binx' Walton (1836–1919)

Sam Newman (1863–1943)

rural song, as a cultural resource and source of cultural meanings, and the social experience of the rural labouring class in Victorian England, that 'downtrodden class of men' (and women) who were treated with such scant respect by their capitalist masters.

The two claims made in the ballad – firstly, for the indispensability of agricultural producers, and secondly for the virtues of a wholesome rural way of life over the decadence of life in town – have been recurrent themes in both polite and popular literature since the Middle Ages. Despite the persistence of such themes, the perception of their moral and political 'truths' has always been dependent on the historically and socially situated consciousness, knowledge and experience of specific individuals and groups. The moral and ideological significance of this ballad at the time of its first production cannot therefore be equated with its significance in those respects in the contexts of later social and cultural formations.[21] The opposed values manifest in the ballad, speaking in the early seventeenth century to the deep divisions between 'court' and 'country', cannot be assumed to have been carried at some implicit level within the ballad across a succession of generations, like coins in a casket, which periodically could be extracted and cashed for some absolute value. This was not the case precisely because the currency of moral and ideological 'truths' changes over time. The perception of values in the symbolic discourse of the ballad would have been mediated by the orientations of historically variable meaning-systems influencing the socio-cultural outlook and attitudes of members of the subordinate class. Moreover, as I hope to show, the fact of the ballad's existence in local song traditions during the Victorian period presupposes an active reevaluation of its sense and worth by contemporary performers and audiences, rather than a dumbly compliant acceptance of a pristine original meaning. Yet what would clearly have been involved in that process of reevaluation over time was recognition of the song's pastness, and with that the illusion that in the dialogue and personages of the ballad were voices of the past speaking within the present. What they had to say was evaluated in the context of a locally experienced social life, but inevitably affected as well in a dialectical process by the contrast between that life in a given present and a sense of how things used to be, in some imprecisely located past. The continuance and/or adoption of this ballad within rural song traditions is, then, only finally explicable in relation to the pattern of rural social change in England, and any explanation of its abiding popularity has therefore to be lodged in the fact of its reference, in spirit and substance, to an older social order.

In approaching the question of the ballad's reevaluated significance in this manner, it is important to avoid too sharp a distinction of cleavage between that older social order and its structural successions, for in ruralist retrospect this has characteristically been the first stage basis upon which has rested the myth of a subsequent fall from Arcadian grace. There is a sense in which the ballad's significance as historical representation (rather than record) can be said to have supported resistance to this aspect of folkist amnesia, for there, in the past with which it was associated, when farmers were not capitalists and gentlemen, was the presence of human greed and pride along with its moral and social opposition. On the other hand the articulation of that opposition was made by a countryman who, as a social type, had suffered considerable relative decline by the late nineteenth century. This was likely to bolster a temptation to romanticize the extent to which independence and socially responsible values had actually existed, prior to the capitalist rationalization of greed and appropriation, arrogance and display. The class society which was then produced grew out of the class divisions already in existence, in whatever period the ballad would have been variably located. Yet my argument is that the ballad remained active as a residual element in vernacular culture because its representation of the past implied the registration of a tension between that which was represented, and its historical and political significations in the determinate conditions and circumstances of a quite different, succeeding period (or periods). The conditions and circumstances of the *durée* of everyday life in which the ballad's significance was felt and understood were the outcome of a longer-term pattern of socio-economic change which institutionalized and consolidated values of a historically different social order than that associated with the ballad's pastness. Before we can examine the ballad's reevaluated significance in the Victorian period, we need therefore to look at the actual pattern of social transformation in the village and its immediate region, over the preceding century or so, for it was within the changed historical context thus produced that the ballad's structural oppositions would have been understood, and the process of reevaluation undertaken. Without some such account of rural social change in the locality, any assessment of the ballad's worth *as* historical representation would be spavined from the start.

The orthodox view in contemporary English historiography of rural social change over the past two centuries is that by at least the second quarter of the nineteenth century an agricultural proletariat had become well established and that, in the main, farming was then being conducted along capitalist business lines in a three-fold structure of landlords, tenant-farmers and a wage-dependent labour force. This was undoubtedly the tendential pattern of development in North Oxfordshire in that by the second half of the nineteenth century a capitalist agriculture had become the dominant mode of crop and livestock production, but the pattern nevertheless was by no means uniform in advance or comprehensive in extent. This can be viewed in two ways. Elements of captialist logic and practice of course predate its general establishment in agriculture, and the birth-pangs of capitalist agriculture as a system of organization and socio-economic conduct were felt long before the Georgian enclosures. Howard Gray's assertion that parliamentary enclosure in Oxfordshire was 'the registering of a *fait accompli*' is probably beyond question.[22] Gray showed that the major period of decline in Oxfordshire of small independent farmers preceded the mid-eighteenth century, and this decline resulted in, rather than caused, the enclosures which followed. It is significant as well that in Oxfordshire 'husbandman' became devalued as a status category in the early eighteenth century, while that of 'yeoman' became upgraded, though use of this latter term in turn declined during the late eighteenth century in line with a further restructuring of rural social relations.[23] But just as examples of capitalist agrarian practice can be cited from periods antecedent to those in which the signs and symbols of its ascendancy had become prevalent, so the persistence of peasant-type farming, and more broadly of a peasant-orientated outlook, can be found in the county, as elsewhere, long after the consolidation of a market economy.[24]

It is difficult to know precisely how to describe that outlook, but it can at least be conceived as distinct from – if not contrary to – that which was supportive of the pursuit of captialistic practice in farming and the productive and social relations which were of necessity embroiled in that practice. It is also difficult to assess the extent to which the distinctiveness of this alternative outlook was conscious and developed. Yet evidence of it was palpable nevertheless. Arthur Young for instance, in a famous passage, observed it clearly in North Oxfordshire in the early nineteenth century. He spoke of the 'ebullition' of change in ideas, knowledge and practice evinced by the new-fashioned farmer, and contrasted this starkly with the 'Goths and Vandels' of the open fields. Both, he said, could be found any Thursday in Banbury market. But moving from the former to the latter seemed to him like losing a century in time, or moving a thousand miles in a day.

I have discussed Young's philippics elsewhere.[25] All we need note here is the fact of division and antagonism between two kinds of mentality. Young singled out a local exemplar of the improver's mentality in John Davis of Bloxham, a village neighbouring on Adderbury, canonizing him as 'an excellent practical farmer' who had farmed 'many years on a large scale'. He had long been an energetic enclosure commissioner when Young met him, and is cited as having once been employed as a commissioner upon twenty-six cases at the same time.[26] Bloxham had been enclosed in 1802; 2,773 acres were allotted, 173 of which had been common land and the rest open fields.[27] Rents, according to Davis, had been doubled after enclosure 'at the first letting', and had risen 'much more after ten or twelve years'. This, he said, made 'very little difference to the poor'.[28] Davis typically viewed the social effects of enclosure as synonymous with its effect upon his own economic and technical advance, seeing public good through the optic of private gain. Enclosure was praised for having led to a decline in 'pilfering', and as being generally 'far better' for the 'morals' of the poor than the old commonfield system. To enclose and cultivate was to tame and civilize. Young's justification for his proposal to enclose Wychwood Forest in Oxfordshire was that, apart from the question of productiveness, it harboured 'poachers, deer-stealers, thieves and pilferers of every kind' and was 'a terror to all quiet and well-disposed persons.'[29] The same reasons were often given for the enclosure of commons.[30] Virtue, respectability, industry and law and order were all at various times invoked in pursuit of the cause of enclosure. Cottagers in Bloxham with common rights previous to enclosure had been able to keep cows and gather fuel, but in Davis's opinion the allotments they had been given in lieu of these rights were a 'much better' arrangement, 'and the people in a better situation' generally as a result of enclosure. One might easily imagine an absence of grievance, suffering and distress, yet in Bloxham that was not the case and continued not to be the case. A pamphlet printed by Cheney of Banbury, in 1834, and addressed to the people of Bloxham, spoke of the inadequate supply of allotments, of pauperisation and the general ill-effects of enclosure. On one occasion the Court House was stormed and a meeting of the feoffees broken up.[31] The Goths and Vandels had retaliated.

The new mentality of local farmers like Davis and Warriner (another Bloxham farmer lauded by Young[32]) did not come out of the blue, develop precipitously or expand all-pervasively. One can for instance detect its presence several decades earlier in the movement to enclose the parish of Adderbury itself. This took place in 1768, a relatively early parliamentary enclosure. Adderbury was also one of the few Redland villages of Banburyshire where a certain amount of enclosing had been accomplished before the award – 965 acres in all – though this was still only one fifth of the total acreage of the villages in the parish enclosed by that award. It is important to note as well that, before the main enclosure movement, progress towards flexibility and variation in open field husbandry in Oxfordshire had been made by the novel sowing of leys (at Adderbury in 1628 the proportion was 16% of the land) and the growing of sainfoin.[33] There was also improvement in livestock husbandry, 'the remaining arable land was given the advantage of better rotations and more manure', and the introduction of four-wheeled farm wagons in place of the two-wheeled long-cart suggests that harvests were becoming heavier during the seventeenth and early eighteenth centuries: by 1720, 34% of Oxfordshire farmers possessed wagons.[34] There were five-field systems at Adderbury as early as 1628, and Grey estimated that in North Oxfordshire, while not being widespread, 'an eight course rotation of crops or something similar must have been well known at the very time when parliamentary enclosure was beginning'.[35] These details are pointers to the agricultural progress which, in Gray's opinion, spurred on the advent of parliamentary enclosure.

Proceedings were instigated by the large landowners, who anticipated a substantial rise in rents.[36] These landlords included New College, Oxford, the Dukes of Argyll and Buccleuch, and Charles Townshend, the Chancellor of the Exchequer. Warden Hayward of New College spoke of enclosure in the parish being supported by the most respectable farmers, but the intention to enclose was opposed by numerous smallholders who in a petition adjudged enclosure as 'extremely detrimental and disadvantageous to us'. Enclosure in their view would lead 'to the Ruin and Destruction of the Inhabitants of this Populous Village.'[37] (See illustration, page 52.) This prospect led one man in the village to desperate remedies. In August 1767, as the enclosures were beginning, it was reported that 'a poor labouring man of Adderbury had hanged himself from an apprehendsion [sic] that he and his family should want bread'.[38]

The enclosure of Adderbury was calculated from the first as a device for increasing the wealth and power of the aristocratic Argyll-Buccleuch-Dalkeith dynasty and the 'great affluence and ample station' of Townshend (aka 'Champagne Charley'), who had married the Duke of Buccleuch's mother and who acted as trustee to the Duke until the latter achieved his majority in 1770.[39]

It having been represented to us, that a Bill will be brought into the House Commons, at the next Meeting of the Parliament for the Enclosing the Open Field of the Parish of Adderbury West We Whose Names are hereunto Subscribed, being near two Thirds of the Principal part of the Landholders, of the said Parish, upon the most Mature, and deliberate Consideration are very Clearly, and strictly of Opinion, that Enclosing the said Field, will be Extreamly detrimental and disadvantageous to us, and also tend to the Ruin and Destruction of the Inhabitants at this Populous Village. Dated at Adderbury the 19th day of October 1765.

J: Cox Vic:
George Pottinger
Benjamin Lamb
George Barrett
John Gaulhorn
John Wyatt
Thomas Cornocks
Willm Shenston
Thomas Cox

John Barber
John Bellow
Elisha Simco
Phillip Turner
Thomas Bagley
Choss Mellor
John Swift
Thos Marshall Wm
William Wyly
John Clark for Danl
Josiah Cox
Messenger
Zachary
Wm Goff
Rich Austin
Mary Mayo

The Adderbury West anti-enclosure petition, 1765, published by permission of the Warden and Fellows of New College, Oxford. The wording of the petition for Adderbury is identical, though (obviously) with different signatories.

The precedent of enclosure for the creation of residential estates had of course been set before this time: thirty four townships had been enclosed in Oxfordshire, chiefly in the sixteenth century, for this purpose. In following this pattern of procedure, the Duke of Argyll and, in turn, his son-in-law Townshend engrossed and consolidated the family's estate and holdings, these moves being a typical 'indispensable preliminary' to enclosure proposals.[40] Between 1717 and 1767 at least £12,000 was spent in the acquisition of local land and property which included the acres of small yeomen and cottagers.[41] The number of freeholders, which had been high since the seventeenth century, declined as a result of these purchases. Some of the land bought in the common fields went into the park of Adderbury House, to the design of which Capability Brown contributed.[42] The stables were altered and extended and many coverts planted to cater for nobility enamoured of riding-to-hounds.[43] The Duke of Buccleuch was a keen huntsman. The site of his kennels in Adderbury West (where the baying of the dogs would not disturb the peace of his lordship) is marked by what is still known today as Dog Close.[44] The mansion in Adderbury East was comprehensively redesigned. In 1774 it contained fifty six rooms, including a lofty entrance hall, three drawing rooms, a library and a billiard room. It was later described as worthy of royalty.[45]

As for the park, it was a question of holding a mirror up to art, of realizing in material form a composition derived directly from an established model, or set of requisite principles, for the transmutation of nature into landscape. Adderbury Mill was removed from the park because it was considered unsightly, and a new mill and millstream were constructed below the church with 'picturesque banks and bridges'.[46] Such features as did conform to the correct conception of a 'pretty landskip' were the flower gardens and parkland enclosed with evergreens and forest trees, the 'fine serpentine stream of water ... in full view of the house', the 'fertile grounds pleasingly diversified with hill and valley', the ponds for fishing and boating, and the then exotic weeping willow and acacia, introduced into this country by the Duke of Argyll.[47] Yet such delights were spoilt by the highway adjacent to the house which might have brought nobility into direct contact with the '*misera contribuens plebs.*[48] The course of the Oxford Road, turnpiked from 1755 to 1875, instead of passing near the Duke's kitchen garden through to the Aynho Road where the toll gate was sited, was therefore altered to its present course. The minor road off it at the junction just north of the village became after enclosure the Banbury-Buckingham road, which previously had run from Weeping Cross at Bodicote south-east to Nell Bridge, following the ancient Saltway.[49]

The green in the East was also subject to aristocratic depradation. In the late fourteenth century it had been expansive enough for the village to be known as Adderbury-on-the-Green, and though perhaps somewhat encroached upon up to the death of the poet Rochester, whose country seat was at Adderbury, it was reduced to its present dimension of half an acre as a result of enclosure. Much of it was appropriated into the purlieu of Adderbury House. The vicar in 1796 wrote that as many as ninety cottages had gone 'to embellish the environs of the heavy pile', a wave of demolition that would have displaced at least a quarter of those living in East Adderbury.[50] Added to this, that part of the village known as the East End became sundered from the rest of the community and left in a state of isolation. Yet there is an ironic footnote to all this. The scent of old Reynard had apparently led the Argyll-Buccleuch family to reside at Adderbury, but enclosure of the open fields spoilt the chase and caused the Duke of Buccleuch to leave North Oxfordshire, hoist with his own petard.[51] Two other big landowning champions of enclosure, Paul Methuen and John Blagrave, also left the parish.[52] But the park and house remained, as did the enclosed fields, 'a visible sign and symbol that rampant family and individual power had gained a complete victory over the civic community'.[53]

It has to be said, though, that enclosure does not seem to have caused any immediate deterioration in yeoman farming. Agrarian reform, as we have seen, had been proceeding for many years before enclosure took place, and in the early eighteenth century it appears that in the country as a whole, the number of farms over a hundred acres increased while those of the small farmer, under a hundred acres in size, declined as a result of landowners buying up small properties (usually done as at Adderbury on the death of such farmers). Other factors, such as low prices and heavy taxation, also contributed to their decline in the early eighteenth century.[54] The engrossing of the Duke's estate at Adderbury had already caused a depreciation in the numbers of small farmers and cottagers in the open fields, and some smallholders in the parish do appear to have been squeezed out as a result of the expenses of enclosure, which were probably disproportionate to the size of their holdings. (There were allotments made in the enclosure award to twenty-nine small farmers (twenty to a hundred acres) as well as ninety-seven allotments of under twenty acres.[55]) Gray found that the yeoman farm was nevertheless much in evidence in Adderbury, Milton and Bodicote at the time of the enclosure, and certain evidence suggests that the majority of smallholders survived the change. Small farmers were not evenly spread throughout the country, but one of the regions where they were concentrated was that around Banbury. In 1785, owner-occupiers in Oxfordshire paid 27% of the land tax in forty eight parishes, and in ninety parishes none were found.[56] In Adderbury they paid 20% of the tax.[57] Arthur Ashby, the eldest son of Joseph Ashby of Tysoe, explained in his survey of smallholdings that those areas where eighteenth century small farmers were most numerous in Oxfordshire were also where smallholdings were chiefly to be found early in the twentieth century. But while this might be true of the neighbourhood of Otmoor and the district directly south east of Oxford, by 1910 the Banbury district, which had been a stronghold of small farmers in 1800, had fallen into line with the national trend, and 'genuine peasant cultivators' had virtually disappeared.[58] Though the period 1770–1813 may have afforded a respite from the gradual pre-enclosure decline of yeoman farmers, because of rising prices for food products and general prosperity for farmers, especially during the war years, this situation altered radically after Waterloo. Farmers who had mortgaged their land in order to buy more, who had ceased to use a more moderate mete-wand of conduct and life-style, became bankrupt when prices slumped.[59] Thousands of small farmers in England failed as well, and the number of landless labourers increased. This depression seems to have taken its toll of small farmers in Adderbury: by 1831 the number of landowners and owner occupiers in the parish had declined considerably.[60] Gray shows a similar pattern of decline in yeomen throughout the county as a whole. The land they were forced to sell went into the hands of 'the more stable of the independent farmers, who thus increased their holdings'.[61] Chambers and Mingay suggest that, in the long run, 'what really counted in the survival of small farmers were the levels of prices and costs'.[62] The gradual abandonment of yeoman farming in the district after 1815 appears to have continued throughout the ninetheenth century. At the beginning of the present century, Oxfordshire contained 16% more large farms (of 300 acres or more) and 6% less smallholdings (of 55 acres) than any other county of England or Wales.[63]

In terms of general pattern, then, the pull was predominantly in the direction of the '"feelosophy" of improvement', farming on a 'free' market basis, establishing a landless, pauperised rural labour force and gradually expanding the size of farm holdings. 'If husbandry improves, it will demand more labour', wrote Young: 'small farms with their universal attendant poor farmers, can never form such a system of employ as richer farmers, for ... improvements in husbandry are but another word for increases of labour'.[64] With these trends went a rigidifying of the class structure, a decline in rural paternalism and a stricter labour discipline. Richard Davis, in an agricultural survey of Oxfordshire fifteen years previous to Young's, had advocated a small-is-beautiful ethos; but in subsequent years it was Young's views which were 'adopted most generally by those who determined the agricultural policy of the county'.[65] There was no uniform wave of change sweeping across the land, but rather a tendential pattern of development the fear of which, and of all it entailed, was manifest in the Adderbury counter-enclosure petition, signed in the main by small farmers and husbandmen on behalf of the whole village community (see illustration, page 52).[66] Enclosures represented a signal victory of one world over another. The conflict, for instance, between legalistic distinctions and customary rights exemplified the pattern of which enclosure was a part, which had been long developing and which enclosure served in many ways to formalize. Enclosure, in this sense, constituted a symbolic triumph. As Mabel Ashby has put it, 'the ordinary man's vision of a sound co-operative village of free men, free to get a living, free to say yea and nay in their own affairs, was less clear-cut, and he found no way to project it clearly for himself and others'.[67] This is what enclosure symbolized: 'the cultivation', in E. P. Thompson's estimation, 'of a long secular process by which men's customary relations to the agrarian means of production were undermined', and 'of profound social consequence because it illuminates, both backwards and forwards, the destruction of the traditional elements in English peasant society'.[68]

I realize that any lengthier and more sustained treatment of this particular example of enclosure would need to take on board the general debate on the historical account of primitive accumulation, and the development of capitalist relations in agriculture, and that we need to discard the quest for a master mechanism of rural proletarianization, or indeed of the formation of a proletariat-in-general.[69] I have concentrated on it as symbolically characteristic (rather than directly causal) of a wider pattern of rural social change in the late eighteenth and nineteenth centuries through which, it seems to me, the reproduction of the ballad of 'The Husbandman and the Servantman' towards the end of the that period has to be understood. My approach is predicated on the assumption that if a popular text is not to be regarded as an autonomous object existing outside the social structural contexts of its performance, monologically yielding an everlasting essence, then the production of its meanings and significances within different periods is necessarily informed by the specific historical conditions which make it possible. I have tried to provide an outline of the pattern of change which generated those conditions for one particular case, for unless we develop some knowledge of limiting and enabling conditions as a constituent part of the task of analysis then we are likely to slip back towards an endorsement of further essentialist conceptions, such as those of a text's possession of a single correct meaning, and of transhistorical or 'ideal' performers and their auditors. It is in order to avoid such critical retrenchments that I have sought to offer an account of certain local manifestations of the antagonism of interests and values sustaining a sense of the contemporary significance of the opposed views regarding the evaluation of the worth of agricultural labour to individual and collectivity which are manifest in the ballad.

Supporting the social and material changes in the countryside which I have outlined were the ascendant bourgeois values of competitive individualism, self-gain, and the aspiration to 'refined' tastes. It is these values which are symbolically represented in the ballad by the servantman, and which are counterposed by the alternative values represented by his adversary in debate. In these terms it is not so much the persistence of pockets of peasant-style farming in the county during the nineteenth century which counts, but rather the continuing prevalence of a traditionalist mentality that involved adherence to those alternative values. The disposition perceived and understood as symbolically represented by the servantman, compounded with a belief in progress and often an anti-popular moralism, became associated with the 'improving' and 'respectable' type of farmer and thus, in the nineteenth century, stood in contrast with the alternative values represented by an alternative type of farmer. During the late eighteenth century, 'farming' became quite distinct from 'husbanding' as a characterization of agricultural activity, the former being realised primarily in terms of the 'supervision of argicultural labour rather than its regular performance'.[70] This distinction became allied as well with complaints from people such as Cobbett concerning firstly, a decline in the mutuality of interests and obligations between masters and men, and secondly, the gentrification of farmers – their elevation to what he called 'a species of mock gentlefolk'.[71] Mary Smith, the daughter of a nonconformist boot and shoemaker of Cropredy in North Oxfordshire, confirmed this pattern locally when she wrote in her autobiography:

> The southern farmers were men of wealth. They sat in their parlours, and were waited upon by servants. They knew little or nothing of farm work, and their children were educated by governesses, and sent to the best boarding schools.[72]

The upward nobility and *folie de grandeur* of 'respectable' farmers was seen by Cobbett (among many others) as having been bought at the expense of the pauperization of the farm labourer, and his complaint rested representatively upon moral grounds that were compatible with those underpinning the dialogue between husbandman and servantman. The view of farmer gentrification taken by labouring villagers is suggested by a popular Oxfordshire saying referring to farmers' children: 'It used to be Mam and Dad and Porridge, and then 'twas Father and Mother and Broth, and now 'tis *Pa* and *Ma* and *Soup*'.[73] The village commoner and the labourer, by contrast, sold his or her birthright for a mess of very thin pottage. At no time between the repeal of the Corn Laws and the First World War did the Oxfordshire agricultural labourer's wages exceed the average English wage for that occupation. Wages in the county invariably fell somewhere between ten and twelve shillings a week, a figure well below Canon Tuckwell's and B. S. Rowntree's estimates for a subsistence wage.[74] (See figure 3, page 58.) As they said in Adderbury, 'we don't live, we linger'.

Villagers did not, however, simply acquiesce or pass sardonic comments in the face of oppression and want. The period from the late eighteenth century to the emergence of unionism in the 1870s is marked by sporadic attempts in the countryside to reestablish a moral economy and to challenge the denial of social responsibility by agrarian capitalist practice. Morally the ballad is of a piece with those attempts and supportive of the traditionalist working class mentality of the time. As Peter Stearns has put it, traditionalism 'describes more ... than a working class avoidance of values associated with a middle class mentality. It describes an effort to preserve standards retained from a peasant or artisanal past'. It involves 'an attachment to certain values associated with a stereotypic peasantry, including a susbstantial amount of fatalism and preference for stability over change ...'[75] What is also implicated in these values is a vision of social equality, justice and common welfare based on what George Foster has called the image of limited good: the view that 'all of the desired things in life... exist in finite quantity and are always in short supply'; in addition 'there is no way directly within peasant power to increase the available quantities'.[76] This is the traditionalist value to which the ballad of 'The Husbandman and Servantman' speaks. A harmonious relation between 'Man and Nature' is represented in the personage of the husbandman, the man who husbands rather than capitalizes on the providence of Nature; this relation was dependent upon the defining and maintenance of measured limits. What destroyed its 'quality' in the nineteenth century was the casting asunder of those limits by 'quantity', the limitless capitalist demand to produce and consume which seemed to be unsettling everything once regarded as stable and assured. The past to which the ballad husbandman belonged would thus have been idealized – and recovered thus in historical imagination – as a time when 'the human being appears as the aim of production' rather than 'where production appears as the aim of mankind and wealth as the aim of production'.[77]

We should not, as Stearns very properly reminds us, think of traditionalism 'as a statement of some eternal peasantness or of working class homogeneity',

1824	8s.
1833	10s.1d.
1837	8s.6d.
1850–2	9s.
1861	10s.
1871	10s.
1879–81	12s.9d. (Wage at Banbury=11s.)
1892	12s. (Wage at Banbury=11s.)
1898	12s.1d.
1901	12s.
1910	12s.

N.B.: 'The local variations in the rate of wages are often very remarkable'. (J. Ashby and B. King, 'Statistics of Some Midland Villages', *Economic Journal*, Vol. 3, 1893, p. 5.)

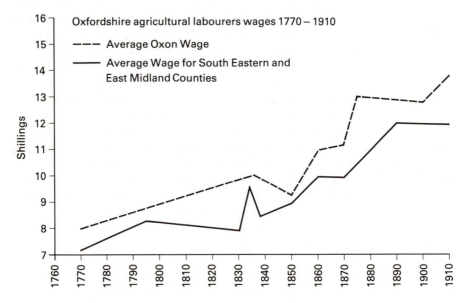

Oxfordshire agricultural labourers wages 1770 – 1910

– – – Average Oxon Wage

——— Average Wage for South Eastern and East Midland Counties

Shillings

Sources:
(i)   A. Wilson Fox, 'Agricultural Wages in England and Wales During the Last Fifty Years', *Journal of the Royal Statistical Society*, Vol. LXVI, 1903, pp. 273–359.
(ii) C. S. Orwin and B. I. Felton, 'A Century of Wages & Earnings in Agriculture', *Journal of the Royal Agricultural Society of England*, Vol. 92, 1931, pp. 231–57.
(iii) R. E. Prothero, *English Farming Past & Present*, London, 1912, Appendix X.
(iv) R. Groves, *Sharpen the Sickle*, London, 1949, p. 252.

Ordinary agricultural labourers wages in Oxfordshire 1824–1910

yet despite regional and occupational cultural differences, we should nevertheless recognize traditionalism as continuing 'to form a unifying motif in terms of values and even some behaviours'.[78] Workers in nineteenth-century English villages generally had few resources with which to fashion and develop any new, radical popular culture, and therefore of necessity cleaved to traditionalism as a moral and cultural anchorage, celebrating the past in the face of 'the development of clearly novel patterns' which 'the middle class was so urgently recommending', striving 'to recall and use the past to react to an unassimilable present'.[79] The conservative or traditionalist tendency running against the grain of the up-and-coming mentality identified by Young was expressive of a desire for social stability compounded with an antagonism to the impoverishment of one class as a consequence of the improvement of another, and was rooted in a belief in the validity of past knowledge, and past patterns of conduct, as a blueprint for action in the present. During the course of the nineteenth century, traditionalism in the country retained greatest strength, and power to sustain a sense of integrity and morale, among the labouring class, not because they were culturally 'backward', but because of a fundamental outlook and orientation that engendered and reinforced an inclination to aspire to the past. It was precisely because the characteristics of a traditionalist outlook and pattern of conduct were seen as virtues, emanating from what Sturt memorably called 'the home-made civilization of the rural English', that people were reluctant to allow them to be swept clean away by the new broom of progress.[80] To the advocate of political economy and utilitarianism, however, 'precedent, prescriptive right, ancient privilege, the pieties induced by habit and time, were no argument, or were even a negative argument: "the wisdom of our ancestors" was Bentham's particular abhorrence'.[81]

Dobrowolski has claimed that in all forms of social life there are 'two fundamental, though contrasting tendencies which manifest themselves with varying intensity in different phases of historical development':

> Firstly, there is a tendency which is essentially conservative and stabilizing, which is expressed in a propensity for the preservation and maintenance of the existing social order. It is always based on the acknowledgement of previous experience and is essentially focused on the past. The past, here, supplies a pattern for living and provides a model for human action. Conversely, there exists a tendency which has grown out of doubt and dissatisfaction and which is invariably conducive to social change. This tendency is often destructive and revolutionary *vis-à-vis* the existing social order, and has often been expressed in terms of a more or less violent opposition to, and negation of, the surrounding reality. This tendency is usually born out of the deep human craving for new and better forms of social life, new moral truths and more adequate technical innovations.[82]

Traditionalist orientations towards the past reflect a need for 'the regulation and ordering of human relationships founded on a set of established values, skills and capabilities, truths and experiences'.[83] Clearly, this kind of cognitive orientation can have opposed origins and ends, being manifest for instance in both a reactionary primitivism and in the radical contestation of a destructive progressivism; similarly, the will to change can be mobilized both in challenge to a backward-looking authoritarianism and to popular conceptions of a moral economy. It was those conceptions, held to in the face of the increasing entrenchment of capitalist social relations, which marked working class culture in the English countryside for most of the nineteenth century as traditionalist. It was essentially an anti-progress culture: things should instead go on as they used to go on. But when? In the past, simply; or in any period sufficiently distant to the present? As Francis Hearn says of English working class culture generally in the early nineteenth century: 'The past was imaginatively reconstructed as a Golden Age and used to critically evaluate the present.'[84] This stance and perspective was retained over a longer period in the countryside, for a variety of reasons, and continued to characterize the political – or proto-political – responses of rural labourers when their counterparts in the industrial cities had developed a more class-conscious political outlook and a more original vision of the future. As Mabel Ashby has put it, for the North Oxfordshire labourer in the Victorian period, a sense of tradition remained 'implicit in his attitudes and customs and speech ... in his cultural blood and bones'.[85]

The husbandman hero is himself very much of a traditionalist in approach and outlook, and as such stood ideologically in contrast to the tendency exhibited by the 'improving' farmer with an eye for technical, economic and social advance for his own farm and family, or the servant dazzled and duped by his (or her) master's wealth, finery, graces and authority. He represented a type, a composite and stock representative of the old-fashioned farmer. But the historical elements of idealization in him did not thereby lose their force: they were part and parcel of a general view of the past in 'an unassimilable present', which those workers in the present, with moral and emotional investments in the values he represented, tended to revere in the possibility of their resurrection. The ballad husbandman was a symbolic figure and was valued as such. His self-determination, his life-style, his relative well-being were worthy of aspiration to those deprived of them, his implicit appeal to a moral economy and to due recognition of the worth of the landworker were worthy of every support in an age witnessing their erosion. His comments and stance in the debate reflected values which, in a song seen as handed down from the past, would in that respect have been understood as inherited from the village past and speaking critically in the present to the 'rigs of the times' in which the continued singing took place. He refuses to avail himself of the more easeful situation to be gained as a lackey to a lord, duke, or any such like thing. His habits are modest, his tastes plain, his pleasures simple, his sense of independence relatively assured and his sense of social purpose confidently held. He is at one with Shakespeare's Corin or Fuller's Edmund Grindell.[86] The ballad husbandman was thus, for many rural workers, an uncorrupted hero in a corrupt age, an adherent of a primitive communism in a fundamentally divided society, a figure associated with 'the social myth of the golden age of the village community before enclosure and before the Wars' which E. P. Thompson accurately calls 'a montage of memories': 'The savage penal code, the privations, the bridewells, of old England were forgotten; but the myth of a lost paternalist community became a force in its own right – perhaps as powerful a force as the utopian projections of Owen and the Socialists'.[87] This tendency among rural workers towards retrospective idealization is of course recurrent in a range of ways, though periodically revised in relation to the past time lamented, so that the general process can be identified as operating not only in relation to the era before enclosure, but subsequently in relation to the time before the Wars, before the New Poor Law, before the 'Great Depression', before the First World War, before the tractor, before the Common Market, before the emergence of a transnational agribusiness ... But this general process of idealizing the past in relation to the perceived comparative inadequacies of the present can only be properly understood in the contexts of particular social and historical conditions, and in the Victorian period, midlands agricultural labourers had, with very few exceptions, only the past to which they could aspire, only the past to which they could validly turn in seeking alternatives to their contemporary position as the 'toad beneath the harrow'.

The insistence among the poor in looking back could be upon the basic equality of all:

> When Adam delved and Eve span
> Who was then the gentleman?

In 1877, eight miles or so from Adderbury, these words, the text for John Ball's famous sermon to the rebelling peasants at Blackheath, appeared as a slogan on a marquee at a N.A.L.U. meeting.[88] But the retrospect could be to a much less distant time, to when this old hat was new, or when grandfather was a boy. 'The Honest Ploughman' laments how the 'times are very different now to ninety year ago' and explains why; 'Eight Shillings a Week' looks back fondly to the good times in 'the reign of old George' that are now 'gone by complete', but which can be clearly remembered by 'our venerable fathers'. This is to give just two other examples.[89] But the actual historical locations of that 'old England' are not what fundamentally counted: it was the retrospective vision – the past as a source of aspiration – that mattered.

The lowliness of the husbandman is important in that it was shared by his admirers, the singers and listeners, but for them it was the virtues of his character in relation to his modest place in the world which basically counted, rather than his specific historical status. In a song from the Hammond and Gardiner manuscripts, an equally idealized husbandman evinces the same values when he declares:

> Let the wealthy and great roll in splendour and state,
> I envy them not I declare it,
> I'll eat my own lamb, my own chicken and ham,
> I'll shear my own sheep, and I'll wear it,
> Was it not for my seeding you'd get poor feeding,
> I am sure you would all starve without me,
> I am always content when I've paid my rent,
> And happy when friends are about me.[90]

This connects with another of the moral values celebrated by the ballad. Those who by the sweat of their brows tended the crops that would feed the populace at large are to be given due recognition and reward:

> And let us all forever, use our best endeavour
> For to defend the husbandman.

Some acknowledgement was paid. Late seventeenth-century writers generally regarded the labouring poor as non-productive, but as the eighteenth century progressed social philosophers began to express a growing appreciation of them, and the importance of husbandmen to the life of the nation became increasingly recognized in print. 'Instead of being non-productive', writes G. E. Fussell, 'they came to be regarded as the foundation and prop of society, the people who produced all the wealth that others consumed'.[91] James Thomson's advice to the masters to

> Be mindful of the rough laborious hand
> That sinks you soft in elegance and ease[92]

was a relatively early literary realization of how the poor ploughman made the money that bought the power that enabled the masters to live in the house of luxury that materialized the order that God built. Within popular rural culture, the claim may well have had a longer pedigree. The point to emphasize here, though, is that during a period of increasing demoralization among rural labourers, this dialectic between hard-working independence and easeful servility, between gainful labour and the non-productive existence of what Cobbett called Dead Weight, gave structure to the indignation and hostility felt by many working people. From it, according to E. P. Thompson, 'the sociology of post-war Radicalism was to be derived, which divided society between "Useful" or "Productive Classes" on the one hand, and courtiers, sinecurists, fund-holders, speculators and parasitic middlemen on the other'.[93] The self-image of the male rural labourer as the king of the land did much to preserve his pride at a time when, in the words of a popular rural song of the 1830s and 40s:

> The Nobs of Old England, of shameful renown
> Are striving to crush a poor man to the ground.[94]

An awareness of the labourer's denied importance and manifold skills acted as a counterweight to the inclination towards loss of self-respect, and resignation to the folly of despair.

While one finds at times a tacit acquiescence in the class society of their childhood and youth, among old villagers one speaks to today, those who grew the nation's food, though exploited and (as they saw it themselves) downtrodden, nevertheless also saw themselves as the 'prop of the land', and their labour as the source of all wealth. The idea of that was never lost. The king of the Norfolk Poachers put it like this:

> But I think the Tiller of the soil is the highest and oldest workman of all. No one can do without him and the product of his hands. The Gold miner cannot eat his gold, nor the Coal miner his coal, nor the Iron miner his iron. All and every one is dependent upon the tiller of the Soil. He is the Father of all Workers, like the old saying has it:
>> The king he governs all,
>> The Parson pray for all,
>> The Lawer plead for all,
>> The Ploughman pay for all
>> And feed all.[95]

The case for labour power is characteristically argued for on the basis of occupation rather than class, for it is class which divides, class which denies a proper sense of mutual obligations and community among people. Later songs repeat this point of insistence on the indispensability of the landworker, often more emphatically; 'The Painful Plough', 'The Ploughshare' and 'We Poor Labouring Men' are examples.[96]

The traditionalist values represented in the rejection of the servantman's argument – the rejection of borrowed plumage, of comfort and prestige bought with the coin of flattery and servility, of needless excess and frivolous consumption – were recurrent in rural culture, and in this sense as well the ballad was part of and helped sustain a customary moral code. Dressing up beyond one's means and social station, for example, continued to be condemned in the countryside throughout the Victorian period. While such a normative reaction against social pretension can be said to have been supportive of the status quo, it could be directed just as much at the gentry-apeing farmer or the artisan's wife with a penchant for white kid gloves. As part of a moral code it was rooted in the harsh pragmatics of measuring one's wants by one's means. There were, then, at least two fundamental areas of value-conflict associated with the ballad: the dialectic between useful toil and parasitism, on the one hand; and on the other the conflict between traditionalist values and practice, and those generated by and through the logic and process of 'Petty's Law', as well as by the widening pattern of social emulation which Harold Perkin, among others, identifies as among the central, constitutive features of industrialization. These moral and ideological conflicts continued into the late nineteenth century in the countryside primarily because of the fact that farm labourers and villagers generally were among the last to be drawn into the new industrial and social system growing, from the late eighteenth century, 'like a vortex within the old, and gradually pulling into its orbit of production and demand circle after circle of producers and consumers'.[97]

While the hero of the song can be said to have corresponded increasingly to a marginalized contemporary social group, during the Victorian period, his contrasting figure continued to exist and to be readily identifiable as a social type: one who served those who neither spun nor toiled. This protagonist was a figure of the present, the ballad husbandman an idealized historical stereotype. This supports the idea that synchronically (taking the song as existing in performance), two chronologies may have been at work: the first historical, whereby a situation was projected in which servantry compared unfavourably with husbandry in the past; the second contemporary, whereby one of the two participating in the debate had to a great extent disappeared from society, leaving the servant as the only actual referent outside the song's own realm of signification. This was clear enough to ordinary people at the time. A Bloxham farmer, in the early years of the twentieth century, considered My Lord Capital to have 'seized on every inch of land', and to have 'thrown the husbandman on the parish'.[98] Historically, the servantman's view was thus seen to have prevailed. All the more weight would thereby have been added to the moral and symbolic significance of the husbandman as idealized type, and his argument as a critique upon the rigs of the time.

The continued singing of the ballad was, then, a response to the social and historical changes which denied its hero and his moral code a real and contemporary context. That is why the song outlived its origins, why it continued to have a specific resonance and force. The ballad's longevity in tradition (whether assumed or actual) cannot be explained by reference to 'absolute truths', or by recourse to such functionalist and determinist notions as that of 'cultural lag'; its continued relevance was lodged in a sense of the discrepancies between the song's moral value and the denial of that moral value in the present by 'those who have plenty', or who were driven by desire to attain plenty at the expense of an already 'downtrodden class of men'. In 1900, as Stearns has it, 'few workers believed that, in its essentials, life had not deteriorated from some vaguely perceived past.'[99] How that past was conceived by workers as images and conceptions of the right order of society, and how the quality of past time was assessed, was inclined to be highly selective – thematically ordered arrangements of a jumble of bits and pieces in the construction of which every participant in cultural tradition, from generation to generation, was in some sense a *bricoleur's* apprentice. In relation to cultural meanings and moral values, then, the historicity of oral tradition and the songs of 'tradition' is beside the point.

To say this is not to imply an indifferent attitude to the historical record, or the absence of an aesthetic feeling for verisimilitude in songs of and about the past. Far from it. But that feeling was important primarily in informing and supporting what was, for singers and listeners, a moral and ethical truth in the song or ballad. If a song did not accord with the value system of a group or community, then it is unlikely, by and large, to have passed into the oral traditions associated with that group or community. But the meanings and significance of 'traditional' elements of a vernacular culture do not remain static through time; they are modified by – and always exist in relation to – contemporary social relations and evolving class formations. The ballad studied in this chapter constituted a key resource in the cultural stock available to villagers with roots in the local community, through which they could evaluate the social pattern of the present, and articulate certain aspirations for the future. The appeal of the ballad and the values it appeared to embody were sanctified by its pastness and by a consensual receptivity to past values and beliefs. This was also bound up with a more general process of retrospective idealization which continued to be characteristic of village culture through most of the nineteenth century. It can be said as well that it is this kind of process that gives weight to the priority of moral over historical truth in vernacular cultures with regard to songs of the past.

This view is supported by other studies, such as David Buchan's analysis of the ballad of 'Red Harlaw', and Tony Green's examination of several variants of the ballad 'McCaffrey'.[100] Buchan talks of the historical detail in songs of tradition existing 'in a Hall of Mirrors fashion' and yet precisely because of this indicating how ordinary people 'reacted to, moulded, and used' for their 'own emotional purposes the raw material of historical event' or historical process. Tony Green has reached similar conclusions. The narrative of 'McCaffrey' is in fact based on an historical event.[101] The singers from whom it was collected were not cognizant of the actual and specific details surrounding this event, nor could they give correct historical information as to date, place-names or whatever. They all nevertheless understood the ballad to be true.[102] Green suggests that 'when a singer talks of "truth", he [or she] is basically referring to morality rather than to historical facts, or to historical facts of such a general kind that their application is more likely to be ethical than documentary'.[103]

I would posit this as a general tendency in vernacular culture. When a song seems to be historically accurate or possible, it will convince singer and audience of its historical veracity, even though analysis may reveal little or no grounds for such veracity. But where a song sounds morally untrue, where it does not accord with the moral codes and value system of a group or community, then it will not become popular, even though investigation may reveal it to be, indeed, historically accurate. And when a song is about and from the past, its ability to outlive its origins, and to have any validity as a contemporary statement, depends upon the satisfaction of these evaluative criteria. Songs of 'tradition' thus stand to tell us more about those who sing and listen to them, in any given present, than they do of the past to which they relate. It is in this sense that they should be appreciated and understood as a historical resource.

Notes

1   *Banbury Guardian*: 30 January 1873.
2   Marx 1977: 110–11. Jauss's claim that historical materialism needs aesthetic idealism seems to me theoretically unconvincing, but to argue this point through would require a detailed treatment inappropirate in the present context. See Jauss 1975.
3   Fischer 1981: 12.
4   Belsey 1983: 17–27.
5   Hawthorn 1973: 4.
6   Cit. Eagleton 1976: 13.
7   Easthope 1977: 60–65. Cf. Trilling 1976.
8   This edition was republished in 1850. See Halliwell-Phillips, 1850: 66–69.
9   Halliwell-Phillips purchased his copy in 1847, and knew of only one extant copy, an imperfect one preserved in the Douce collection at Oxford.See Halliwell-Phillips 1850.
10   *The Roxburghe Ballads*, VI: 520–23. A possibly earlier version of the ballad than that of 1665 has quite different wording, suggesting perhaps that one or other broadside publisher appropriated the idea and rewrote rather than merely reprinted the text. See I, 1873: 385–93. The 1665 version was printed by W. Gilbertson, the one with quite different wording by F. Coles, both of London. For these printers, see Blagden 1954.
11   On this difficult topic, see Harker 1971: v-liii, and Green 1972. Also Elbourne 1980: 90–114.

12   See Dean-Smith 1954: 74 for a list of these sources. See also Holloway 1972: 195; Kennedy 1975: 508; Tiddy 1923: 82.

13   The detailed treatment the ballad requires was prevented by the plenitude of other material with which I had to deal in my monograph on the song tradition of Victorian Adderbury: see Pickering 1982. (For the Blunt mss., contact the Vaughan Williams Memorial Library, Cecil Sharp House, London.)

14   See Pickering 1982.

15   'Binx' Walton provided three times as many songs as the other major contributor to the Blunt manuscript collection. This pattern is common in 'folk' song collections, with the majority of singers providing only a few songs, and a minority providing many. In view of the difficulties posed by collectors' mediations of vernacular song, it would be unwise to draw any hard-and-fast conclusion from this pattern.

16   'Binx' Walton as the servant sang tenor, while his brother John in the persona of the husbandman sang bass. For the Walton brothers, see Pickering 1982, particularly chapters two and six.

17   See Pickering 1982: 51–3, 60, 175, and Pickering 1983.

18   Williams 1923: 112.

19   *Jackson's Oxford Journal*: 18 June 1881. The song was cited in this report as 'The Serving-maid and the Husbandman', by which we can either suppose a mistakenly heard song by an outsider, or a differently adapted text more directly appropriate to an age of predominantly female domestic servantry. The argument would have been essentially the same.

20   Dixon 1846, XVII: 42. Such long-lived popularity seems to have been true of Oxon generally, as well as other counties. How much its durable appeal in Adderbury – never mind anywhere else – was to do with the tune is an extremely tricky question. While interesting and valuable attempts exist to explain and analyse the social meanings of music, both generally and in relation to verbal texts, these operate at so general a level that anyone not a musicologist – and I am not – is bound to suffer the gravest difficulty in applying their findings to a specific and local case. There are in any case, as Tony Green observes elsewhere in this volume, substantial methodological problems involved in the analysis of the music of vernacular popular song, which would not be solved even were Janet Blunt alive to give her description of singing styles in Adderbury, or the Walton brothers still here to offer their own account of what the music meant to them. In the absence of a solution to these problems, my observations on the song's meanings, locally, must rely on my reading of the text.

21   For two slightly earlier examples of dialogues expressing the same ideological opposition as in the ballad, see Greene 1871 edn., and Breton's *Court and Country*, 'a brief discourse' between a courtier and a countryman, 1879 edn., II: 1–16. See also Chambers 1925, I: 79–81 on *debats* and *estrifs*.

22   Gray 1909–10: 317.

23   Stone 1969: 107–108. In his celebrated dictionary, Dr Johnson defines a husbandman as 'a man in a low position of life, who supports himself by the use of the plough', whereas a yeoman is discribed as 'a gentleman farmer'.

24   Otmoor is one of the best documented local cases, but note Headington Quarry and Baldon also: Ashby 1917: 104; Reaney 1970; Samuel, 1975: 139–263. See also Reed 1984: 53–76.

25   See Pickering 1981.

26   Young 1813: 109.

27   Gray 1959: 536.

28 Young 1813: 94–5.
29 Young 1813: 239.
30 Hasbach 1920: 102.
31 Lobel and Crossley 1969: 70.
32 Young 1813: 106, 148, 153, 175, 184, 218, 263.
33 Havinden 1968, I: 151–4.
34 Havinden 1968: 155–6, 158–9. See also Jenkins 1972: 50–7, 182–7, 233.
35 Ballard 1908: 28; Gray 1959: 130.
36 Lobel and Crossley 1969: 26–27.
37 New College Archives: 2864.
38 Henderson 1902: 126.
39 See Montague II: 292 for an adverse response of a member of the nobility to this match. Also, Namier 1959, and Namier and Brooke 1964.
40 Tate 1967: 172.
41 Lobel and Crossley 1969: 27; Gray 1909–10: 317.
42 Stroud 1975: 214.
43 Lobel and Crossley 1969: 5; Hoskins 1977: 197.
44 *Adderbury Parish Magazine*: July 1891.
45 Lobel and Crossley 1969: 9.
46 *Adderbury Parish Magazine*: July 1891; Gepp 1924: 63.
47 Lobel and Crossley 1969: 9; *Banbury Guardian*: 4 June 1891; Plumb 1971: 19. Pope nicknamed the Duke 'the tree-monger'. Bean 1921, I: 6.
48 Marx borrowed this phrase from Horace in commenting on a similar case; see Prawer 1978: 267.
49 Beesley 1841: 4.
50 Lobel and Crossley 1969: 27.
51 Gepp 1924: 62.
52 Lobel and Crossley 1969: 27.
53 Ashby 1974: 282.
54 Mingay 1968: 28–32.
55 Lobel and Crossley 1969: 27–8.
56 Ashby 1917: 103. The percentage of land tax paid by the owner occupiers is normally taken by economic historians as an index of the number of small freeholders. Large estates were often parcelled into tenancies for which by contrast only one gross annual sum was paid in land tax.
57 Gray 1909–10: 301.
58 Ashby 1917: 127.
59 Hasbach 1920: 106.
60 Lobel and Crossley 1969: 28.
61 Gray 1909–10: 306.
62 Chambers and Mingay 1966: 96.
63 Ashby 1917: 125.
64 Cit. Hasbach 1920: 131.
65 Ashby 1917: 110. It should be noted that Young, at the outset, genuinely believed his ideas would prove beneficial to all, but he lived to see them go sour and, like Oppenhimer, had the grace to admit how mistaken he was.
66 The local case of Merton, enclosed in 1763, provided every justification for this fear. See Dunkin 1823, II: 2–3.
67 Ashby 1974: 281.
68 Thompson 1968: 239.

69   Tribe 1981: ch. two.

70   Tribe 1981: 77.

71   Cobbett 1973: 227.

72   Smith 1892: 108–9.

73   Parker 1876: 90. See also Baker 1854, I: p. 169.

74   Green 1820: 103–110, 337; Rowntree and Kendall 1913; 22, 30; Prothero 1912: 469; *Banbury Guardian*: 23 May 1918, referring to 1907.

75   Stearns 1980: 627–28.

76   Foster 1965: 296.

77   Marx 1977: 487–88.

78   Stearns 1980: 631–32.

79   Stearns 1980: 639, 647.

80   Sturt 1966: 76.

81   Burrow 1978: 125. Note also Burrow's distinction between traditionalism and social nostalgia or reaction (120–38).

82   Dobrowolski 1975: 278.

83   Dobrowolski 1975: 278.

84   Hearn 1978; 129.

85   Ashby 1974: 285.

86   *As You Like It*, III, ii, 1.71; Fuller 1840, I: 342–43.

87   Thompson 1968: 254–55.

88   *Banbury Advertiser*: 16 April 1877.

89   Barrett 1891: 32; Palmer 1973: 32.

90   Purslow 1965: 31. This verse has, incidentally, been found printed on two-handled mugs or loving-cups, dating from around the late eighteenth century; the reverse side of the mug bears a coat of arms, part of which consists of scrolls bearing the inscription: TRUST IN GOD, DILIGENCE, THE HUSBANDMAN PROVIDES BREAD (Rawlinson 1979: 18).

91   Fussell 1949: 39.

92   Thomson 1908, see 'The Seasons: Autumn', ll. 351–2.

93   Thompson 1968: 108. The point is made with reference to Volney's *Ruins of Empire*. an influential book among nineteenth century freethinkers.

94   Henderson 1937: 112.

95   Haggard 1974: 102–3.

96   Barrett 1891: 5; Copper 1975: 208–9; Palmer 1973: 22–3.

97   Perkin 1978: 141.

98   Gretton 1914: 106.

99   Stearns 1980: 655.

100   Buchan 168: 58–67, reprinted in Lyle 1976: 29–40; Green 1970–71. See also Halpert and Herzog 1939: xiii-xx, and Ashton 1977.

101   A feature in the *Lancashire Evening Post*: 17 December 1973, retells the reporting of the event in the *Preston Mercury*: 16 September 1861. A chapbook, published in the same year (?) by John White of Preston quotes from the *Preston Mercury* report and adds verses on the 'dreadful tragedy'. (Thanks to Tony Green for this information.)

102   Cf Motherwell: 'I have, unfortunately for myself, once or twice notably affronted certain aged virgins by impertinent dubitations touching the veracity of their songs, an offence which bitter experience will teach me to avoid repeating, as it has, long ere this, made me rue the day of its commission'. Motherwell 1827: xxvii.

103   It is interesting to note here that Steblin-Kamenskij 1973 has argued that the distinction we make between 'historical' and 'artistic' truth does not apply at all to the early Icelandic sagas.

3   *Parody and Performance*

IAN RUSSELL

The yeoman culture whose disappearance in the south midlands provoked, in Michael Pickering's analysis, a symbolic reaction in the invocation of one of its members as a metaphorical counterweight to the capitalization of agrarian society, did not disappear all over Britain. In some areas, geomorphology, low population density, and the demands of local industries, have combined to preserve it into the twentieth century – now crucially complemented by the Common Market's policy of protecting farmers on marginal land. One such area is the mid-Pennine region where, on the borders of Yorkshire and Derbyshire, Ian Russell has been engaged in field-research for over a decade and a half. Here, the unsuitability of terrain and weather for mechanized farming on a large scale, coupled with the West Riding's historical demand for wool and meat, and more recently with EEC subsidies, have provided the basis for a continuing pastoral economy. It may seem paradoxical to call a man a small farmer when he runs a thousand sheep on as many moorland acres; but those acres are likely to be rented from a large public corporation such as the local electricity board, and he and his wife farm them with a Land-Rover, a couple of dogs, and little or no hired help: a far cry from the highly capitalized agricultural labour-market of the southern and eastern counties.

It is this pastoral economy, fundamentally an old-fashioned mode of subsistence, but now maintained by its being keyed into a multi-national market and financial infrastructure – just as through the last century it was maintained by a major growth-industry on its doorstep – which provides the basis of the lively popular culture which Ian Russell discusses. For men and women leading relatively isolated working lives, the crack and the singing on a Saturday night are more than usually important; and big social occasions such as hunt-suppers and the twice-yearly business meetings of the Shepherds' Society, which from a wide area draw people together who have interests in common but may otherwise rarely meet, provide the context for informal performances of long duration and great vigour. It is to an aspect of these performances that Ian Russell addresses himself. It is worthy of note that, drawing his methodology largely from synchronic ethnography (with an increasingly detailed concentration on the dynamics of public performance), he takes 'tradition' as having a virtually self-evident meaning, viz., the set of behaviour patterns which has coalesced in the situation which he studies in the present. At the same time, he makes it clear that, for him, a performance-tradition of singing and recitation is a dynamic, eclectic, and contextually defined phenomenon subject to its own internal dialectic.

In concentrating on the 'transgressive' art of parody, Russell moves beyond literary definitions of the artistic mode to a communicative conception in which the handsome progenitor and its deformed and raspberry-blowing offspring are seen in relationship to each other, not in any abstract and universal sense, but within the particular sequence of events and network of personal and social relationships which make up a singing evening in a moorland pub.

The performance of parodies is a phenomenon of vernacular singing that has been largely overlooked. I wish to examine from my own fieldwork experience not merely the parodies themselves, but their contexts of performance, in order to establish a rationale for their existence in tradition.[1] Initially I was attracted to the genre by three paradoxes that posed fundamental questions. Firstly, why is it that, at least in my experience, amateur singers, all country men, should relish and revel in songs that mock their own kind, bumpkin songs? Secondly, why is it that such a vital and popular part of the traditional repertoire in the public houses as parody is almost entirely overlooked by commentators and scholars, many of whom have conducted fieldwork at some time? Thirdly, how is it that the song and the parody can exist side by side in the performed repertoire, when the ostensible purpose of the parody is to render the original ridiculous? It will be a primary purpose of this essay to try and answer these three questions.

The paucity of direct references to parody in vernacular song makes the second question a useful starting point and provides the opportunity for a brief ground-clearing exercise. English folksong scholars such as Sharp have even less to say about parody than obscene songs.[2] Following Motherwell's aspersions there are a few references to the sacred parodies of the Puritans[3] and to William Hone's defence of parody in his trials of 1817,[4] but nothing much that is contemporary. Lloyd and, more recently, Watson refer to workers' home-made political/protest lyrics being parodies. Whereas Watson states that most of the best satirical songs are parodies and cites 'Doctor Beeching' (a parody of 'The Bonnie Lass of Fyvie'),[5] Lloyd adopts a more pejorative tone:

> Often, ironic point was given to these parodies by setting words of harsh, even coarse realism to appallingly sentimental melodies, which had the effect of radically transforming the originals and making a jeering comment on the whole stupefying genre of bourgeois popular song ... a few scraps of this kind linger on ... others sank without trace almost as soon as they appeared.[6]

It is regretable that Lloyd's feelings for parody prevented him from discussing this aspect more objectively or from tackling the subject head-on. Such gut-reaction is fortunately not shared by the Opies who quote numerous examples of children's parodies but confine analysis to specific examples, prefacing their chapter with the observation that, 'Parody, that most refined form of jeering, gives an intelligent child a way of showing independence without having to rebel'.[7] Similarly Green observes that through parody, 'working class people were able to distance themselves to some extent from the powerful institutions which all but owned their bodies and wanted their minds as well'.[8] His example, a hymn parody from the forces, represents an important and vital subgenre which compares with another parodic oral tradition, that of rugby songs.[9]

It is to North American scholars, however, that we must go in order to find more substantial statements. Herbert Halpert recognized that the existence of parodies was a factor that helped to preserve the life-in-tradition of the parodied songs and commented:

> I want to suggest that parody is the true test of popularity ... I believe that the presence or absence of parodies or local songs is a test of the vitality of a folk song tradition. If singers do not make up new songs, or manipulate the old materials, we have one indication that the singing tradition in that area has become fossilised.[10]

Abrahams and Foss support this view:

> Parodies seem to have infused new life into the otherwise moribund tradition of such songs as 'Springfield Mountain', 'Bangum and the Boar' and perhaps 'Lord Lovel'. A fine case in point is 'The Three Ravens'.[11]

Although the authors point out the difficulties in distinguishing local songs, imitations, and parodies, the fact that these remarks appear in a section devoted to creation and re-creation shows a marked difference in tone to that adopted by Lloyd. Peter Narvaez sees the element of plagiarism in parody, at odds with individuality and originality, as the primary cause for scholarly disinterest. He identifies parody in terms of audience responses:

> Two polar types of folk parody may be distinguished along with intermediate forms: firstly, humorous folk parody (intention of laughter), and secondly, serious folk parody (intention of reflection).[12]

Whilst his first type is acceptable, his second is not. His concept of parody as illustrated by such 'parodic cycles' as 'The Wabash Cannon Ball' and supported by an editorial tail-piece of further examples, demonstrates his confusion with straight imitation, typified by localized reworking of songs. Without any element of humour at the expense of the original, an imitation cannot be termed parody. This distinction is one with which John Greenway, in his seminal work on protest songs, would concur.[13]

Tony Barrand's provocative piece suggests that parody has survived in tradition because 'it provides easy access to anyone who writes to generate a *pertinent* song'. On adaptation in tradition he comments: 'Parody ... is the most overt demonstration of this basic process', and adds, 'A successful parody should stand on its own'. However, his suggested morphology is flawed by the same misconception as Narvaez demonstrates: that is, the inclusion of serious reworkings of traditional songs.[14]

It would be easy to write off this lack of concern on the part of scholarship as evidence of a puritanical approach which argues that parodies are a degenerate form that corrupt and subvert the tradition. Whilst we have seen there is clearly some support for this negative view, other points might usefully be considered.[15] In the first place the singers with whom folksong collectors worked were invariably elderly people who, in the process of reminiscing, were reconstructing their image of themselves: 'Singing songs of high seriousness reinforces certain images of one's life and character: singing parodies doesn't.'[16] The process of selection was further reinforced by the dictates of the singer/collector relationship for much the same reason as bawdy was withheld; that is, not wishing to offend the incomer's sense of propriety and respectability. This process of selection, or rather censorship, was further compounded by the fact that most songs were (and still are?) recorded in an artificial situation dictated by the presence of the collector/researcher rather than created in context.[17] Few fieldworkers since the 1900s have made a study of what was being sung in the taproom of an English public house (nor cared it seems);[18] similarly their ignorance of what was sung at a Harvest Home, coming-of-age party, wedding celebration, Christmas, family gathering and suchlike is a scholarly disgrace.[19] One consequence of their approach was that most of the material recorded was primarily from the private family repertoire rather than the stuff of public performance.

Whether or not this neglect of parody is the result of anathema, it contrasts strongly with the status accorded to it by traditional singers and their audiences.[20] Singers go to great pains to obtain versions; limp and worn handwritten copies are carefully stored inside the pages of a pocket diary or in a wallet. During the course of an evening's socializing in the pub these treasures may be proudly exhibited by the singer to an associate – in strict confidence of course. Later one may be performed during the round of singing and this precious private possession becomes the meat of outrageous public performance subject to the overwhelming approval of the audience. Such a description accurately epitomizes the attitude Arthur Howard had towards parodies and the hilarity caused by his regular performance of them. At this point it will be appropriate to examine some specific examples of parodies in performance chosen from the singing of Arthur Howard because he, of all the singers I have recorded, had the most examples in his repertoire.

Arthur Howard (1902–82; see photograph) was a Pennine sheep farmer and guardian of the rare-breed Woodland Whiteface sheep,[21] who worked and farmed on the moorland to the south-west of Holmfirth on the boundaries of West Yorkshire, South Yorkshire, and Derbyshire. An extrovert by nature and teetotaller by preference, he was one of the leading singers and entertainers in his district with an extensive repertoire approaching 200 songs. He was much in demand at the Saturday-night singsongs in the local pubs and often acted as MC for the socials that followed the meetings of the local Shepherds' Society, hare hunt, and the local branch of the National Farmers' Union. Arthur's sense of fun was well known within his locality; besides the comic songs and parodies, he had a fund of humorous tales and anecdotes, rhymes, monologues, and jokes. In the pub, all of these featured in the entertainment from time to time. Typically on 5 November 1974 at the social that followed the twice yearly

Arthur Howard (1902–1982)   *[Photograph by Ian Russell]*

Shepherds' Meet at the Stanhope Arms, Dunford Bridge, Arthur performed his parody of the sentimental parlour ballad, 'Thora'. There had been several comic and risque items performed during the course of the evening. For instance, Ian Siswick, a young sheep farmer from Marsden, had led the company in a bawdy version of 'Old King Cole', and Arthur himself had earlier given three scatalogical monologues ('Piddling Pete' or 'The Farmer's Dog',[22]

'The Dogs' Party', and 'Sonia Snell') as well as a boisterous chorus song of cuckoldry revenged, 'The German Clockmender'. However, the evening was getting late and had taken a rather sombre turn with a sentimental rendition of 'The Mountains of Mourne' and a concert-style tenor's performance of 'Oh my Papa'. This was quickly followed by that ultimate of sacred parlour ballads, 'The Holy City'. Then when some members of the audience suggested more of the same and another classic, 'Thora', was mentioned, Arthur stepped in and burst the bubble with his parody.

The intervention strategy Arthur Howard adopted was not only noisily appreciated and applauded but restored the holiday atmosphere to the final part of the evening. Ian Siswick quickly followed with two risqué and rowdy songs loaded with innuendo, 'The Soldier and the Female' ('For she loved to hear the waters rattle and the nightingale sing') and 'The Nutting Girl' ('"Young man", said she, "I think I feel/The world go round and round"'.) Other humorous items followed until the proceedings were wound up with the traditional song of farewell, 'Bless this House'.

In almost every particular, Arthur's parody conforms to the late nineteenth/ early twentieth-century conception of literary parody.[23] It will help if I summarize the main elements identified in literary parody and then establish how each aspect relates to Arthur's parody of 'Thora':

1 A parody is an imitation, usually comic, of an original work and as such it is a reflexive and backward-looking form.[24]
2 Parody is a form of criticism that is usually achieved by means of ironic inversion, ranging from playful mockery to biting ridicule. Hence the heroic become, prosaic, good sense becomes nonsense and vice versa.[25]
3 Parody depends for its effect upon the competence of the reader to appreciate the nature of the allusions. This presupposes a level of cultural sophistication and awareness.[26]
4 Parody demonstrates a conservative function as it reinforces the form of the original, and thereby perpetuates its tradition. This has been referred to as oblique homage.[27]
5 Normally, when the original is the 'target' of parody, a negative ethos is encountered in the use of such terms as denigration, contempt, and scorn. (In fact it is a corollary of this somewhat condemnatory approach that certain critics have adjudged parody to be essentially parasitical, derivative, and malicious.[28]) Sometimes, however, the original is chosen as the 'weapon' of parody in order to satirize fashions and practices.[29] Here the parody is not at the expense of the original, which is afforded respect and generates a positive ethos.[30]
6 Parody has, besides its main critical function, an interpretive one, such that it may shed new light on the meaning of the original.[31]

It is not difficult to see that the parody of 'Thora' embodies several of these ideas. In the first place the original song, popularized by John McCormack in 1907,[32] is afforded a great deal of respect by singers. Stanley Marsden, a farmer from Lodge Moor, Sheffield, whose father Arthur sang it, performed an incomplete version and commented 'It's a good song!', and showed admiration towards another singer, Ted Wragg, who knew both verses, 'I want to get 'im to write words down'.[33] Another singer, Jack Couldwell, observed that you have to be an exceptional singer to do the song justice 'It's a classic!'[34] This attitude undoubtedly is generated by the lofty sentiments typical of such parlour balladry:

> I live in a land of roses but I dream of a land of snow,
> Where you and I were happy in the days of long ago.
> Nightingales in the branches, tralalalalala,
> I only could 'ear you singing, I only could 'ear your song,
> I only could 'ear you singing, I only could 'ear your song.
> Speak, speak to me Thora, speak from your heaven to me,
> Child of my dreams, light of my life, angel of love to me,
> Child of my dreams, light of my life, angel of love to me, angel of
> love to me.[35]

Parody of 'Thora'   Arthur Howard

I was standing in a police court,
But in silence and in fear.
'Are you the father of this child?'
The old judge said with a sneer.
'Am I the father? No, Sir!'
I said without a doubt.
And the child who was only six months old
Began to bawl and shout,
The child who was only six months old
Began to bawl and shout:

'Speak, speak, speak to me father!
Speak to your only child!
Speak to me Daddy!
Speak to me Dad!
Speak to your only lad!'
'One pound a week you'll pay, one pound a week I'll say
To that angel of love to me!(T)

The convention of the dream, the flashback, the premature death that ended the romance, reach their climax in a hopeless attempt to communicate with the dearly departed. It is tempting to assume a spiritualist influence in the song's composition. The melody carries the tone of high seriousness well with tonal inflections, modulations into the minor, clearly defined phrases that call for crescendo and diminuendo, as well as pauses, accelerando and decelerando. In fact, in Stanley Marsden's rendition, the piece is performed with a rhythmic complexity amounting to rubato, though his style is not declamatory, rather it is contemplative and subtle in his use of dynamics. To summarize then, 'Thora' is a song of great stature among singers, some of whom aspire to perform it, and when performed it is handled with great respect and sensitivity. Arthur's parody is a comic imitation that uses ironic inversion to achieve its effect and so fulfils points one and two.

In the parody the dream world has become downtown Piccadilly (in Manchester?), the angel of love is a prostitute who robs him. The hopeless attempt at contacting the dead in heaven is given stark reality in the context of a police court, where the communicating is done by an infant (far too young to talk) but here miraculously speaking out to identify the unhearing and perjuring father. The case for parenthood is thereby proven and the persona of the song ends up paying alimony to 'That angel of love to me!' The 'angel' is, of course, far from innocent and the deeply spiritual relationship of the original here is transposed to a sordid sexual contract. The ironic inversion is successfully completed. Without some familiarity with the original (point three) the audience would fail to appreciate the way that the text is closely paralleled. For example, the mock-heroic exclamations that mark her disappearance have clear echoes in the original, but are thrown into sharp comic relief by the pathetic aside 'so had my watch and chain'. Similarly the pathetic appeals of the babe echo the unanswered appeals to the dead Thora. It is doubtful, however, if the humour of the parody would be completely lost on an audience unfamiliar with the original. The sense of melodrama, given weight by the melodic structure, the absurdity of the talking infant, the bathos, the sordid reality of a chance romantic encounter, and the cynical ending can all be taken at face value without reference to 'Thora'. Moreover, the parodist (whoever *he* was) chose a recognizable traditional theme – the young man lured by the bright lights of the city avails himself of the services of a woman of easy virtue and pays the consequences.[36] In this conservative function point four is fulfilled.

Arthur believed he learnt the parody from a single hearing at a hunt social at Slaithwaite. He found it especially easy to learn because he knew the original song. He associated the singing of the parody with 'good times', with pleasing his audience, and with the intention of gently shocking or mildly offending some of its members in a good-natured way. This he had masterfully accomplished on 5 November 1974 in a performance that captured the mood of the evening. Whereas his rendition was outwardly serious and straight, and gave no clue as to the content of the piece, his audience, familiar with the knowing look in his eye and tuned in to his keen sense of humour, were quick to seize on and relish every comic aspect.

While there seems to be little about Arthur's parody that relates to points five and six, he did say quite emphatically that people never objected to him singing it, nor did he feel it detracted from the original at all, either through his eyes or through his audience's – 'There's no harm in it at all'.[37] Whereas on paper the purpose of the parodist would seem to have been to ridicule and shock, to deflate and expose the pomposity of the original, in the reality of the social evening of the Shepherds' Society, no great or obvious offence was caused, on the contrary the audience was greatly amused and pleased by its performance. Similarly the fun may have been at the expense of the original but its status was not intentionally diminished especially in the eyes of the singer.

The three qualities in particular that distinguish 'Thora' are the emotionally-intense lyrics, the dramatic melody, and the esteem afforded it by audience and singers. Moreover, the song forms part of the common core repertoire of familiar songs that singers in South Yorkshire can either sing or join in with. This is equally true of another 'tear-jerker' of which Arthur sang a parody.[38]

Arthur knew two versions of 'The Irish Emigrant', the one 'that everybody knows', and a second, longer version that he learnt from his eldest sister, Mary.[39] It was the familiarity of 'The Irish Emigrant', along with the other features mentioned above, that made the song particularly suitable for parody. The emigrant, having lost his wife, is forced to leave his native land for reasons unstated. The song is laden with grief, nostalgia, and homesickness. The version Arthur learnt from his sister (which I have not encountered in tradition elsewhere) is in several details more explicit.[40] These aspects serve to heighten the emotional intensity with harsh reality, as can be seen in the second verse:

'Tis but a step down yonder lane, the little church stands near.
The church where we were wed, Mary, I see its spires from here;
But the graveyard lies between, Mary, and my step might break your rest,
For I've laid you darling down to sleep with your baby on your breast.

I thank you for the patient smile when your heart was fit to break,
When the hungry pain was gnawing there and you hid it for my sake.
I bless you for the pleasant word when your heart was sad and sore.
Oh I'm thankful you are gone, Mary, where grief can't reach you more,
Where grief can't reach you more.

Here we learn the specific plight of the emigrant, namely that both his wife and his child have died from starvation. The grief and nostalgia are given further momentum by the use once again of the device of a dream or vision. The flashback in the final verse is particularly poignant as the separation is now both of time and of distance. The motifs recalled from the first stanza hark back to the idealised setting of the lovers' original meeting.

Although I never heard a public performance of the parody, others had and have commented favourably on its merits.[41] Just like 'Thora' the song had touched on extremely emotive and sensitive subjects (in this case widowerhood and exile) that were held in reverence and were respected by both singers and audience. It is not hard to see that the parody might make capital out of such sentimentality. In fact, I cannot think of a more suitable comic deflationary statement than that which opens the parody.

This is the only parody in Arthur's repertoire for which he had a printed source.[42] Among the large collection of songs, songsters, and sheet music that Arthur had acquired was a bundle of very tatty songsheets which he had labelled 'old songs of father's still to tape'. Understandably Arthur never did work his way through the thousands of songs contained in the sheets. The collection dates from 1870–1900 and includes several similar volumes (nearly all published in Manchester), among them the Number 59 edition of Hibbert's *Grand Song Book*, published by Edward Hibbert, Green Street, Manchester. It sold for a penny, dates from the early 1890s, and includes '"I Sat Upon a Pin Mary: Parody of the Irish Emigrant", written by George Hopkinson, composed by W. Strickland, and sung by Geo. H. Leslie, Negro Comedian'. A full score of the song is given as being available from George Hopkinson (the parodist?), 24 Alma Street, Harpurhey, Manchester. It is possible that Arthur's father, Haigh, had taken out a subscription with Hibbert and other publishers of songs; for it was unlikely that he, a farmer and gamekeeper, was able to visit Manchester on a regular basis so as to acquire the sheets directly. Of course, a stationers in Holmfirth might have stocked the sheets but it is more likely that they had been hawked by cheapjacks. Certainly Arthur remembered cheapjacks coming to the village of Holme where he had been brought up and selling and singing songs, as well as collecting them.[43] However, Arthur never heard his father perform this parody and the copy in number seven of Arthur's handwritten songbooks is in his own hand, and does not occur in the songbooks written out by his father. It seems reasonable to conclude that Arthur's source was the Hibbert's sheet especially as the text in his songbook is the same word for word. Even Arthur's performed version adheres faithfully to the text of the printed copy with only one minor variation – 'while' for 'whilst'.

The humour of the parody is very similar to that employed by the 'Thora'

Parody of 'The Irish Emigrant'

Arthur Howard

The doctor came to me, Mary, but when he saw the stab,
He whispered unto me, Mary, 'It must have been a dab'.
I told him he was right, Mary, and then he gave me some stuff.
I dashed it from my sight, Mary, the smell was quite enough.
I am a hopeless case, Mary, the doctor says so wise.
I lie here on my face, Mary, I can't lie otherwise.
Though your face I may not see, Mary, while here I'm strapped so tight;
So do not wait for me, Mary, we cannot meet tonight,
We cannot meet tonight.(T)

parody. The ironic inversion of sitting on a pin rather than a stile, the risque innuendo contained in the fact that the location of the wound is unmentionable, the mock-heroic of such phrases as 'my race was nearly run', and the bathos of 'they took their hook again' – slang for 'went away'. The bereavement is mocked in that the persona is convinced he is going to die from the pinprick; and so is the exile, for he cannot see her face or keep his rendezvous because he must lie on his stomach on account of the pain. In terms of our six points of literary parody, the correlation is much as before. However, it is worth stressing points three and four. Firstly, Arthur performed not one, but two different versions of the original; secondly, his songbook number seven contained two copies of the original text as well as the parody; and thirdly, the Hibbert's songsheet contained a copy of the original text as well as the parody. Besides reinforcing the original text by following its structure and metre, to be of course sung to the original tune, the parody depends largely for its humour on an audience's familiarity with the original. Because the success of the parody may depend on this fact it presupposes regular performances of the original, which can be interpreted as a force to promote the original especially if the singer is the same for both. Arthur's parody is unashamedly irreverent and ridiculous, but obvious as the target is, it does not damage the original. The 'send-up' is just a momentary hiatus that is forgotten until the next time it is heard.

The two parodies described above were distinguished by their mock-heroics and their touch of risque humour set to the original dramatic melodies. Our next two parodies are unashamedly vulgar, openly risque, and fitted to much more rumbustious music-hall tunes.

Neither the parody of 'My Home in Tennesee'[44] nor that of 'Show Me the Way to Go Home'[45] were part of Arthur's 'private family' repertoire. However, he did treat them as 'private and confidential' in as much as handwritten copies were interleaved with other loose sheets in his pocket diary, as mentioned above, and only shown discreetly to companions at predominantly male social gatherings. Later in the evening they would be performed when all inhibitions had long been overcome, and the company were in the mood for ribald songs such as 'Put my Hand on Myself' and 'Allouette',[46] as well as monologues, jokes, verses, and anecdotes that enlivened the evening entertainment. The advantage of this mix was that it allowed farmers, farmworkers, and shepherds, men who normally lead a solitary life, to participate even though they might not be recognized as singers. Often spoken items were more noisily applauded than the songs, with the notable exception of parodies. In this respect, the parodies were regarded by the audiences as musical jokes.

It is hard to separate our two parodies, especially as both celebrate a fairground visit to view the delights of the tattooed lady, a classic butt of music-hall humour.[47] They both follow similar tours of the lady's topography with descriptions of the sights; the erotic destination is glimpsed and hinted at in the double-entendre of 'home' in their respective titles. The mention of Germany, battleships, the Army Service Corps, and troops suggests that both originated in the armed forces, which seems likely as Arthur had many acquaintances who had served in one or other World War, although he himself had been too young for the first and classed as a reserved occupation for the second.

Parody of 'My Home in Tennessee'   Arthur Howard

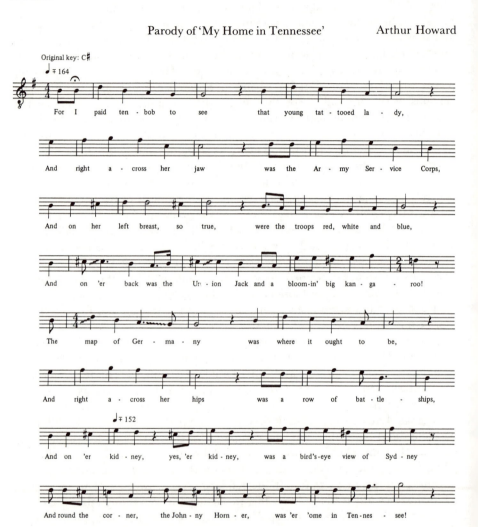

Back home in Tennessee, she threw her legs at me.
I saw her housemaid's knee; that's all she showed to me.
All I could think of that night was her skirts of snowy white.
She was haughty, fat and forty, what a glorious sight!

The stage she tried to trip, when something it went rip;
And the audience, they did grin when she asked them for a pin,
And the orchestra of eleven played a little bit of heaven,
And I'm certain they pulled the curtain to hide her home in Tennessee!(T)

Parody of 'Show Me the Way to Go Home' (Standard tune)

For I'm so happy, oh so happy! I went to the fair.
I paid eighteen pence to see the tattooed lady there;
And of all the sights I saw, the thing that pleased me best
Was when they pulled the curtains and she lifted up her vest:

And she showed me a picture of 'er home;
She'd a battleship tattooed on 'er chest;
Underneath her arms were the 'Babes in the Wood';
Down 'er back was the 'Scotch Express';
And the next thing I was shown,
As round her knees she began to roam
I said, 'Mother have mercy on a fellow like me!
Will you show me the way to go home?'

I'm so sorry, oh so sorry! I got mixed in a fight.
I got rudely wakened in the middle of the night.
Someone knocking at my door, before the night was through,
And when I went to open it, there stood two men in blue,

And they took me away from my home
To a hard wooden log for me bed.
There weren't any pansies or roses round the door;
There were bars down the door instead.
I said, 'I've one request, my wife she is all on 'er own,
And if the lodger comes in while I'm away,
Will you show him the way to go home?' (T)

In neither example does the humour openly ridicule the original, rather the original melody and form is used as a vehicle for the risque humour. That is not to imply that close knowledge of the original is not important to the appreciation of the humour for it gives the double-entendre an extra layer of meaning. However, there is little chance that any pub audience that participates in singing or whose average age is such that they have had first hand experience of variety and vaudeville shows, could be unfamiliar with the originals. If criticism is intended in the parodies, then it is directed at the hackneyed image of the original pieces.

Over-familiarity must be one of the primary reasons for the success of Arthur's parody of 'Grandfather's Clock'.[48] The original is a great favourite of public houses if not as a complete song, at least the first verse and chorus as part of a piano or organ medley of choruses. Arthur noted, 'You hear it too often but you never hear it through'. Needless to say, Arthur knew 'it through' and he was fond of the words and the sentiment expressed by them.

Above I have mentioned how the success of the parody depended in part on the regular performance of the original. In the case of 'Grandfather's Clock', familiarity is better described as close proximity, such that Arthur regularly followed up a rendition of the original with the parody. At the social evening of the Shepherd's Meet on 5 November 1975, Arthur followed 'Jerusalem' with 'Grandfather's Clock' and then the parody of it, followed by the 'German Clockmender'. The parody was understandably better received than the original and yet, for all this, it was an instance of oblique homage (see point four). The members of the audience were at one with Arthur's feelings towards the song: they loved its infectious melody and identified with the lyrics, but they were all too familiar with it. Thus when Arthur ignored the polite applause that followed his rendition of the original and broke into the less familiar parody, he gave the audience a pleasant surprise and an opportunity to reflect back on the qualities of the original. This was greatly helped by the tonic of humour.

Parody of 'Grandfather's Clock'   Arthur Howard

Ninety years without slumbering, tick-tock tick-tock
His life's second numbering, tick-tock tick-tock,
It stopped short, never to go again,
When the old man died.

Now me grandfather's clock was me mother's p'rambulator
And in it round the park we used to ride.
There was me and Brother Benny, Squeaking Tom and Justice Parking,
Screaming Jimmy and the twins all stuck inside.
Now me grandad, who was dead, changed 'is mind, got up instead,
And the sight that he saw gave 'im a shock:
For the man 'at brought the coal couldn't get it down the hole,
So he put it in me grandfather's clock.

And we didn't need a shovel as the pendulum swung higher;
For everytime it swung it knocked some coal into the fire;
And at nine o'clock the crank used to chime a double blank,
So Grandad had to knock, he couldn't go. Tick-tock!

Ninety years without slumbering, tick-tock tick-tock,
His life's second numbering, tick-tock tick-tock,
It stopped short, never to go again,
When the old man died.(T)

There are several instances here of the parody mocking the original and the use of ironic inversion. Thus the large clock becomes a pocket watch on the one hand, and food cupboard-cum-coal store-cum-perambulator (large enough for seven children) on the other. The watch has nonsensical animal properties – 'it could go ninety days without food' (a Waterbury watch took several minutes to wind up everyday!) – and because it goes wrong on account of the butter, poor Grandad is unable to die until it's repaired. In fact, the piece reaches complete absurdity when Grandad changes his mind and gets up from the 'dead'. The conclusion is a painful pun on the game of dominoes where the double-blank puts a stop to the game and Grandad 'knocks' to say he cannot go (as well the dead might, were it a séance). The use of such nonsense and non-sequiturs is a departure from the form of the parodies so far examined, as is the absence of risque humour. However, the linking of such ludicrous and non-sequential ideas into a comic unity was not unusual in the patter of music-hall comedians,[50] while miraculous shifts of shape, size, and function are found in the works of Rabelais and others.[51] In this sense the parody strikes at the universal appeal of the original song and the notion that it has come to mean all things to all people. Despite all the targetting of the humour, the original seems only to gain by it, perhaps because the real object of criticism is not the song but the attitude to death it portrayed, encountered among countless Victorian songs and granted royal approval following the death of Prince Albert (see point five). Although Arthur had sung the parody for most of his life, it was not until a chance hearing of a programme on television about the life and songs of George Formby, senior, that he realized who had popularized the parody.

One final observation on the form of this parody is that there is an additional strain of melody for the chorus. It appears to be from a source that is almost as familiar as 'Grandfather's Clock', that is 'The Death of Poor Cock Robin',[52] and specifically from the couplet that begins, 'All the birds of the air ...' Not only does the borrowed phrase fit into the overall musical contour without any awkwardness, but also provides a refreshing variation that brings to the parody a measure of originality and independence. An even stronger element of originality is found in the next of Arthur's parodies.

The 'song of songs' form or *cento*, [53] an ancient literary genre, is not unusual in music hall songs and parlour balladry; a famous example is 'The Song that Reached my Heart',[54] which pays homage to 'Home Sweet Home' by incorporating it into the chorus; to a lesser extent the parody of 'Grandfather's Clock' is also a *cento*. Arthur's song of 'The Egg' is essentially a succession of parodies strung together around the bizarre theme that 'eggs are never quite new laid'.[55] It delights audiences through its ingenuity, with eclecticism as the governing principle of composition, and is such a tour de force that it might be described as the 'parodist's parody'. As it works its way through the sequence, the parody changes tune and adopts the appropriate strain of each melody. A priori, it seems like a recipe for confusion and a hotchpotch of disjointed fragments. However, as Arthur performed it, each part transferred to the next with great ease and fluidity, such that a unity of form was achieved, and attested to by an audience that were appreciative of its originality. Following the parody is a list of the well-known songs from which it was constructed:

'The Egg'   Arthur Howard

It's birth cer - ti - fi - cate's been de - layed for months and months and months;

I think per - haps 'twas laid _____ by some ex - tinct do - do

♩ = 120

Ten, twen - ty, thir - ty, for - ty, fif - ty years a - go.'

♩. = 98

And then a small chick - en jumped out and cried, 'Par - lez - vous?'

In my best French I then re - plied, 'The same _____ to you!'

He said, 'I think I've come ov - er here with Ma - de - mai - selle from you know where.'

♩ = 86

So we threw it through the win - dow,

We threw it through the win - dow,

We threw it through the win - dow.

♩ = 104

Then the wai - ter went _____ to the gro - cer's shop

Just to find the fel - low who'd sup - plied him;

With 'is fa - ther's sword _____ that he'd gird - ed on

He _____ slew the egg which ran be - side him.

There it — lay, all that — day, till the dust-man came to clear the bits a · way.

♩ = 120

Egg shells 'e saw, egg shells 'e saw.

♩ = 150

He wrapped them up in 'is old sta · ble jack · et

And thought for 'is tea they would do,

So 'e ate them and ear · ly next morn · ing

His wi · dow 'is club mon · ey drew!

♩ = 152

Then it's 'Rule Bri · tan · nia, what · ev · er might be paid,

Eggs are nev · er, nev · er, nev · er, quite new laid!'

© 1921 EMI Music Publishing Ltd, London WC2H 0LD Reproduced by permission of EMI Music Publishing Ltd and International Music Publications.

1 Lines 1–2 'Annie Laurie'[56]
2 Lines 3–4 'The Boys of the Old Brigade' or 'The Old Brigade'[57]
3 Lines 5–6 'Poor Old Joe' or 'Old Black Joe'[58]
4 Lines 7–9 'For Months and Months and Months'[59]
5 Line 10 'I Mind the Day' or 'My Old Shako' or 'Hey ho many a year ago'[60]
6 Lines 11–13 'Mademoiselle from Armentieres'[61]
7 Lines 14–16 'In and Out the Windows'[62]
8 Lines 17–20 'The Minstrel Boy'[63]
9 Line 21 'The Bay of Biscay'[64]
10 Line 22 'Excelsior'[65]
11 Lines 23–26 'The Tarpaulin Jacket'[66]
12 Lines 27–28 'Rule, Britannia!'[67]

I am full of admiration for the ingenuity of the parodist, Greatrex Newman, for in each section he has imitated the original so effectively as to incorporate either the title or a key phrase, or a pun on it, and yet keep the narrative flowing. Not only do each of the twelve sections follow on effectively in narrative terms, in that each song parodied is carefully ordered for greatest effect, but also the individual melodic phrases fit together with surprising ease. The harmonic progression modulates seven times between the keys of G and C until line 23 (Section 11), when it moves into a coda of F and and finishes in C for the 'Rule Britannia' finale. The humour too has a flow that is constantly revitalized as each new section is commenced. Bathos, hyperbole, and absurdity characterize the humour. For example, the opening line brings an audience down with a thump, and the preposterous notion of a talking or rather humming egg (colloquially meaning 'stinking') possibly a dodo's, which then hatches, takes the theme of staleness to ridiculous extremes. When the waiter girds on his sword and goes in search of the grocer, some sort of revenge might be expected. However, he finds (to his horror?) that the 'egg' won't go away and is following him. In desperation he slays it. The pun on 'Excelsior' provides a comic climax, only to be capped with bathos by the entrance of the dustman whose subsequent food poisoning enables his widow to collect the life insurance money from the Sick Club. Finally there is the adage, and the audience is left with the feeling that never a truer word was sung in jest.

Arthur's song of 'The Egg' is not a send-up in the same sense as the parody of 'Thora'. The steady procession of songs that pass before the audience's ears deny the possibility of focusing on the target of the original songs (with the possible exception of 'Excelsior').[68] Clearly they provide a vehicle (point five), but for what is open to question. The mundane choice of a bad egg is a suitably humorous and earthy topic, and provides a clue to the target. In each section the abstract, metaphysical language of the original lyrics is set against the everyday, concrete language of the parody.[69] The pastoral image of 'Maxwelton Braes' is displaced by the grotesque Victorian reality of a 'Grand Hotel', just as the ludicrous sentiment of the protagonist's intention to die for love (only true to the lyrics of songs), is offset by the uninspired complaint of a belly-ache caused by food poisoning. Nor is bathos the only technique used; hyperboles found in most of the original songs are here extended to surreal lengths – the egg is so old it came from a dodo, it is so high-smelling that it is not only on the move but it can run, it is such a threat that it must be put to the sword. There is also a sideways dig at the misleading language of advertising. The redundancy of such a term as 'new laid' is exposed with the aid of literalism, rather in the manner of Jerome K. Jerome.[70] While I am sure that Arthur himself was aware of the literal truth of the adage, this was not the aspect he chose to remark on:

> I rather fancied it with all the bits in 'cos I knew practically all the songs belonging it.(T)

Thus the ingenuity of the piece was what appealed to him, and so was the opportunity to gain the admiration of the audience for the ingenuity of the artist who could perform such a complex item.[71] The parody also had a personal meaning, for it had been performed at Arthur's wedding reception (7 February 1929) by a friend, Ernest Jackson, from whom he had learnt the piece.

Although 'The Egg' like the parody of 'Grandfather's Clock' does not employ any risqué humour, Arthur obviously had an attraction towards 'summat a bit more spicey'.(T) One such parody which Arthur performed in the pub with two friends is a variant of 'Old MacDonald Had a Farm' in much the same vein as 'Old King Cole', i.e. it is cumulative and unashamedly vulgar. In both pieces any shadow of doubt as to the connotation of each verse is forcefully dispelled by the blatant use of reinforcing gestures and actions. Thus the force of the parody completely turns the innocence of the original on its head. (Was it ever really innocent?) The parody is further compounded by the stitching on of the chorus from 'The Farmer's Boy'.[72] Although the use of a 'double-barrelled' parody appears to re-echo the principle of 'The Egg', it compares more accurately in form with the parody of 'Grandfather's Clock', for it too keeps the serious, well-known chorus and incorporates a strain of melody from another source. However, there is an element beyond the humour of the bawdry and the spoofing of the songs; that is the way the parody appears to be holding up a mirror to its performers. The singers are farmers and farmworkers; their parody is a vehicle for the satire of country songs and country bumpkins, farmlife and stock-breeding in particular. This outrageous song presents a caricature of the singers themselves which they find outrageously funny. Nor is this self-reflexive humour unique in the target of its satire among the repertoires of singers in the Pennines of South and West Yorkshire. A much better known example is 'Gossip John'.

Gossip John

Arthur Howard and others

Ma petticoit, A've lost, A've lost,
A've left it at me granny's,
But A'll fetch it back int' morning,
A'll fetch it back int' morning, Gossip John.
(Verse form follows that of the first verse.)

'Na then!' (Spoken.)
Ya brand new care (cow) 'as corved, (calved) 'as corved
Reet under parlour winda; (Sound of mooing)
And its corf (calf) it will not suck,
Thou'll 'af ta give it finga, Gossip John.

Ya duck 'as swallowed a snail, quack-quack!
Now isn't that a wonda?
And it all came out its tail
And split its tail assunder, Gossip John.
'Yer very polite, aren't yer?' (Spoken.) ('Arse' is usually sung.)

Oh, Kate A've seen thee ... (Whistled.)
Na aren't A a lying ol' rascal?
Thar's nobbut seen me armoil,
Thar's nobbut seen me armoil, Gossip John!

There's a lot more verses ta this song,
But we aren't barn ta sing them,
'They aren't fit t'ear! (Spoken.)
So we'll bid you all goodnight,
We'll bid you all goodnight, goodnight, goodnight! (Loud applause.)
'More! More!' (Spoken.) [73]

The overwhelming popularity of this piece is hard to reconcile with the observation made by Frank Purslow,[74] that the song is a townsman's send-up of the ways and speech of the countryman/woman, for clearly it is held in abiding affection by the very group it is intended to satirize. If there is any doubt as to the truth of this paradox, the reader should consider the following points as s/he listens to a recording of the song:[75]

1 It is performed in unison by a group of men, who each put on their own 'act' as they sing.
2 The dialect of the song is crudely exaggerated.
3 The melodic frills are deliberately over-emphasized and hammed.
4 Full play is made of gestures, asides, and innuendoes.
5 Audiences participate in and encourage the general licence afforded by the song.

Compounded with these performance aspects are those inherent in the text: that country people are notorious gossips and that the substance of their prattle is inconsequential trivia.

Such a song has been in tradition for a long time.[76] The parodox here can be reconciled by the fact that in its present form it represents an attempt to come to terms with what is a rather odd and idiomatic inheritance.[77] When such a piece is no longer tenable as a straight song, the predictable outcome is that it is dropped from the traditional repertoire. However, in the case of 'Gossip John', an alternative has been found through the remedy of parody. Harking back to the words of Abrahams and Foss and other American scholars, it is an example of parody extending the life in tradition of the original in a modified form, a restatement of point four.[78]

Traditional singing has, like all forms of cultural expression, developed its own form of self-criticism, in terms of repertoire as well as style. Parody is a form of control from within the culture,[79] and 'Gossip John' fulfils such a function. Its performance indicates the type of song (and style of singing) that can no longer be taken seriously.

There is, however, one notable absence that sets 'Gossip John' apart from the other parodies under discussion. There is no evidence of an original in tradition. Even the version in *Pills to Purge Melancholy* of 1720 already appears to have the form of parody built in. The tune John Gay incorporated into *The Beggar's Opera* of 1727–28 with its exaggerated melodic leaps and staccato runs was clearly intended as part of his overall parody of Italian operatic conventions.[80] The fact that an original may never have existed calls into question the assumption that such a song is a parody at all. But I would argue it is and, in support of this claim, suggest that parody can be understood by two distinct but inter-related concepts. Firstly there are items of repertoire that loosely constitute the genre such as the parody of 'Grandfather's Clock' and secondly there are techniques of performance that parody songs or styles of singing or even aspects of life, such as 'Gossip John'.[81] This latter concept is what is generally understood by the term 'burlesquing', and a classic example from the music hall is the treatment of 'Villikins and his Dinah' by Frederick Robson and by Sam Cowell.[82] Their text was not so much imitated as distorted: extra bits were inserted, the lines were delivered nonsensically, words were deliberately mispronounced and speech affected, while slang and cant terms supplanted more innocent speech. There can be no doubt that what was performed in the London music halls of the 1850s and 1860s to great acclaim was a parody, based on a technique that E. L. Blanchard had worked out, originally for Robson. When G. A. Sala, the critic, wrote in 1864 about there being an 'original ballad' it is quite obvious that he was educating his readership to a little known fact.[83] In other words most of the Victorian audiences that found 'Villikins and his Dinah' so excruciatingly funny did so without reference to any original, like the case in point 'Gossip John'.

It is worthwhile pursuing the subject of 'Villikins' a little bit further in order to shed light on one aspect of the tradition that deserves consideration. As most scholars now realize, the original is a ballad, that existed on countless broadsheets, called 'William and Dinah'.[84] Despite the devasting popularity of the parody, the original has survived in tradition. Frank Hinchliffe of Lodge Moor, near Sheffield, sings a version, which line for line closely resembles the parody.[85] Surprisingly, he had not (at the time I interviewed him) connected the two pieces, as the one being a parody of the other, even though the hero of

Frank's song is called Wilkins. Perhaps in the serious side of the original he saw nothing that related to the corny humour of the parody, especially as melodically the two pieces are expressed so differently. Frank is a discerning and discriminating singer who is not naive in such matters and yet the connection simply had not been made. I think it would be wrong to read overmuch into this particular instance. However, it does serve indirectly to reinforce several points already made; that enjoyment of a parody by audience and singers is not necessarily based on an appreciation of the original text (see point three); that the success of the parody is not normally at the expense of the original; that, where the success of parody is not dependent on an audience's knowledge of the original, it is the technique of parodying rather than the genre of parody that is the source of appeal.

Arthur Howard sang two versions of 'Old Johnny Bugger', a song which is well-known throughout South Yorkshire.[86] Essentially he kept the text the same but had two variants of the tune, a fact of which he was unaware. He would also append some of his verses to the renditions of other singers, if the verses had not already been included. In fact, the piece was often sung as a dialogue with different singers contributing verses:

> It's always been a favourite in the pubs. First one sang one (verse) and then one sang another (verse).

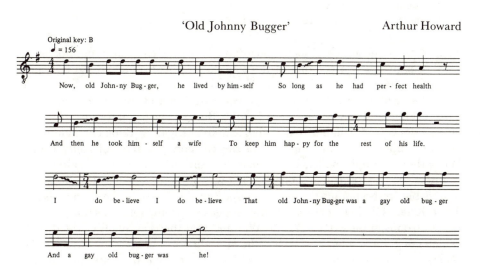

'Old Johnny Bugger' Arthur Howard

Now, old Mrs Bugger, she had a bad leg.
The doctor ordered her to bed.
He told Johnny Bugger, he'd better begin
To rub his wife's left leg with gin.

Now, old Johnny Bugger, he thought it was a sin
To rub his wife's left leg with gin;
So he up with the bottle and he poured it down his throttle,
So he rubbed his wife's left leg with the bottle.

Now, old Johnny Bugger went riding one day.
His horse broke down so he walked all the way,
He came to a hill and reached a full stop,
So he walked right up from the bottom to the top.

Now, the Lord made the bees, the bees made honey.
The Lord made man and man made money.
The devil made Hitler, Hitler made sin;
So Johnny made a hole just to put the bugger in.

Now, old Johnny Bugger, he joined a submarine crew
To sink a German ship or two;
So all you little Nazis, you'd better look out;
Johnny doesn't scuttle, no, he fights the bugger out.

Now, the war is over, Hitler is dead.
He thought he'd go to heaven with a crown upon his head.
But the Lord said, 'No, you're going down below.
'There's only room for Churchill here so off to hell you go!'

Now, little Mrs Bugger went a-swimming in the river,
And that was the end of a perfect figure.
She could have been saved, there wasn't any doubt.
But there was nobody there just to pull the bugger out.(T)

The song's comic appeal is its vulgarity caused by the constant repetition of the word 'bugger'.[87] The persona of the song is an unconventional figure, whose zany exploits range from sinking U-boats to downing his wife's bottle of medicinal gin: an anti-hero in the perverse tradition of 'Brian O'Lynn'[88] but more callous and bloody-minded. Johnny Bugger encapsulates an attitude of independence and defiance that finds great favour with working class audiences in public houses. (I am reminded of the cartoon character of Andy Capp.) While there is ample evidence that he is anti-authority, he is not a traitor to his country for his unconventionality allows him to achieve the ludicrous impossible by becoming the secret weapon of the British Tommy against the Third Reich. Obvious textual evidence suggests that the song was taken over by British troops in the Second World War and that they had readily added to the exploits of Johnny Bugger. In fact, the episodic form of the song (like 'Cosher Bailey'[89]) invites its performers to add new and topical verses, and update others:

Now, the Americans went to the moon one day
To beat the Russians so they say;
But when they got there they found instead,
Oh, little Johnny Bugger was lying in bed.[90]

Moreover, the stanza has a straightforward metre and rhyme scheme with an uncomplicated melodic formula (ABAC+DE) set to a tune whose contour is based on phrases commonly encountered in well-known songs such as 'Little Brown Jug'. Perhaps as a result of a semantic shift in the meaning of the word 'bugger' and its connotations, the probability that a performance will raise eyebrows is low and hence the song now lacks some of the notoriety of other examples mentioned above. Often in my own experience the piece is performed as a matter of course, alongside such songs as 'The Village Pump' and 'She'll Be Coming Round the Mountain When She Comes'. It would appear that the potency of the parody over a period of time has been dissipated. Reasons for this changing perception are difficult to substantiate but one line of development would take account of the following:

1 The original was a 'black-face' minstrel song called 'Old Johnny Boker', popularized by Joe Sweeney, one of the earliest stage banjo players.[91]
2 Like 'Jim Crow' it presented a caricature of the negro.
3 As the song became parodied in tradition, the spotlight moved from a racial focus to impropriety through the distortion of 'Boker' to 'Bugger'.
4 Singers in South Yorkshire do not perceive any racist links in 'Old Johnny Bugger' as it is performed today. Rather they identify with its humour and vulgarity, and the defiant figure of Johnny Bugger, which is no longer a mere caricature, but a positive working-class hero.

If we take into account our racist heritage over the past 100 years, it is all the more surprising that 'Old Johnny Bugger' should have lost its racial overtones. After all there are other songs sung in the South Yorkshire tradition that are blatantly racist.[92] I would conjecture that in the contemporary singing tradition the original song of 'Old Johnny Boker' would prove to be far more controversial than the parody that has outlived it. One might expect that audiences would react with embarrassment to the racial overtones and would discourage its performance. If this interpretation is acceptable, then the parody can be seen as successfully extending the life in tradition of the song form. Ironically, a 100 years ago the use of vulgarities would have earned the song universal condemnation by polite society. However, it was the success in shocking their social superiors that recommended the parody, to working class people, and led to the popularity of the piece as a general repository for their humorous sketches. It is a remarkable example of how a song can change along with the attitudes and perceptions of its audience. It has shed new light on the original text, re-interpreted it, and embellished it, and as such approximates to point six of our original list. Moreover, the notion of change in meaning, in terms of denotation and connotation, is one that can be followed through in the next example.

When Arthur performed 'Three Crows', he knew that the piece was widely sung and ubiquitously popular but was unaware that it was a parody of a song of great antiquity.[93] He realized that there were many closely related versions of the song in tradition, especially in his district, and he had added verses in the version of it in his songbook as well as noting two alternatives for the final verse, from which he selected according to the company.

'Three Crows'   Arthur Howard

Original key: F

♩ ± 144

Spoken: There were three crows sat on a tree,
And they were as black as crows could be.

There were three crows sat on a tree

Faster

And they were as black as crows could be, And they were as black as crows could be,

Slower

And they were as black as——crows could be.

(The pattern is repeated for the remaining verses.)
Then one old crow said to his mate,
'What shall we have this day to ate?'

They flew across the burning plain
To where an old horse had been slain.

They perched along his old backbone
And pecked his eyes out one by one.

Then one old crow said unto t'other
'By gow! He is a tough old bugger!'

Up came the farmer with his gun
And he shot them all excepting one.

This one flew up into a tree
And said, 'You old farmer (usually 'bugger'), you can't shoot me!'

Amen.(T)

(Of the two final verses in his notebook he usually performed the second. The
censored expletive is 'buggery'.)

Then farmer cocked his gun at tree
And he blew that crow to b------.

The farmer then threw up his gun
And blew that crow to Kingdom Come.[94]

His version was intentionally comic and like 'Old Johnny Bugger' was relatively
noncontroversial and trivial, even though it contained the same obscenity in
three places. It was, however, the technique of parodying in performance that
brought to the piece its main element of humour and not simply the text. Arthur
would recite the words of each stanza prior to singing them in chorus. This

technique, which insured maximum participation, was in imitation of the 'lining out' of hymns by country parsons dating from the time before standard hymnbooks were commonplace and literacy was the norm.[95] Arthur used the piece to parody the hymn form; he adopted a pious stance and maintained seriousness throughout appending a mock 'Amen'. Also, he would sometimes intone, as do others who perform it,[96] a liturgical 'All sing!' before each verse to exhort his 'congregation' to join in with him.

Arthur had a penchant for such anti-clericalism and relished every opportunity to have-a-go at the institution of the clergy. Among the many items in his active repertoire, one of his favourite songs was a version of 'The Sucking Pig', an attack on the greed of the clergy under the tithe system. He also sang 'The Darkies' Sunday School', which poked fun at evangelical preachers, and 'Doctor Mack', which was directed at an unscrupulous priest who was obsessed with hunting. 'Muffin Man', another favourite, is an attack on the sexual laxity of the clergy and has the parson and the curate boasting to each other about the number of female parishioners they have compromised.

Although Arthur's anti-clericalism was good-humoured, it had its roots in an instinctive distrust of the clergy and the tithe system. He would discuss the topic as if the injustice had only recently been removed (in fact, it was not totally abolished until 1977[97]), and would relish anecdotes such as the following:

> These tithemen, never same came round twice. They'd send word on when he were coming. They'd be waiting on him at the back of the wall with this here dog – they'd all a dog that'd face anything. (Arthur whistles the dog.) Keep out sight theeself and let this dog go! They say that were never same chap came twice! The law didn't reach every place then!(T)

Arthur had no deep commitment to religion for he was essentially a pragmatist and a humanist.

In his use of 'Three Crows' as a vehicle of anti-clerical parody (see point five), Arthur was following a traditional formula and not offering a distinctive or new interpretation. Although other examples of anti-clerical songs have been recorded in the tradition such as 'The Soldier and the Sailor'[98] and 'The Parson and the Clerk',[99] their satire is explicit in the text. 'Three Crows', however, relies solely on the performer to bring to the text a parodic interpretation that satirizes the singing of hymns. Even though 'Three Crows' may have started life as a parody of 'The Three Ravens', as is generally accepted,[100] present audiences unlike scholars have no knowledge of the original target of the humour. The comedy of the action, the simple two-line verse with repetitions, and the harmonic and rhythmic underlay lend themselves to a hymn-like rendition. Thus the target of the parody has switched from an original ballad text to a particular practice, a ritual of the Anglican Church. This shift can be seen in other terms such that the meaning of the parody has changed from a denotative to a connotative expression. Like 'Villikins and his Dinah' the parody is in the style of performance suggested by and not explicit in the text.

From all our examples a pattern has now emerged that distinguishes the extent to which a parody is dependent on explicit meaning and form, or on implicit meaning and technique. Such explicit parodies include 'I Sat Upon a Pin Mary' and 'My Grandfather's Watch', with 'The Egg' as a tour de force. Examples of implicit parodies, which depend for their full effect on performance, are 'Gossip John' and 'Three Crows'.

At this point I want to move on from the studies of individual examples and to look beyond the 'literary criticism' approach embodied in the six points. Other analyses of parody are possible, employing a variety of current critical perspectives from the structuralist terms of form, through the hermeneutic context of response and the semiotic-ideological framework, to a post-structuralist notion of textuality.[101] Whereas carnival is interpreted as 'festive inversion',[102] song parody occupies a less formalized, mundane slot that can be termed 'everyday inversion'.[103] Parodies are performed on a regular basis within the context of pub-singing in South Yorkshire and elsewhere. The performance of a parody such as that of 'Grandfather's Clock' implies a shared process of coding.[104] The singer encodes the parody: not only has he chosen it and memorized it, but he also has decided to perform it at that precise moment. His audience decodes the piece: the success of the message will depend on whether or not the members of the audience agree that he has judged the moment right, whether or not they recognize the form as parody, and whether or not they are able to appreciate the component parts. Thus an audience hearing a singer like Arthur Howard strike up 'My grandfather's clock was a Waterbury Watch ...' quickly recognizes the familiar tune, reads the singer's deadpan expression, realizes that the words are not the standard set, and signals that the song is therefore a parody. This in turn prompts the message that parodies are usually comic and that there is humour to be shared. At the same time the audience makes immediate allowances: 'anything goes' in the text of parody from nonsense to obscenity. Parody is a transgression that subverts the normal conventions associated with songs: that they should make sense and be sensible, that they should not use 'bad language', that they should be performed uninterrupted, and that the delivery should not be exaggerated or affected. However, as long as an audience demonstrates its approval of the parody through laughter and applause, the performance reinforces the conventions of traditional singing which at the same time it seemingly transgresses. These conventions are numerous and include such notions as; singing should take place in an appropriate context; singers take turns to sing; they sing in tune to a recognizable melody; they do not sing a song that is normally performed by another singer; they sing to or with an audience; they sing to entertain, to share meaning, and to show fellowship;[105] they select their repertoire according to custom and practice. In fact, the act of singing in pubs is itself the primary convention that is reinforced.

This essay started with three paradoxes and the point has now been reached where explanations are possible. Firstly, the lack of interest of scholarship is an élitist attitude which partly stems from a semantic legacy of dictionary definitions of parody that stress ridicule; ridicule is trivial, and hence parody is trivia. Coupled with this is the artistic concept of mere imitation bordering on plagiarism which is denied the cultural kudos of true creative originality.[106]

Together with the dearth of evidence from field recording, these factors make for a negative ethos. By contrast, the singing of parodies generates a positive ethos. The singer is apparently freed from the normalizing conventions of 'good' songs to perform the parody. His audience approve the piece and reaffirm the conventions. Singers like to sing parodies and audiences enjoy hearing them. In infrequent doses they provide the opportunity to let hair down, to relax, to bend the rules, but not to break them. Just as carnival provides an invigorating tonic to reconcile us to normal existence, so parody momentarily licenses all sorts of breaches of song etiquette in order to reassert the equilibrium more effectively. However, during performance itself there are clear instances when an audience is held in suspense believing, perhaps even hoping, that the parody will go too far. The performance of parody carries risks and it is the tension between these risks and the accepted norms of song performance that provide for the essential vigour and vitality, manifested by the obvious excitement of the audience.

Within such parameters, bumpkin songs are particularly relished. Although they cut near to the bone, as caricatures they can never ring true. In holding up a mirror to their performers, they afford a form of self-criticism that is control from within the group. But the performers do not laugh at themselves. Rather they relish the excesses their performance creates.

It has been shown in several instance that the singing of a parody such as that of 'Thora' reinforces the original song, as well as its traditional theme and the conventions governing the singing of such songs. As long as the apparent destabilizing of the text within the singing context wins the approval of the audience, it results in the reaffirmation rather than the rejection of the unwritten laws that control such public performance. It is therefore predictable and reasonable that parodies and originals should appear side by side in order to function more vigorously and effectively.

At a textual level parody can have, beside the conservative and normative function, a transformative one. This has been observed in 'Gossip John', 'Old Johnny Bugger', and 'Three Crows'. Moreover, a distinction has been drawn between the 'genre of parody' and the 'technique of parodying'. One valid lesson that has emerged from the analyses is that parody in song is not a simple, easily definable form, even if an audience experiences little trouble in recognizing it as such; it is multiformed and multifaceted, and occupies ranges of expression even within this one mode of cultural expression – traditional song. It is not surprising that such terms as paradox, parameter, and parallel should readily spring to mind in a discussion of parody, for all share the same Greek root of 'para' meaning 'beside'.[107] Thus parody is referential and reflexive, it imitates and parallels, it breaks the conventions and yet the extent of its licence is limited, it implies contradictions that ultimately serve to reinforce the norm.

I would propose that it is through the presence of targeting above all else that parody can be recognized; and for each example that I have analysed, this aspect has been identified. It will have become obvious that only in extreme cases is it demonstrated by ridicule; it equally well describes such gentle fun as that poked at the universality of 'Grandfather's Clock'. The targetting may be seemingly offensive, even racist, but more likely it is sexist, risque, and perhaps obscene.[108] Such conclusions could not have been drawn from an examination of the printed page with any semblance of conviction. They demand a contextual examination of parody in which the performance of everyday inversion can be studied through the vigorous form of traditional song.

Notes

1 The main repository for my fieldwork is the Centre for English Cultural Tradition and Language (CECTAL) at the University of Sheffield. All transcriptions are from my field recordings and were recorded between September and October 1980, and these are shown in the text by a 'T' in parentheses. I am grateful to the many people who have unselfishly offered help and advice with this essay. In particular, I would like to thank John Foreman, Roger D. Abrahams, Peter Narvaez, Roger de V. Renwick, David Buchan, Edward D. Ives, Jacky Bratton, and the volume editors. Unfortunately James Porter's study, 1985, of satire and parody in the repertoire of Belle Stewart was not available to me until after this essay had been substantially written. Finally, I would like to thank Marjorie Wood for permission to reproduce her father's songs.

2 There is no reference to parody in Sharp, 1907 (1972 edition). For a discussion of obscene songs, see Cray 1970: 86–89.

3 Wederburn 1578, Motherwell 1827, Gilchrist 1938, Legman 1964: 230 and 232–33, and Howes 1969: 146–47.

4 Hone 1818, Thompson 1963: 792–95, and Robinson 1978: 121–44.

5 Watson 1983: 129; for other examples see Richards and Stubbs, 1979: 14, 69, 149, 175, 184–85.

6 Lloyd 1967: 392.

7 Opie 1959: 107–17 (107); for recorded examples see *An English Folk Music Anthology*, two 12-inch L.P.s, recorded by Sam Richards and Tish Stubbs.

8 Green 1978: 153.

9 See, for example, Pegg 1976: 87–88.

10 Halpert 1951: 39 and 40.

11 Abrahams and Foss 1968: 34.

12 Narvaez 1977: 32–37 (33).

13 Greenway 1953: 13–14.

14 Barrand 1978–79: 24–34. Compare Porter 1985: 303–38.

15 Narvaez 1977: 32. For examples of such 'pertinent' songs see Glassie, Ives and Szwed (no date): 147–69, and Ives 1965: 163–68.

16 Roger D. Abrahams, private communication, July 1985. Consider also Dundes' 'Devolutionary Premise' in Dundes 1969, passim.

17 ibid

18 Sharp 1907 (1972 edition): 175.

19 An exception is Williams 1923: 20–21; see also *The Elliots of Birtley*, 12-inch L.P., recorded by Ewan MacColl and Peggy Seeger.

20 Compare Hone's evidence for the popularity of parody as a radical working class tradition of the early nineteenth century and before in Hone, 1818, cited in Thompson 1963: 792–95.

21 Moreton Thomas, 'Sheep of the Peaks', *Livestock Heritage*, 1981:7–9.

22 Arthur Howard can be heard performing this monologue on *Merry Mountain Child*, privately-produced 12-inch L.P., HD006, available from Bridge House, Unstone, Sheffield S18 5AF.

23 Stone 1914; Adam and White 1912; Hamilton 1884–89, I, introduction; Jerrold 1913; and Kitchin 1931. See also *OED*, *Grove*, and Hone 1818.

24 Macdonald 1960: 567.

25 Hutcheon 1985: 6, 15–16; Stewart 1978: 185–86.

26 Hutcheon 1985: 19; Rose 1979: 27.

27 Green 1982: 46. See also Porter 1985: 328–29.

28 F. R. Leavis cited in Amis 1978: xv.

29 Markiewicz 1967: 1265. Compare Porter 1985: 329.

30 Hutcheon 1985: 58.

31 Bakhtin 1981: 76.

32 'Thora', words by Fred E. Weatherly and music by Stephen Adams, Boosey and Company, London, 1905, to which is appended the copyright warning, 'The Public Performance of any parodied version of this composition is strictly prohibited.' John McCormack's 1907 recording can be heard on *John McCormack sings 'Panis Angelicus'*, Pearl Historical, 12-inch L.P., GEMM 176E, 1979. I am grateful to L. R. Reynolds for this last reference.

33 Russell 1977: III, Mar 36.

34 Russell 1977: III, Mar 36.

35 Russell 1977: III, Mar 36.

36 See for example 'The Oyster Girl', in Kennedy 1975 no. 234.

37 Compare William Hone's defence of parody at this trial in 1817, cited in Robinson 1978: 122.

38 Russell 1977 I: 218. For a discussion of the sentimental mode, see Pickering 1986: 12–21.

39 The words were written by Lady Dufferin and the music by George Barker, see for example Graves 1847: no. 119, and Turner: 1972 116–20.

40 The second part of both Arthur's stanzas two and three have not been located in print.

41 Arthur Deakin and Wright Cooper recorded 5 November 1982.

42 Copies of other parodies were printed, but Arthur did not know of their existence.

43 Recorded 15 September 1980.

44 The original song was written by Cyrus Dare, with a tune composed by M. P. Hunter, and published by Herman Darewski, London 1901, Cray 1971: 161 refers, I think, to the song by its American title 'In Bohunkus Tennessee'. For a version of Arthur's parody, see 'The Tattooed Lady' in Fahey 1970: 230.

45 The original song is by Irving King, London: Campbell Connelly, 1925.

46 The first is also known as 'Nicky-Nacky-Noo', I have only seen bowdlerised versions in print, see Curry 1981: 70.

47 See for example, *Rawtenstall Annual Fair*, which Arthur also sang. There is a version in Harding 1980: 70–72.

48 The original song is by Henry Clay Work (1832–84), see Turner, 1972: 165–69. The parody is by George Formby, senior, (and Hargreaves?), and was recorded by him in 1916 on Xonophone 1696 (matrix no. Y20054e). I am grateful to Bob Davenport, Reg Hall, and Earnie Bayly for this information.

49 The Waterbury Watch was the first mass-produced cheap pocket watch. It was designed by D. A. A. Buck in 1878 for the Waterbury Watch Company of Connecticut, USA. Because of its long wind (140 half turns), it became the subject

of many jokes, especially in the music hall where Waterbury was known as 'the land of eternal spring'. It was also given to couples for their honeymoon and as a free gift with purchases like a suit. See Carl and Maria-Luise Sifakis, *Beginner's Guide to Antique Watches*, New York and London, 1978: 82, and E. J. Tyler, *Clocks and Watches*, Maidenhead, New York, 1975: 58–59. I am grateful to John Swain for this information.

50   See for example, Dan Leno, T. E. Dunville, Frederick Robson, and Little Tich, in Davison 1971: passim and Billy Bennett in Marshall 1981: pp. 2–3.

51   See for example, Gargantua's birth in *Gargantua and Pantagruel*.

52   *Scottish Students' Song Book*: 248–49. The technique used here is not unlike that used during improvization in jazz where extraneous strains of melody are sometimes 'quoted'. I am grateful to Richard Middleton for this point.

53   *Brewer's Dictionary of Phrase and Fable*, 1978 edition: 232.

54   Turner 1972: 144.

55   'The Egg: A Mournful Medley', written by Greatrex Newman, arranged by Wolsely Charles, and sung by Leslie Henson, London: Reynolds 1921. I am grateful to John Foreman for this information. The technique used by Greatrex Newman echoes that used by Ned Corvan. See Harker, 1981 26–56: 47–55).

56   *'Daily Express' Community Song Book*: 14, and *'News Chronicle' Song Book*: 24.

57   Turner 1972: 88–93.

58   *'News Chronicle' Song Book*: 114, *'Daily Express' Community Song Book*: 130, and *Scottish Students' Song Book*: 289.

59   By Joseph Tabrar, London: Francis, Day and Hunter 1909 originally sung by Jack Smiles. There is a version by Georgia Brown on Decca SKL 4143. I am grateful to Steve Race and John Foreman for this information.

60   By Francis Barron, see 'Monologues and Comic Songs', *This England*, 19, no. 4 1986: 12. It is stated that it was a popular favourite among military-minded gentlemen years ago, and was recorded by Peter Dawson among others. A 'shako' was a round peaked hat with a plume. I am grateful to William Noble for this reference. 'My Old Shako' was also used as a model for hunting songs in the Yorkshire Pennines, see Holme Valley Beagles Hunt: 38–39.

61   *'Daily Express' Community Song Book*: 45. See also 'The History of Mademoiselle' in de Witt 1970: 60–65.

62   See Opie 1985: 360–64.

63   *'Daily Express' Community Song Book*: 120.

64   *'Daily Express' Community Song Book*: 23, and *'News Chronicle' Song Book*: 45.

65   Turner 1972: 337–49.

66   *Scottish Students' Song Book*: 104.

67   *'News Chronicle' Song Book*: 46, and *Scottish Students' Song Book*: 66.

68   It was a favourite target. Hamilton 1884 I: 81–101, gives 25 parodies including one from 1876 called 'Egg-Shell she o'er'.

69   I am grateful to A. E. Green for this point.

70   See for example, the episode in *Three Men on the Bummel*, where they try to buy 'good' shoes.

71   Compare Greenway 1953: 14.

72   See Pickering 1983: 44–64 (especially note 13). There is a polite version of the song called 'The Farmyard Song' in Gardham 1982: 17.

73   Recorded 6 November 1973.

74   Purslow 1965: 106. Compare Harker 1985a: 73–74.

75 Arthur is one of the singers on *A Fine Hunting Day*, 12-inch L.P., recorded by David Bland.

76 D'Urfey, 1720, VI, pp. 315–16; Chappell 1859 II: 672–73; and *Journal of the Folk Song Society*, no. 34, 1930: 235–36.

77 Bate 1971: 4.

78 Abrahams and Foss 1968: 34.

79 Hutcheon 1985: 1. See also Green 1978: 152–53.

80 See Chappell 1859 II: 672–73; and Booth 1981: 116–24.

81 Nash 1985: 21; Bernard Dupriez, *Gradus: les Procédés Littéraires*, Paris, 1977, cited in Hutcheon 1985: 18.

82 Davison 1971: 20–25.

83 Scott 1946: 68.

84 Catnach included it in his 1832 catalogue, see Roud and Smith 1985; see also *Journal of American Folklore*, 29, 1916: 190–91, and Creighton 1932: 34–37.

85 Russell 1977 I: 78–79, and II Hin 70; see also *Frank Hinchliffe: 'In Sheffield Park'*, 12-inch LP, recorded by Mike Yates. Compare the account of an Adderbury version in Pickering, 1982: 170–72.

86 Noted 6 November 1973. Versions have been recorded at Dungworth, Wadsley, Ingbirchworth, and Oughtibridge.

87 Compare the use of profanities in 'Samuel Hall', see Legman, 1964: 197.

88 See, for example, Richards and Stubbs, 1979: 61 and Buchan, 1984: 115–16.

89 See, for example, MacColl, 1954: 17–18.

90 John and Betty Dawson, recorded 14 November 1970.

91 I am grateful to Michael Pickering for this information. See Williams, 1923: 304. Note that there is a sea shanty of the same title which is otherwise unrelated.

92 At the Fountain, Ingbirchworth, I have recorded 'The C.R.E. March', which is performed with lines such as 'I caught a nigger boy ... Hold him down while I get at him!' (20 December 1970).

93 The earliest version is dated 1611. Child numbered it 26 in his canon, see Child, 1882–84, I: 253–54; see also *Journal of American Folklore*, 31, 1918: 273, Wells, 1950: 147, and Bronson, 1959, I: 308.

94 Arthur Howard's Notebook 4: 66–67.

95 See La Trobe 1831: 198, Lightwood 1905: 80–81, Temperley 1979: 89, and Gammon 1985: 35.

96 Barry Bridgewater, recorded 8 September 1984, and Tal Clark recorded 2 December 1974.

97 Finance Act 1977, c.36 s.56, s.59, and Schedule 9, Part V.

98 See, for example, Hamer 1967: 22.

99 See the note by Roy Palmer in *Folk Music Journal*, 4, 1982: 276–79.

100 Abrahams and Foss 1968: 34 and 172–76: Bronson, 1959 I: 191.

101 The two most significant contemporary studies are Rose 1979, and Hutcheon 1985.

102 Bakhtin 1968, Ladurie 1981, Babcock 1984.

103 Roger D. Abrahams, private communication, July 1985; see also Stewart 1978: 76 and 185–86. Dundes' concept of metafolklore is helpful here: 'Such parodies ... can be useful sources of the folk's own attitudes towards their folklore'. See Dundes 1966: 510.

104 Eco 1984: 5–6.

105 Dunn 1980: passim.

106 Narvaez 1977: 32–33; Barrand 1978–79: 24–25.

107 Rose 1979: 18; Gilman 1974: 144.
108 Although there has been no direct consideration of sexism, the reader should note
      that two of the most successful performances of parodies that I have recorded have
      been by women, and that their songs have been blatantly obscene. See also the
      discussion of Belle Stewart's 'parodies' in Porter 1985: 303–38.

4 *James Lyons: Singer and Story-teller: His Repertory and Aesthetic*

TONY GREEN

In comparison to Ian Russell's highly detailed and sophisticated fieldwork of recent date, Tony Green's work in the industrial West Riding, now over twenty years old, looks old-fashioned in its concentration on the relationship between a repertory of songs and stories and the life-history and opinions of the singer-storyteller. Nevertheless, it remains interesting in two ways. First, historically, in that it shows that more than two decades ago the old folkloristic paradigm was beginning to crumble under pressure from functionalist ethnography and the Scandinavian-based 'folk life' movement: the very term, enshrined in the titles of Leeds University's Institute of Dialect and Folk Life Studies and of the ethnographic journal Folk Life, has always sounded odd in English – it is in fact a literal translation from the Swedish, in a conscious attempt to shift the study of popular traditions in Britain from its cultural evolutionist base towards a holistic and contextual methodology. Second, in that even now the questions it raises have yet to be satisfactorily answered, except with reference to particular, empirical cases. Questions of the relationship between the individual and the society in which he or she lives, as presented in and arguably mediated through local artistic practice; of the application of diachronic and synchronic, and cognitive and rhetorical perspectives, to that practice; of the contribution of different artistic genres to an individual's expression in performance; and of the sociological analysis of music, particularly in conjunction with sung texts, at a microscopic level; all these are still only possible to pose in a crude and theoretically flimsy manner. And even this does not touch on the bluntly practical problem that it is exceptionally difficult to analyse – much less compare – the content of repertories outside a publication-format which is, under most contemporary circumstances, impossibly lavish.

Three things, however, are clear. First, and most simply, that it is inadequate to approach the individual's repertory (recorded, after all, wholly accidentally at a particular point in time) as a synchronic whole, without reference, in the first instance, to the chronolgocial perspective of the individual's biography, and, in the second, to the historical circumstances pertaining to different junctures in that biography. Second – just as is implied in Russell's discussion of parody – that it is simply wrong to refer an English working-class repertory of song and story in the twentieth century to a single, unified 'tradition'. James Lyons' repertory was highly eclectic in its derivation, and its acquisition owed, if anything, more to a concern with the immediate and topical than to an atavistic interest in the past. Its unity, in so far as it had one, was not given by 'tradition' but created by the man himself, in selecting songs and stories which orbited around particular thematic and stylistic preoccupations. Finally, that, at least as far as this man is concerned, it is fair to speak of an 'aesthetic' as a consciously conceived and articulated set of artistic aims and predispositions; which may, by inference and analogy, add further substance to Pickering's claims about the historical meanings of a ballad whose singers are no longer with us to be questioned.

I

The repertory is a key unit in cultural analysis. Whatever the methodological problems in approaching it, it is a cultural fact not a theorist's construct. Whatever reference points it has in psychology, intellectual disposition, ethics and aesthetics are those of the person or group who has assembled and possesses it, not those of the observer. As such, it lies at the heart of ethnographic study. This is not to say that it is unproblematic. This essay attempts to confront some of the problems, through the discussion of one man. It is the individual's repertory, rather than the group's, to which subsequent remarks are addressed.[1]

First, while the observer perceives it, with hindsight, as a synchronic whole, because that is in one sense what it is – all its elements coexist simultaneously – it is also the product of an historical process in two distinct senses. It has been created over a period of years, through a process of learning, invention, forgetting and discarding, which may not have been a regular and uninterrupted one; and at no point, even late in the artistic career or natural life of its owner, can we be sure that it is static. And its various elements, whether acquired or invented, have each their independent existence within processes of production and distribution which may be very old or very new.

Second, it is never manifest as a whole, but in its operations is highly sensitive to contexts. Only under the exotic circumstances of fieldwork will a performer attempt to realise his or her whole repertory in performance, though of course the opportunity to do so may be a source of unusual satisfaction. Normally, under the performance-circumstances which gave rise to it in the first place, the repertory is the *langue* from which the *parole* appropriate to a particular discourse is selected. However, as that analogy implies, it would be wrong to argue that a repertory is no more than the sum of its parts, for those parts are, in greater or lesser degree, mutually referential and, in so far as they are may at any occasion prompt each other into action.

Third, there may be within the repertory a hierarchy of importance among the elements, whether in absolute terms of personal taste, in frequency of use in response to demand, or of course diachronically in changes of fashion or preference during the repertory's existence. Other criteria could be adduced, but the general point is made.

The study of repertory militates against the idealization of popular culture. Whole repertories are likely to be as complicated and internally contradictory as the individual man or woman who amasses them and his or her experience of life, and to bear the marks of whatever cultural phenomena he or she has brushed up against. Only in a very simple and isolated society might we expect repertories to be consistent in tone, style and content; outside such societies, we had best be alert to attempts to create consistency, but not expect its achievement. In a society such as England in the twentieth century, with its long history of literacy and print, and its virtually equally long history of the industrial production and distribution of cultural artefacts, manifesting in broad terms (though always unevenly) an underlying pluralism of social and artistic attitudes, it is unlikely that a popular song and story repertory would be other than eclectic, drawing not upon any single, unified tradition, but rather upon a number of strands of cultural activity of varying length and strength. So it proves in practice, as any number of collections now show. The task is to find what holds these disparate items together within the individuated mode of cultural practice, and, further, to determine as precisely as possible what is meant by the appeal to the past that is commonly voiced with regard to them by their performers. It has often been noticed that there is ideological profit to be made by attributing recent creations to a real or imagined past (the Ploughman's Lunch effect in culture) and in its general outlines that process is well understood.[2] What is interesting, and possibly special, about repertories is that they are in their very form the manifestation of an historical process, which may give them a particular potency, in this respect, for the performer.

II

I am sending you a song I learned when I was a boy of about 12 I am now 68 hoping this will help. I have been one who has always followed songs like these and I hope it will add to your collection.[3]

An unpretentious letter from an unpretentious man, in response to an appeal in a local evening newspaper, enclosing a hand-written text of 'The West Stanley Disaster'. It tells us three things about James Lyons, and raises one question. It tells us that he was likely to be accurate, or as nearly so as makes no matter (he was probably thirteen when he learned the song); that songs had been a life-long interest; and that he thought them worth communicating, as an act of personal generosity, even through the post. The question is, what is meant by 'always followed', which is not the simple matter it might seem. Finally, I quote it as a reminder – to myself as much as anyone else – that my relationship with this man began with a song, and existed largely within the framework of a mutual interest in singing. My knowledge of him is necessarily skewed by that interest, and there is no doubt much about him that I do not know.

He was born in Batley, in the West Riding, in 1896, and died there eighty-three years later, having spent the last few years of his life in an old people's home. He left school in 1909, at the age of thirteen, and immediately began work at a local colliery, Soot Hill, as a pony-driver:

I left school o' Friday, I was down t' bloody pit o' Monday. When I were a lad, when you left school, if they'd a pair o' boots to fit you, they dropped you straight down t' pit.

The language is typical of him, like his letter: terse, concrete, the sentences short and well constructed, and with a dash of poker-faced irony.

Early in 1914, before the Great War began, he joined the Royal Navy; not, he insisted, out of any particular desire to serve King and Country; he was not unpatriotic, but, he maintained, he was then ignorant of international politics, and did not really believe that war was about to break out. His decision was pragmatic:

> As soon as you were old enough you went into the army or the navy to get out o' the pit. It were out o' the fryin' pan into the fire.

His choice of proverb has a precise referent. Not only had his need to escape from the hole into which he had been dropped five years before, thrust him into a situation where explosive projectiles were being lobbed at him – notably at Jutland in 1916 – but also he had failed to get access to the fresh air which he had thought of as the seaman's daily fare. He had merely exchanged the heat and narrowness and shovel-work of the pit (he was by then filling) for the same commodities in the boiler-room of a cruiser. He served through the war as a stoker, and detested the experience. At the earliest opportunity, when his six years were up in 1920, he left the navy and went home to Yorkshire. Initially, unable to find work in Batley, and feeling footloose after six years at sea, he travelled south, working the pits in south Yorkshire and north Derbyshire, living in lodgings and staying nowhere long. In 1926 he returned to Batley, just in time for the General Strike and what was to be, for the miners, its seven-month aftermath. Later that year he married a local girl. Sick of pit-work, and sickened by the experience of that spring and summer's defeat, he quit it for good and took a job as a fitter at Taylor's, the largest of Batley's woollen mills. There he remained for twenty-five years, until a period of short-time working persuaded him to look elsewhere, and the GPO took him on as a postman, an outdoor job (at last) which he enjoyed until his retirement in 1961.

Throughout their marriage, he and his wife, who died in 1965, lived near Taylor's mill, initially in a rented through-terrace, subsequently in a pleasant post-war council house with a garden. Here they raised their family of three sons and a daughter.

It is not an unusual career, taking in the two basic Calder Valley productive industries, plus a nationalized service industry, and military service in a major war; and, on the domestic side, marriage, a family, and life in rented accommodation both private and public. There is no such thing as a typical working man, but there are common patterns of experience. In their broad outlines, James Lyons' working and family life were not unusual for their time and place. Sometimes we sense from the literature that performers of oral genres are eccentric beyond their predisposition for performance (if that is an eccentricity)[4]; there is no evidence that this man was, or that the culture which nurtured him expected eccentricity of its performers.

It is true that James Lyons was an intelligent man, who took an informed interest in the world around him, thought about it, and liked to discuss it, characteristically in language accurate and economical. He also had a good memory for historical dates (e.g. the rising of the United Irishmen, 1798, which is well known; the battle of Majuba Hill, 1881, and the accidental sinking of

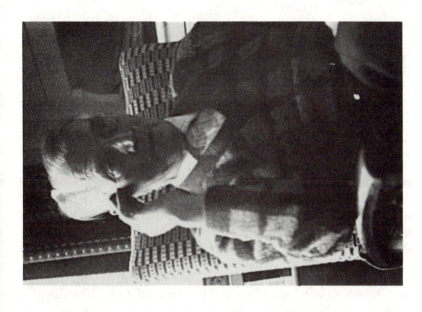

James Lyons, singing

James Lyons telling a story

[Photographs by K.R.Green, 1966]

HMS Victoria, 1893, which are not – all of these, note, before he was born). But it would be as unfair to him as to his peers to suggest that this informed interest in the world was particularly unusual. It is likely that he was one of that large number of working men and women for whom the Education Act of 1944 came too late: given the opportunity, his intellect and articulacy would probably have taken him out of the working class. It is no accident that three out of his four children are professional workers. He himself spoke feelingly about the importance of the 1944 Act – and sometimes scathingly of those of his acquaintance who failed to recognize it and 'wanted all for their kids to get out and addle some brass' – and could be a stern and uncompromising advocate of book-learning at the expense of other skills.

By descent Mr Lyons was Irish, and a devout Roman Catholic. He believed that all his grandparents had come to Batley from Charlestown, Co. Mayo, during the great famine or just before. The only one of them he knew was bilingual in English and Gaelic. His parents understood some Gaelic but did not speak it, and he himself knew only a handful of words. In his life-expereince, and in his speech, he was thoroughly a West Riding man, yet his cultural connections with Ireland were important to him. In this too he was not atypical. As has been observed, what is striking about the Irish migration to Britain from 1825 onward is not how much conflict it generated but how little.[5] To a large extent the Irish integrated with and were accepted by the indigenous population – the speed with which Gaelic was abandoned by immigrants from the Gaeltacht being both index and mechansim. What was retained was their religion (in any case not exclusively Irish) and a substantial part of their English-language song-repertory, which, in Mr Lyons' case, was consciously reinforced by reference to both printed sources and subsequent generations of immigrants. There is a sense in which Mr Lyons' singing points to a dual cultural identity: both his Irish and his English credentials were manifest in the performance of songs about Ireland in a medium which included English listeners.

James' father (married 1883) was likewise a collier, and his career was even less happy than his son's. Lucky to emerge unscathed from a disaster at Bruntcliffe, he was on strike for nearly two years (1905–1907) against the lowering of prices at Hemsworth, and his career ended not long before World War I when, as men's check-weighman at West End, he was sacked for the reprimandable offence of putting his lamp on the ground, and blacklisted.[6] These injustices, and consequent hardship, left a lasting impression on James: 'It's a scar that's allus there, is poverty.' Laconic in speech and usually quite reserved in manner, he could become vehement when discussing the living and working conditions of his youth:

> There were no baths in them days, no pit-head baths. And no bath in the house, one up and one down. You were brought up like bloody cattle.

Throughout his life he was a firm grass-roots trade unionist and an unswerving though unaffiliated socialist. Not that his politics had any elaborate theoretical dimension: they were the politics of experience, expressed, as for so many working men of his generation, in supporting his union, voting Labour, mistrusting anyone who might be classified as a boss (even priests), and maintaining a staunchly egalitarian attitude in the face of an unequal society –

> Them people, they think they've a right to rule everything, and they're only common clay.[7]

We have, then, a West Riding man of Irish descent, fascinated by the Ireland in which he had never lived and only briefly visited, and conscious of family ties in north America with people he had never met; a convinced Christian and church-goer who was suspicious of priests; a trade unionist who mistrusted the union hierarchy; a man dedicated to collective action and profoundly egalitarian in his beliefs, who encouraged and sometimes bullied his children into social mobility, into becoming, in principle, the kind of people whom he would wish to remind that they were 'only common clay'; a life-long manual worker whose mind was never satisfied by his job; one who tried to kill foreigners he did not hate in the interests of English people he neither knew nor approved of ('It were a bosses' war'). A stern, tough, dogmatic and sometimes difficult man, and a moralist; at the same time a humorist, fond of children, a lover of conversation and good company, the songs, the yarns, the crack; fond of his beer, but contemptuous of drunkards, yet, paradoxically, sensitive to the social context of vice: 'What was there for a fellow to do when he were laid off, but to go supping beer?'

A very ordinary man. All that made him unusual for me, in Batley late in 1964, was that he knew a lot of 'old songs'.

Figure 1: James Lyons' Repertory[8]

SONGS

1   Billy Boy
2   Bonny Bunch of Roses, The
3   Botany Bay
4   'Can't you spare me one?' the Letter ran
5   Come all you young Fellows (The Soldier's Warning)
6   Croppy Boy, The
7   Deep in Canadian Woods (Ireland Boys Hooray)
8   Down by the Tanyard Side
9   Empty Sleeve, The
10 Erin's green Shore
11 Flagship Victoria, The
12 Foggy Dew, The (i.e. the Easter 1916 ballad)
13 He was ashamed of his poor old Dad
14 Here we come a-wesselin' (the Wassail Song)
15 He's been a long time gone for the Wood
16 If the Blarney Stone stood out on Sydney Harbour (Ireland over here)
17 Irish are just like the wild creeping Flower, The
18 Little Stowaway, The
19 McCaffery
20 Meet the Boys from Kerry (The Boys from the County Cork)
21 Mr McAdam and Co.
22 Night Express, The

23   *One of the best*
24   *Pack of Cards, The*
25   *Pardon came too late, The*
26   *Patrick Shiernan (Patrick Sheehan)*
27   *Robin-a-Bobbin (Hunting the Wren)*
28   *Shamrock, the Thistle and Rose, The*
29   *She Moved through the Fair*
30   *Skibbereen*
31   *There was a Lady lived in Leeds (The Cruel Mother)*
32   *The Titanic*
33   *Two old Crows (The Three Ravens)*
34   *West Stanley Disaster, The*
35   *Wild Colonial Boy, The*
36   *Young Sailor cut down in his Prime, The*

FRAGMENTS

37   *Connaught Ranger, The*
38   *Fox, The*
39   *He works down below in the dark dreary Pit*
40   *Heroes British Heroes*
41   *How Paddy stole the Rope*
42   *I gave her a call (?Cruising round Yarmouth)*
43   *I was sold that afternoon (Napoleon's Farewell to Paris)*
44   *In a Cottage by the Sea*
45   *In an old Australian homestead (Suvla Bay)*
46   *It's the Poor that helps the Poor*
47   *Lord Nelson and Lord Howe (The Deeds of Napoleon)*
48   *Mrs Napoleon*
49   *Oh Josephine my Josephine*
50   *Remember I'm his Mother*
51   *Spare the old mud Cabin*
52   *Trooper, The (The bold Trooper)*
53   *When the Hills and the Dales are all covered in white (Remember the Poor)*
54   *Young Jack Crawford*

JINGLES

55   *I am a Man of great Influence*
56   *I do believe I will believe that Bugs are bigger than Fleas*
57   *John get up and light the Fire*
58   *Look on the Wall, a great big Spider*
59   *Old Roger is dead*
60   *Reight dahn in our Cellar-'oil (un 1.) Oh we're reight down in't' Coal-'ole)*
61   *Reight dahn in our Cellar-'oil (vn2.)*
62   *Ship that struck a Match, The*
63   *Up yond' Hill, a long Way off*
64   *Wheel goes round, The*
65   *Wheer'st'a bin Lad? Hawkin' Papers*

STORIES

66   *Chalk and the bald Head, The*
67   *Clinking Toad, The (The Watch mistaken for the Devil's Eye. Aa.Th 1319*)*
68   *Communal Marriage, The*
69   *God and the Gardener*

70   Russian Bear, The
71   Tubs of Seagulls
72   Uncle Jim's Pit Story (*?Lie: remarkable Carrier, Motif X942(b), or Mighty Lifter F624*)

Note: The reference numbers to 67 and 72 are to the standard reference works on oral narrative, respectively Aarne, A. and Thompson, S., *The Types of the Folktale*, Helsinki 1973, and Thompson, S., *Motif Index of Folk Literature*, Copenhagen 1955–8.

III

Figure 1 lists James Lyons' repertory, divided into four categories based on genre and function and deriving from his perception of it, insofar as the distinctions are not self-evident. A *song* is a polystrophic sung poem which he regarded as complete and suitable for performance to adults. A *fragment* is a song which he regarded as incomplete and therefore unsuitable for performance under normal circumstances. A *jingle* (his usual term) is a sung poem, usually of a single stanza and regarded as complete in itself, generally unsuitable for performance to adults and ideal for amusing or consoling young children, or for singing to oneself while working.[9] (Two items, 59 and 64, belong to this category functionally, despite their polystrophic structure, and are so assigned on the grounds that function overrides form; both originally belong to children's games.) A *story* is a spoken prose narrative. The listing is of titles only, most of them adequate in themselves to identify the item. The title used by Mr Lyons (or, for the stories, to which he gave no titles, invented by me) is supplemented, wherever necessary and possible, by an alternative title, scholarly or otherwise, by which the item is commonly known. Of the songs and fragments listed here, those which have appeared in the folksong literature are almost all well known to students of that bibliography; for the most part, titles not instantly identifiable belong to commercial popular songs of the late nineteenth and early twentieth centuries.

The breakdown of the repertory shows a number of striking features.

1   *Songs* outnumber *fragments* by precisely two to one. It is possible that Mr Lyons knew far more fragments than were recorded, but I doubt it: throughout our working relationship he volunteered items which he knew only in part, in case they might be of interest to me. It would be foolish to claim absolutely that he knew only eighteen fragments (scraps of songs easily come and go), but I doubt that the number was greater than that of complete songs. This suggests a consistent effort of selection, learning and memorization (through use, even if in private, and even silently in the singer's head) rather than a random and insecure acquisition of whatever came his way, or a repertory falling into decay through loss of memory.

2   This impression is confirmed by examination of the *fragments*. Although some, such as 'Remember I'm his Mother' and 'Spare the old mud Cabin' are very much the kind of lengthy, sententious, late nineteenth or early twentieth-century ballad which Mr Lyons liked, and their fragmentary condition must be attributed to failure to learn or to remember, others are in the repertory by accident rather than choice. It is reasonably certain that he did not fail to learn 'The Trooper' from his workmate Andrew Judges, but

rather never tried to learn it because its bawdry was not to his taste. The tune, with two inoffensive text-lines and a syllabic refrain, got into his mind unbidden through repeated hearing. Similarly, the group of four Napoleonic fragments (43, 47, 48, 49) are residual items from his father's repertory, and Mr Lyons was sure he had never known them in full. Interestingly, by 1964 'The Bonny Bunch of Roses' was barely clinging to the status of *song*. When he first performed it for recording, Mr Lyons could remember only four of its six stanzas: usually he was confident and word-perfect when he reckoned to know a song; a fragment would be prefaced by a disclaimer. We may infer (i) that Bonaparte was less interesting to James than to his father, and became even less so as he got older, possibly because of lack of reinforcement from his audience; (ii) though less definitely, that the subject was generally declining in interest for British working class singers over the period represented by two generations of the Lyons family: while the 'Bonny Bunch' shows up frequently in the field-record, other Napoleonic ballads printed in the nineteenth century figure much less often. It is possible that, without the intervention of a fieldworker to revive the singer's interest in it, this song would have quietly slipped out of the active category of *songs* and possibly into oblivion.

What these examples suggest is confirmed by the other fragments. They represent, in large part, an early stratum of the singer's experience of songs – probably taking us back to a time before he began to take a serious interest in singing as a worthwhile, adult activity – which he never consolidated; or, subsequently, the rejection of certain items as unsuitable for his purposes. Because they were in the family repertory, or current among his friends, bits of them stuck, but no effort was made to assimilate them. Of the eighteen fragments, I estimate that six (37, 44, 45, 50, 51, 54) represent failure to acquire a chosen song, for reasons which can only be guessed at. In principle it is unsurprising that a singer who has mastered thirty-six songs should have failed to master six: any learning process involves an acceptable level of random failure. If, however, six represent failure, then twelve represent choice; which is why fragments are important methodologically.

3   With two exceptions, the eleven *jingles* also represent an early stratum. Seven of them he learned in childhood from his family or their friends (56, 57, 58, 60, 61, 63, 65). Two, 59 and 64, were learned from and among other children. In contrast, 55 and 62 (the latter known by Mr Lyons to be part of a polystrophic *song*, but used as a *jingle*) were learned in adulthood and assimilated to the same function because they 'tickled' him.

It is surprising that a man who has mastered thirty-six *songs* should recall only eleven *jingles*, which can be memorized quickly by anyone used to listening carefully. Again, this must be a product of choice, though here, probably, as much in preservation as acquisition. It is so unlikely that Mr Lyons learned only two of the songs current among children, that we must assume that he had forgotten a large number of others – which was his own view. No doubt a concerted effort could have dredged others out of his memory; but he did not volunteer them and I did not ask. Methodologically this is perfectly satisfactory. I was not concerned to reconstruct the repertory of West Riding children at the turn of the century, but to describe the singing activities of an adult. We know beyond doubt that these eleven items were actively in use, and we know what for. Hypothetically it might have been useful to identify discards, but we must also bear in mind that these rhymes are bluntly utilitarian: a small number will do as well as a large one for amusing children and grandchildren – especially given the propensity of small children for requesting the same piece repeatedly – and to attribute inclusion or exclusion to aspects of content would be to take a sledge-hammer to a nut. This is not to say that the jingles are somehow content-free. It is to propose a working distinction between those learned in childhood from adults, and *ipso facto* potential elements of an adult repertory (among these there is a striking consistency of content), and children's songs which are, in the first instance, functionally different from jingles, for all that some of them have the capacity to take on the function of the latter.

4   The stories recorded are few in number. This is partly an accident of collection. The work with Mr Lyons was done as part of an investigation of singing traditions in the industrial West Riding, and stories were regarded as incidental material. Though I would no longer defend this procedure, it remains true that Mr Lyons did not see himself as a story-teller, and did see himself as a singer. The latter was a source of pride, seen as calling for special qualities of voice, memory, presence, and emotional commitment. Story-telling was something that all men did, at snap-time or over a pint; it required no skills beyond those of normal conversation, and its proper forum was a small, intimate group rather than the large audience that a singer might call upon for attention. Such, at any rate, was Mr Lyons' declared view, which conformed closely to what could be observed of the culture to which he belonged. The examples we have are, at least, adequately representative of his work in the genre – all brief, humorous tales, with *blason populaire* prominent as content.[10]

5   The archaeology of the repertory has already been touched on. The subject has two dimensions: the history of the repertory's construction, and that of each individual item within it.

The latter is simple in outline. The repertory stretches from a tiny number of *songs* known to exist well before the birth of any of this singer's sources, albeit in late redactions (e.g. Child 20 and 26); through an equally small number originating in the first half of the nineteenth century (e.g. 'The Bonny Bunch of Roses', 'Botany Bay'); to a larger number from the second half of the nineteenth century (e.g. 'The Flagship Victoria', 'The Little Stowaway', 'Patrick Shiernan'); and finally to items of known early twentieth century composition (e.g. 'The Foggy Dew', 'Meet the Boys from Kerry', 'The Titanic'). The weight of the *song* component, then, is very much in the area of Mr Lyons' own early lifetime and that of his parents. The *fragments* broadly reflect this, though 'The Fox', known from the fifteenth century, gives more historical depth, and the Napoleonic texts throw the weight towards the early nineteenth century. Documentary evidence for the age of the *jingles* is not readily available, but on internal grounds it is unlikely that most of them pre-date 1850. The *stories* present a slightly more complicated case. 'The Communal Marriage' seems, in its content, to take us back before Hardwicke's Marriage Act (1753), but the story, as such, seems not to be on record until the twentieth century. The international tale-type represented by 'The Clinking Toad', and possibly motif F624 or X942(b) – the latter is essentially a generic sub-type of the former – which seems to be at the heart of 'Uncle Jim's Pit Story', offer a deeper historical perspective internationally, but not necessarily in English-language culture. Altogether, there are too many variables here, in too small a corpus, to make generalization safe – though if I had to play a hunch, it would be that, overall, the prose repertory has greater historical depth than the poetic. In general, we have a repertory which is historically rather shallow, the more so if we discount the fragments as non-functioning items. For the most part, it is coeval with two generations of the Lyons family.

The former dimension gives an equally clear picture. Two songs are in part the singer's own work, the tunes to 32 and 34, the texts having been learned from 'leaflets'. Otherwise it is a learned repertory. The two tunes were composed when he was in his teens (c.1909 and c.1912), which suggests, not surprisingly, that he began his serious singing career not long after leaving school and entering the adult world of work. Despite some complications with multiple sources, Mr Lyons was normally very clear where he had learned his poetic repertory, fragments included. Interestingly, again, the same was not true of the prose. Of the sixty-five songs, fragments and jingles, he could account with reasonable certainty for the source of sixty; of seven stories, he could attribute only three.

As Figure 2 shows, Mr Lyons' immediate family, particularly his father, account for the largest single portion of his repertory, followed by printed sources. Manuscript sources are probably under-represented: he was sometimes uncertain whether he had learned a piece purely aurally or with the assistance of a hand-written text (he did not read music); Figure 2 records only those cases where he was certain. The history of the repertory is unaffected by it, since in practice learning from a manuscript is tantamount to learning from the person who wrote it out for you, and it is now generally known that working-class singers exchange songs in this way.

To the best of his belief, much or all of the family repertory was assimilated before he joined the navy in 1914, and there seems no reason to doubt it. If he had decided by the age of thirteen to be a singer, as the purchase of a ballad-sheet and the composition of a tune to it suggest (the first act of artistic independence, as it were, by a boy not long out of school) he would already have had the experience of singing in the home to build on, and quite probably knew a number of the songs he subsequently made his own. Further, he was not regularly resident in the parental home between demobilization and marriage.

The printed sources relate mainly to the same period of his life as those items learned from shipmates. Among his mess-mates was a fiddler, who

Figure 2   Sources of the Repertory

FAMILY
Father 17 items	(1, 2, 3, 5, 21, 26, 28, 30, 35, 41, 43, 47, 49, 51, 53, 55, 61)
Mother 6	(1, 30, 31, 35, 49, 54)
Family 5	(56, 57, 58, 63, 65)
Wife 3	(6, 7, 44)
Sister 2	(36, 38)
Uncle 2	(70, 72)

FRIENDS & ACQUAINTANCES
Shipmates 7	(1, 11, 19, 33, 42, 45, 62)
Peergroup of children 4	(14, 27, 59, 64)
Mates in Pit 3	(r, 18, 37)
Irishman from Wigan 2	(12, 20)
Andrew Judges (pit) 2	(15, 52)
Jim Gilbert (pit) 1	(71)
Michael Grogan (Taylor's mill) 1	(8)
Irishman called	
Harrington (Taylor's) 1	(16)
Bob Mullins 1	(43)

OTHERS
Print 11	(3, 7, 10, 13, 22, 23, 24, 25, 29, 32, 34)
Professional 5	(22, 39, 40, 48)
Variety Artists Manuscripts 3	(5, 6, 16)
Own Composition 2	(32, 34: tunes only)
Sound Recording 1	(16: tune only)

Note: The totals do not add up to 72 because (i) the source of nine items is not known; (ii) an item has more than one source, e.g. 5, 'Come all you young Fellows', learned from his father and later synthesised with a variant MS text in the posession of an acquaintance; (iii) text and tune have different sources (so infrequently the case as to be not worthwhile tabling them seperately).

The headings 'family', 'shipmates' and 'mates in pit' mean either that an individual source could not be identified to Mr Lyons' satisfaction, or that the item was in general currency among those performing groups. The same applied to the 'peer group of children', among whom singing was largely choral in any case.

The repertory is heavily dominated by male sources, especially as it came to draw on, and operate among, performing groups outside the nuclear family into which he was born; though note the three items from his wife, deriving from their recreation of the nuclear domestic context of performance in their own home.

would play for them tunes bought in sheet-music form, so that they could learn the songs. Add to this the four items from the peer-group of children (the two ritual songs 14 and 27, acquired in the context of seasonal feastivity, in addition to the two jingles already mentioned); two topical songs learned from ballad-sheets in his early-to-mid teens; two songs from the Wigan Irishman, whom he knew during 1921 and 1922; and three learned from workmates in the pit, where he stopped working after 1926; and it is clear that the bulk of the repertory, including all the stories that can be accounted for, was assembled by the age of thirty, and most before he was twenty-five. Thereafter, we find sporadic additions. 'Down by the Tanyard Side' and 'If the Blarney Stone' were learned from workmates at Taylor's, during or just after World War II. Three songs came from his late wife and were, I believe, latent in his repertory until after her death. Finally, 'Botany

Bay' is a special case: he had it from his father, but modified and expanded it by reference to a printed text at some time in 1965, possibly under the stimulus of fieldwork.[11]

The pattern is clear. A steady acquisition of songs and some stories during childhood and young manhood, through membership of a performing family and exposure to two male peer-groups which encouraged mutual entertainment; thereafter, only the most intermittent concern to expand a repertory evidently regarded as satisfactory, and that not necessarily an active pursuit of new material. The workmates at Taylor's frequently sang in pub and club, as did he, and it would be odd if he had not picked up a couple of songs. His wife sang around the house, and sometimes they sang to each other and to their children. His adoption of two of her songs (one is fragmentary) was a tribute to her, and no doubt part of coming to terms with bereavement, after the initial period of grief (he began to sing them, as far as I know, in 1966, a year after her death).

It may be that this pattern is of some currency in the English-speaking world. Psychosocially it presumably derives from (i) an economy of artistic need among non-professional performers – there is no pressure on them to create novelty; (ii) the more generalized pattern of the use of childhood and young adulthood to acquire skills which are thereafter practised and honed rather than elaborated; (iii) a shift of emphasis, specifically in the direction of mental energy, which comes with marriage and child-rearing.

IV

The compilation of James Lyons' repertory was, to a large extent, complete some forty years before any record was made of his artistic principles. This does not invalidate what he had to say about it, but it does mean that account must be taken of the retrospective nature of his observations. His comments, which I have in part discussed elsewhere,[12] add up to this: he liked long songs, 'true' songs, songs that 'tell a tale', and 'descriptive songs: something what expresses the thought of the song, the thought of the times it were written'; he disliked bawdy songs; stories were 'no'but tales', and not worth serious discussion; likewise jingles, even though they, like songs, could be 'true' (e.g. 'I do believe' he referred explicitly to the often verminous condition of working class housing in his youth). All these generalizations, positive and negative, are concerned with textual content. He never commented spontaneously on literary style or musical content, and, if questioned, his replies were brief and uninformative: 'I like a tune with a bit of a swing to it.' In the first instance, then, at least at a conscious level, his aesthetic was to do with verbal genres and their content.

There is a problem here. Most people are bad at articulating their feelings about music, and James Lyons was no exception; we cannot therefore assume that he had no feelings about it. However, nothing that might be said, objectively, of the melodic content of his repertory would differ significantly from what might be said of many singers like him; nor, musically, do the fragments show any general contrast with the songs, so even that potential negative evidence of taste is denied us. His musical aesthetic, as far as melodic preference is concerned, must be taken as read: it appears to be equatable with a working class musical tradition of the late nineteenth and early twentieth centuries in a particular geographical area (possibly English-speaking Britain), and any useful analysis of it would have to be undertaken, in the first instance, within that framework, not via the individual performer.

There is however a level at which musical considerations enter James Lyons' aesthetic in a heuristically useful way: that of a consciously preferred mode of performance, which, interestingly enough, takes us straight back to the text. On this he had strong and simple views, founded on the principle that 'to be a good singer you have to be a good listener'. Cognitively this is a truism, but he meant more than that. Prepared to listen attentively himself, he saw the singer's task as that of offering the maximum opportunity and reward for attentive listening. In practice, this meant leisurely pace, clear diction, and a minimum of musical frills. In this, it may be argued, he was again located squarely within a particular singing tradition. But here he knew what he was doing and why, and made conscious choices within what that tradition offered. So strong was his wish for 'the voice to stand out' that he rejected accompaniment as a distraction – 'You can leave t' piano alone, I don't need no piano', as he told a pianist at his club. His comments on the popular music of the mid-sixties (including the commercial folk music of such groups as the Spinners) reinforce the point: 'You can't tell what they're on about. You can't hear the words.' For him the tempi were too fast, the diction too loose, and the sound of guitars was noise that got in the way of the information.

There is nothing unusual in such musical conservatism of course; up to a point it is a consequence of changing fashion. But though a common consequence, it is not an inevitable one, and it may tell us more about this man, as an artist, than that he was just set in his ways. For, austere as his own performance-ideal was, he did not see it as unemotional, and nor, apparently, did his peers. As his wife put it, à propos 'The Night Express' (a lugubrious frame-story in which an engine-driver recounts his observation of the sweet sorrows of platform partings): 'He used to have women crying in lumps when he'd sing that one.' For himself, he was quite clear about the need for a sincerely felt emotional commitment:

> Unless you can put feeling in a song, don't sing it. These pop-singers have no feeling, and don't tell me they have.

On the face of it, we might expect a logocentric singer such as Mr Lyons to think that the pathocentric performances of rock-singers suffered, if anything, from an excess of feeling. Challenged on this, he granted that 'they seem to put a lot into it' (like any performer, he recognized performance-energy when he met it, even if he thought it misdirected), but, in the end, such performances 'make no sense: there's no story to them.' Fragmented and anecdotal Mr Lyons' views on the singer's art may have been (and it would be unjust to expect more), but this much is clear, and we do not have to ally ourselves unreservedly with his bewildered aspersions on pop-music to recognize it: for him good singing linked specific events with appropriate emotions. It was a cognitive rather than a simply expressive art, which dealt with 'the thought of the times'.

It is easy to see how the length of a song might contribute to this, in two ways.

Textually, greater length will usually mean elaboration of the all-important narrative – or, to use another of Mr Lyons' criteria, though it probably means the same thing, more opportunity to 'describe'. *In performance*, it enables the singer to let the emotion grow through the detailing of events – a crucial consideration for a performer whose style is highly restrained. It also puts a man one-up in the competition to 'go a verse better', enables him to kid his mates as 'no'but chorus-singers', and wind them up by offering 'a pound for the next verse'. Here, of course, we are moving into status-relationships, and the sociology of banter.[13] It is outside the scope of this essay to discuss the important questions of song-performance and meta-performance as self-presentation, and the range of performance-roles available.[14] But it is a guiding principle that the consciously text-based aesthetic of singers such as Mr Lyons arises out of biographical patterning and realizations of self within a particular historical framework of locality, family-history, and class; and the particular style of adult, male, working class encounters contributes to that aesthetic.

The formal property of the length of *songs*, and its relevance to peer-group prestige, also enables us to understand why this singer's attitude to *jingles* was dismissive, even though they might truthfully reflect actual living conditions. An example may help:

> Reight dahn in our cellar-oil wheer't'muck slarts at winders
> When we've used coil up we start burnin' cinders
> If bum-bailiffs come they'll niver find us
> Dahn in our cellar-oil wheer't'muck slarts at winders.[15]

An observer might rightly comment on the comprehensive integration of subject-matter, style and context in this little lyric. A vignette of working class life is created in local working class language (including vernacular pronunciations in stressed positions, notably in a rhyme)[16], for performance in the home to a child who is expressly included in its terms of reference by first person plural voicing. Functionally, such a rhyme combines with kinship terms, greetings and farewells, and *blason populaire* in inducting the infant into the concentric worlds of family, locality, and class.[17] These are aesthetic propositions, and, insofar as he understood them, Mr Lyons would probably not have disagreed with them. Certainly he would have needed no persuading of what, for him, would have been the most important one: the reality of debt and the threat of eviction, and the need to keep your chin up under conditions of siege. But, in his terms, the 'tale' is only implied here and not told, as McCaffery's story is told, or Patrick Sheehan's, or the fictional Little Stowaway's;[18] and were it told, it would no longer be funny.

James Lyons was not such a dour moralist as to disapprove of humour. He enjoyed it, in others and in himself. He knew perfectly well that true words are spoken in jest, and that jokes can be therapeutic:

> The Irish songs, they're all a lament. Either they're a lament, or they're having a good laugh. Often about same things.

Simply, he prized more highly, and probably always had prized more highly, those works of art which confronted directly, and with the appropriate emotion, situations which made him angry, both in principle and as a result of his own experience – war, tyranny, injustice, poverty, separation, threats to the home and the family. 'Reight dahn in our cellar-'oil' is true enough to 'the times', but arguably not to 'the thought' of them.

What is undeniable is that the generic divisions of his repertory overlap an almost total dichotomy of tone. The jingles and stories are comic without exception. The songs are serious, with only three exceptions, two of them of little weight: the erstwhile ritual song 'Robin-a-Bobbin', which was functionally on the way to being a jingle by 1964 (in my experience, he sang it to his grandchildren, but since, by his own account, he formerly sang it sometimes in convivial company for everyone to join in, it must be defined as a song);[19] and the mildly bawdy 'Two old Crows', which he had learned in the navy as an informal choral piece, and remembered (it has a very simple text) but no longer sang. These two cases are probably attributable to their choral function within a predominantly solo repertory. The only important exception is 'Mr McAdam and Co.', a whimsical Irish bull of a song about a brickie's labourer. There is no need to seek an explanation for this; it is puzzling that a repertory so nearly dichotomized is not wholly so; but no human being is totally consistent, and the general picture is unaffected. The more so since while, at the most generous estimate, only three out of thirty-six songs are comic (8.33%), five out of eighteen fragments are (27.77%), which seems again to indicate a deliberate process of selection.

But why did this dichotomy exist? Comic songs may be rejected, presumably as less worth the effort of learning than serious songs, but why does a man who speaks approvingly of songs that 'tell a tale' dismiss prose narrative as 'no'but tales'? As it happens, Mr Lyons knew only funny stories, and it may be that in his culture most stories were funny – such is my experience as a casual participant-observer, though systematic fieldwork might show otherwise. But there is another relevant criterion, touched on in the discussion of jingles: that of voicing. Just as the repertory splits generically between the serious and the comic, it splits (though in a different place, and not as starkly) between different personal voices. Of thirty-six songs, twenty-six are in the first person or its equivalents of direct address or unreported dialogue, ten in the third person. This is surprising, given the prevailingly narrative mode which substantiates the singer's declared preference. The jingles divide nine to two respectively. The stories reverse the position: five in the third person, two in the first; and so, again, do those methodologically useful fragments, ten in the third person, eight in the first. If comedy is an art of distancing, and the third person the voice of objectivity, so tragedy is an art of empathy and the first person the voice of involvement. Jingles – an important element in Mr Lyons' early aesthetic experience – embody both tendencies, and in doing so sketched out alternative models of artistic emphasis. Both were taken up, but one given pre-eminence over the other, in the repertory and in the artist's explicit evaluation of it. Clearly what matters is the way in which a 'tale' is told.

In an earlier discussion of Mr Lyons' artistic thinking, I analysed one of his songs in terms of a relationship between *history* and *truth*, concluding that he tended to regard as historically true whatever he could see as morally true.[20] I did not then know that the ballad in question, if not wholly accurate, was factually based; but neither, strictly speaking, did Mr Lyons. He *knew* that the battle of Waterloo, and the explosion at Burns Pit in 1909, and the Easter Rising in 1916 were historical facts; the life and death of Patrick McCaffery – and, for that matter, of his compatriot Patrick Sheehan – he only *believed* to be so, because the songs that tell their stories conformed to his view of the relationship between England and Ireland, and between the rulers and the ruled – and of course because, in their transmission to him, those songs had brought with them a tradition of their factual validity, which he felt no need to test or question. His gloss on 'Patrick Shiernan' even included the statement that 'it were in the paper about him', which is correct, though Mr Lyons had never seen *The Freeman's Journal* of 28 September 1857. In principle, then, I would still regard my earlier finding as broadly correct, even if I would wish to give more credence to the historicity of traditions – at least as a working hypothesis – than I then did. However, in relation to Mr Lyons' repertory as a whole, that finding suffers from a misplaced emphasis. Precisely ten songs have – as far as their content is concerned: their date of composition may be another matter, but Mr Lyons was concerned only with the former, and on the whole assumed contemporaneity – dates *post quem* earlier than his lifetime, and four of these are contemporary with his father's life.[21] Most of the repertory will therefore have been topical at the time of its acquisition, either explicitly and factually so (e.g. 'The Titanic', 1912), or, more frequently, fictionally so, understood as such by the singer, and therefore 'true' in a different sense, i.e. in being an accurate account of the state of the world as he knew it.[22]

In short, though the repertory had an historical dimension from the beginning, it was a relatively small one and, in fact, largely devoted to Ireland (seven out of ten songs), an aesthetic reflection of the family's own history and already a personalization of it – all seven employ the subjective voice. This historical dimension had inevitably grown during the singer's lifetime. What was hot off the press in 1909 was by 1964 a statement about the past, and specifically an objective correlative of Mr Lyons' own past as a young coal-miner, and the son of a man who had experienced the death of work mates in a pit-accident. This is where the 'times' and the 'thought' merge. Those recurrent preoccupations of his song-repertory – the Irish diaspora, military service overseas, emigration and exile, the break-up of the family, the exploitation and abuse of the powerless by the powerful – are, of course, constants in the modern industrial and imperial history of the British Isles, and, equally obviously, James Lyons knew that they were: songs, among other things, had told him so. But their reference points for him were more local, particular and personal than that. That restrained solo voice expressed, in its words, and contained, in its manner, the anger and anxiety of its own early experience.

Notes

1   A number of repertories, or substantial selections from them, are now in published form, and uncounted others lie in archives; but discussions of how to approach them are still not common. For valuable presentations of individual repertories in their social context see Abrahams 1970 and Bringemeier 1931. Goldstein 1972 remains the most important methodological statement. For a pioneering approach to the repertory of a whole community see Brailoiu 1960 (based on fieldwork undertaken between 1929 and 1932). Though constraints of space prevent their giving a full account, Dunn 1980 and Falassi 1980 are important analyses of the dynamics of community repertories – the latter especially interesting because of its consideration of different genres.

2   See especially Hobsbawm and Ranger 1983.

3   Letter from James Lyons to the writer, 28 November 1964. All subsequent quotations from Mr Lyons are excerpted from conversations with him during fieldwork in the Aire and Calder valleys between December 1964 and July 1966.

4   See Blacking 1961; Glassie n.d.; Ives 1964.

5   Kerr 1942–3; Richardson 1968; Thompson 1963: 439.

6   I have very little information on Mr Lyons' mother, and consequently on what influence her experiences and opinions may have had on him. He showed little interest in talking about her, and at that time, in my first experience of fieldwork, my interviewing procedure was permissive to a degree which I would no longer think proper.

7   cf Hoggart 1969: ch. 3.

8   An error in Green 1970–1 concerning the extent of Mr Lyons' repertory was unfortunately perpetuated in Dawney 1974: 10. The responsibility is of course mine, not Mr Dawney's.

9   An analogous distinction between *songs* and *ditties* was made by Henry Dawe, Darrell's Hole, Newfoundland – v. recording of 28 October 1967 by John Tucker, Memorial University of Newfoundland Folklore Archive. For vernacular distinctions between genres, and the intricate relationship between genres and functions, see Ben-Amos, D. 1976a, and especially his important essay 1976b.

10   There is no satisfactory English term for *blason populaire*, despite the attempt by Widdowson 1978: 45 to revive one not apparently in use since the seventeenth century. The term comprehends all conventional or stereotypical descriptions of or references to the characteristics and interactions of different social groups, whether defined by region, occupation, race, nationality, language, religion or any combination of these.

11   The text he used, though from a source unidentifiable owing to loss of cover and title-page, was 'The Boston Burglar', frequently reprinted in Irish and American songsters. See for example *Walton's New Treasury*, 1968: pt 1, 12–13.

12   Green 1970–1.

13   See Green 1978a.

14   See Abrahams 1970b and 1972; Bethke 1976; Green 1976.

15   An attempt has been made to represent orthographically the vernacular which Mr Lyons used in singing this jingle, because it is intrinsic to the text. Standard orthography would not only misrepresent it, but would blur a distinction in Mr Lyons' repertory between items performed in dialect and those (the majority,

including all but two of the *songs* – the two erstwhile ritual songs) performed in modified standard.

16   'find us' pronounced /findəs/. For preliminary considerations of the different registers at play in English working-class singing traditions see Green 1972b.

17   See Widdowson 1976 and 1978.

18   For McCaffery see Corr 1973; and for Sheehan, Zimmerman 1967: 245–7. 'The Little Stowaway', a dramatized song, was the most celebrated act of the serio-comedienne Jenny Hill (1851–96), and very popular during the 1870s. See Pulling 1952: 187.

19   That *songs* are good for singing to adults does not make them, *ipso facto*, bad for singing to children. The relationship of function between *songs* and *jingles* is asymmetrical.

20   Green 1970–1.

21   Viz., 2, 3, 6, 10, 11, 19, 26, 28, 30, 35, ranging from 'The Croppy Boy' (1798) to 'The Flagship Victoria' (1893); the earliest song from his father's lifetime is 'McCaffery' (1861–2).

22   'The West Stanley Disaster' (Burns Pit, Co. Durham, 1909) represents the effective turn-around from historical to topical content. 'One of the Best', learned from print while in the navy, predates it in its content (an unspecified war in South Africa), but it is impossible to tell whether its content predates Mr Lyon's birth in 1896, since it could refer to the Zulu War of 1879, the first Boer War of 1880–1, or the second of 1899–1902. Twenty songs have no demonstrable factual content whatever.

5 Westcountry Gipsies: Key Songs and Community Identity

SAM RICHARDS

Just as Ian Russell insists on the study of what is definably popular with a given social group, as demonstrated by its currency in public performance, and Tony Green makes a case for approaching the repertory through the articulated perceptions and perferences of the performer; so Sam Richards, like Michael Pickering, concentrates on the analysis of a single song whose reiterated performance in a particular context suggests a prima facie *case for its having a special importance for its singers in that context.*

Thereafter, however, an important difference of approach becomes apparent. Pickering, in working with documentary evidence, is necessarily unable to talk to the men and women who sang the ballad of the husbandman, and must therefore find some other point of engagement with his material, essentially that of its reference to changing class-formations. Both Russell and Green, for all that their fieldwork is different in emphasis, adopt the premise that the participant-observer is a neutral and objective figure. Sam Richards challenges this heuristic stance. Taking as his starting point the notion that, willy nilly, the presence of a field-worker – by definition a stranger, and almost always (in the United Kingdom at least) socially distinct from his or her informants – necessarily modifies the interaction of the group which he or she is studying, Richards sees the encounter between the traveller-singer and gaujo-fieldworker as a paradigm of the relationship between the minority and majority cultures. On that basis, he constructs a rhetorical analysis of a particular song, both words and music, as a symbolic statement about both the immediate human situation and its long-standing sociological foundation. Unlike Green, he emphasizes the importance of perceptions which cannot be articulated explicitly at any general level, and which, in his view, find indirect and allusive expression through song.

Ultimately, there is little doubt that all the approaches so far canvassed would need to be brought together, with necessary adjustments, in a methodology for approaching popular song in its vernacular manifestations which synthesized historical and ethnographic considerations so as to avoid the danger of compartmentalizing knowledge through the equivalent fallacies of the ethnographic present on the one hand, and an over-schematic historicism on the other.

One final point should be noted here. The terminological and conceptual debate which is sketched out in the first essay in this book is far from resolved, even among people who share a common concern with locally shaped contexts and the meanings of works of performing art within them. Tacitly, the concept of 'folk-lore', with all its derived terminology, has always been a polemical rather than a scientific one; and the writers represented here differ in their views of how best to engage with it. Pickering and Green are inclined to scrap it altogether; Russell is provisionally content to substitute for it the equally problematic but less sociologically loaded concept of 'tradition' (given its close referral to actual, lived situations); Richards takes the line, similar to that current in American folkloristics over the last two decades, that the concept exists and must be fought for, in order to free it from its cultural evolutionary origins and idealistic tendency and re-invest it with the denotation of a special kind of cultural process proper to and observable in face-to-face interaction.

In a cultural context in which song figures as a folkloric process it will frequently be found that the overall repertoire is built up in three generally discernible layers: diverse, shared, and key songs.

The first are usually the most numerous and provide the fund of varied songs which keeps a repertoire rich and interesting to its performers and listeners.[1] Shared songs are, self-evidently, known and performed by many singers in a tradition, while key songs are the least numerous and the most commonplace. Key songs constitute part of the shared layer of a communal repertoire, but have especial significance for particular groups. These emphases have been found within various folkloric repertoires, and it would seem that a similar breakdown of songs in a local tradition, or group of congruent or overlapping traditions, could be carried out in most cases.[2]

Clearly a numerical count of items encountered in fieldwork gives a good initial guide as to which are key songs, but it is at the same time a loose one. In some cases it may suffice, as when some songs lead by a very wide margin. Russell's researches have shown that this appears to be the case with the song 'Good News' in a group of South Yorkshire carolling traditions.[3] However, there are cases in which a song, although not documented a large number of times, can be regarded by the participants in a tradition as highly significant to the extent that the folklorist might consider it a key song. Firmer understanding of such significance can be provided by knowledge of the immediate context type: how a song is performed, who by, why, when, audience reaction. We also need to consider the wider context, cultural, social, environmental. Likewise we require sustained acquaintance with a tradition for the fieldworker to begin to observe the 'feel' of certain songs and performances. Though fraught with the problems of participant observation, such observation is crucially important to the formulation of questions and hypotheses.

To give detailed evidence concerning the key song which forms the main focus of this study would be, at this stage, to jump the gun. Suffice to say that in the case of 'The Highwayman Outwitted' as sung by Westcountry gypsies, its numerical popularity, and its repeated occurrence in a certain type of context (e.g. the first encounter or first recording session with a singer) together give a degree of incidence which could hardly be *co*-incidence. Just as important, though, were singers' and listeners' attitudes to and comments about the song. Here we are in the field of what Dundes has termed 'oral literary criticism' in which 'folklorists must actively seek to elicit the meaning of folklore from the folk'.[4] This may be quite tricky. In the case of a song whose deeper meanings may be concealed by subtle codes and symbols we move into a difficult area for oral literary criticism. Even so, there are certainly examples of informants offering their reasons why those present, including, of course, the folklorist, should take particular note of a song. Such information can help to determine the importance of a song in a tradition, and may offer clues as to whether it should be regarded as a key song. A group of people, either in a localized or wider context, does not arbitrarily select its key songs, although the selection process is not deliberate and articulated. Unconscious selection is, however, ultimately rational. I have coined the term 'key songs' to suggest that by taking up the challenge of understanding these important items in a repertoire we are engaged in 'unlocking' areas of meaning which give strong pointers to shared attitudes and values held by the people a tradition represents.

It is the intention of this study to combine various analytic methods, using the insights of all where appropriate. These include description derived from fieldwork, sociohistorical and oral historical observations, musical and textual analysis, cantometrics, symbolic analysis, and sociopsychological analysis. In light of the fact that gypsies are a subgroup within a host culture which sometimes (far too frequently) treates them with little sympathy, some observations made in this study will also touch on the roots of racism. This means that we have to approach the subgroup and the host culture not only as separate, but also as interdependant, particualarly so in those areas of contact where differences occur. Consequently in this study of a key song, gypsies and non-gypsies are often presented as they interact.

A song which stays in a key position within a tradition for a long period of time may be presumed to be dealing with matters of lasting import. Such songs are crucial in expressing the identity of a community – insofar as a song tradition can, at least partially, do this. This includes a community's internal values and view of itself, the way it is and the way it would like to be (when these are not the same), the way it thinks others view it, and the way it would like others to view it. I have already maintained that singers and other participants in a tradition gravitate towards key songs for 'ultimately rational' reasons. These reasons involve problem solving through symbols or codes, matters of self-image, the need to confront subjects and ideas not generally or easily discussed in other ways, and group values. It may be that a key song serves one or more of these purposes until the particular problem loses its importance.

Appropriate and available songs are pressed into service. Amongst songs that are available it might seem to the observer that some might be appropriate but do not attain popularity at all. Invariably, though, the key song gives as good an expression of the *insider's* view as it is possible to get. Research amongst Westcountry gypsies has revealed two songs at least which must be regarded as key, and it is one of these which forms the basis of the rest of this study. The song is 'The Highwayman Outwitted' (Laws L2),[5] and is generally known to Westcountry gypsies by a phrase from its first line: 'The Farmer In

Leicester/Chesfield/Sheffield/Yorkshire'. Apparently they are not alone among English gypsies in their liking for this song. Mike Yates recorded a version from a gypsy in Kent and commented: 'For some reason The Farmer of Chester is a song which has proved especially popular among gypsies, and is frequently met with today.'[6] Analysis of songs as key songs brings us a little nearer to what that 'some reason' may be.

Every folklorist, writer, educationalist, sociologist, or researcher has to deal with a complex of myths and misunderstandings as soon as they turn their attention to gypsies. The most frequent question that occurs in conversation with gaujos[7] (non-gypsies) concerns the *bona fides* of the particular group of gypsies under consideration. One example of this can be gleaned from a radio interview in which a Bradford councillor put his view:

> To me a gypsy is a man (sic) who lives a specific way of life with his own caravan, with Romany traditions, and they are great traditions. The people that we are talking about are people who drift from site to site, developing a site into a tip in a very short time – masses of filth, human excretia. And, of course, we get reports from people who live around that the factories, the shops, and the private houses are no longer safe when these people move into the area.[8]

The implication behind many such statements by local officials is that if the particular families to be dealt with are not gypsies they can be moved on with impunity. The convenience factor here is transparent.

For many gypsyologists from the nineteenth century until comparatively recently it has all been a matter of 'blood' of the purity of the "blood line". Even Vesey-Fitzgerald, a romantic but pioneer writer on the subject in 1944, scatters references to 'blood', 'half-bloods', or 'pure blooded families' throughout his *Gypsies Of Britain*.[9]

There is variation of opinion amongst gypsies themselves as to the usage of the word 'gypsy'. Some use the word in reference to themselves, often with pride; others do not, and some disparage it. The only word which meets with understanding, approval, and some level of agreement is 'traveller', although I have one example of a family refusing even this designation, preferring 'travelling hawkers'.[10] In my view the word 'traveller' is ideologically loaded. It implies a self-image of real or imagined nomadism, adaptability, freedom from constraint, and does so because, as an English language word used in other contexts, it carries a range of meanings that are transmutable in the context of meaning 'gypsy'. 'Traveller' being the generally preferred word, I shall use it from here on.

Any attempt to define the 'real' and the 'spurious' amongst travellers raises the whole range of myths about the 'true' gypsy, 'Romany blood', and ethnic purity. Such myths are counterproductive to any effort to gain genuine understanding and are, ultimately, racist. This is not to deny that many travellers themselves are what MacColl and Seeger refer to as 'victims of racist feedback' and 'often contemptuously dismiss members of their own fraternity as *mumpers, poshrats* (half blood), or merely as *not proper gypsies*'. This may come as a surprise when fieldworkers begin making contacts. One traveller told me:

The tinkers are not the really proper traveller. Not the same sort of class as the traveller. I think tinkers were somebody who sort of took to the roads. I can't help feeling that they started off a little bit like tramps in a way. More that type of thing. But they're not the same, 'cause the Irish tinkers do give the travellers a bad name because they're quite untidy. And I do think they're more dirty, whereas the travellers are very clean. So there is a difference.[11]

But, to quote MacColl and Seeger again: 'Even tinkers, those "ultimate whipping-boys" (Acton) in the scapegoat hierarchy, have their lesser breeds, their *bucks, blue-bucks,* and *schulas*.'[12]

The roots of the travellers' internal racism lie in gaujo attitudes. Gaujos rationalize their own dislike of modern day travellers by reference to idealized types. The 'real' gypsy is a gentleman, honest, slightly mysterious, and has 'true' Romany blood. Many of the travellers' most vehement critics claim to have great respect for 'real' Romanies, but will contrast these with the actual group of travellers that happen to be camped or passing through their locality. A good brief account of this negative stereotyping is given by Judith Okely. Travellers, realizing gaujo prejudices, feed the stereotypes back to the gaujo as a means of self-defence, or, as Okely puts it:

> These stereotypes have also been exploited by individual Gypsies in specific circumstances, to reassure officials that they themselves are not to blame, but some other groups.[13]

The quest for the 'real' and the 'spurious' is misguided and ultimately a political convenience. The notion of a race of people sticking together as a gathering of totally endogamous bands throughout their transeuropean travels for nearly 2,000 thousands years, never admitting a single ounce of contaminating gaujo blood, is clearly untenable. It is simply ironic that *gaujo* blood is claimed to contaminate the gypsy race, thus making it possible for *gaujos* themselves to dismiss particular groups as not 'real' gypsies and thus to avoid having to deal with them. None of the evidence supports this curious view, and fieldworkers in recent years have accepted that marriages between travellers and gaujos frequently happen without, in any sense, 'thinning out the gypsy blood'.

With the apparent exception of a brief period in the fifteenth and early sixteenth centuries just after their arrival in Britain, travellers have been a marginal group subject not only to passive discrimination in the senses already described, but also to severe punishments and harassments. At its most harsh this has amounted to capital punishment for the mere 'crime' of being a gypsy, and, indeed, many were hanged. Harassment continues to the present, albeit in less dramatic forms than hanging, and generations of experience have created in travellers degrees of distrust of the host system of authority. With a few travellers this distrust extends to the majority of gaujos. However, it would be wrong to overdramatize this point. In most travellers known to me the distrust is latent, becoming active only when the group is threatened. In the normal course of events policemen are regarded as 'only doing their job', and some travellers have argued to me for a stronger police force to deal with civil disorder. When the representatives of authority are in direct conflict with travellers *as travellers* latent distrust becomes more tangible. Even then, this does not imply violence towards authorities. Generally speaking, even in ugly scenes such as evictions, travellers take only defensive action.

Like MacColl and Seeger before me,[14] I quote Thomas Acton's passage in which he shows how the word 'traveller' is used. It is as *near* to a definition as any writer has so far managed.

> The word may be applied by Gypsies living in England and Wales to the following classes of people: first, any person who is living or has lived on the road, following one or more of the modes of self-employment of casual labour which are perceived as the 'Gypsy trades' or occupations. Second, any person whose parents or other ancestors were Travellers, and who has inherited (i.e., derived from the socialisation practices of his parents, real or adoptive) elements of travelling culture, particularly Romani or Gammon linguistic elements, or Travellers' economic habits, the 'Gypsy occupations' referred to above.[15]

The particular family groups in England's Westcountry that form the basis of my research are mainly settled travellers. That is, they have mobile homes, shacks, trailers, in a few cases bungalows. In the case of trailers – still the majority – they are permanently and legally parked, either paying rent to a farmer, or, in some cases, owning their own patch of land. Their family names are Holland, Birch, Small, Penfold, Sanders, Orchard, Roberts, Hook, Richards, Edwards, Crocker, Isaacs, Packman and Stanley. In all cases they have done some travelling even if only for short periods in their lives. Many have experienced living in a tent, and a few still travel. The older travellers in this group travelled a lot before the 1939–45 war, ranging as many as six counties in the South and Southwest. Some went across much of the south of England.

These families are not the only ones found in the Westcountry. There are other families who do not have such a long history of settlement in the area, or who have visited the area frequently while continuing to travel and have not, therefore, established themselves in local consciousness so much. Perhaps the most important factor here is that of property or a permanent place of residence. The Westcountry families mentioned above often have these; their economically poorer counterparts are longer-range travellers of mixed ancestry – English, Welsh, Irish. Contact between these two groups is minimal and, perhaps predictably, members of both groups can be heard to assert that the others are not real gypsies/travellers.

The Westcountry travellers studied here present relatively few social problems other than a little elemental fisticuffs at country fairs. In many cases this reflects the changing times, their more settled position and higher degree of integration into the host communities.

The Anglo-Romani vocabulary often reflects the travellers' marginal economic status, sharing many words with street traders, fairground people, the criminal fringe and, further back in time, highwaymen. They do not work permanently for outside employers, although there are some exceptions to this rule. They are more usually self-employed with the nuclear family as the basic social and economic unit. The most typical trades amongst the male travellers are scrap-dealing, tarmac-laying, and roofing. Some deal in second-hand cars, buy and sell a range of commodities, and a few do casual agricultural work. Some of the younger generation of both sexes now work in factories, and while unusual, this may be evidence of a gradual drift from travellers' culture. As for the women, work with the men on heavy labouring does take place but is exceptional. Some sell flowers on the streets, take a basket of lace, charms, and other trinkets round shopping centres, but the majority known to me seem to have settled into a more conventional domestic housewife's role. This appears to happen alongside settlement and greater economic security. Those who do sell from door to door or in the streets have a highly developed, insistent, almost theatrical patter, exploiting gaujo myths about 'lucky gypsies', fortune-telling, charms, and curses. A traveller woman in her fifties recalled how she worked as a teenager:

> You'd go up to a person and ask them if they'd buy a charm for luck. You wouldn't put a price on it. Just ask 'em to give you something for luck. If you was lucky you might get a pound, and you might get a penny ... Some days you'd earn good money and another day you might not earn enough for bread.[16]

In a frank interview one traveller women put it this way:

> Fortune telling? There's a lot of it done. A hell of a lot. That's how the money's got as well. It's just diddling people out of money. People that's foolish enough to part with it ... Charm selling. In a summer like this (very hot). Beaches. Holiday places. Beaches, things like that. Charms, key rings – People fall over themselves to get it. Why? I don't know ... They just go and tell a load of fibs. Lead the people on just for the money. They'll tell you anything to get your money out of you. It's just a fight for survival.[17]

The same woman admitted that this means of survival was a hard one which put youngsters in the way of many rebuffs.

> When you get bawled off at the door, see, you get immune to it. People shouting at you. It doesn't worry you. When you're younger it hurts, you know. But as you get older ... if they're rough to me I don't mind because I'm used to people bawling at me. I don't mind people shouting at me because I'm quite used to it. You get hardened to it.[18]

All who were born before the 1950s remember such things. Indeed, many refer to the 1939–45 war as a watershed in their life style, changes rapidly happening thereafter. One of the most profound changes for many families was the shift in roles in the division of labour between the sexes. At one time traveller women went out for the day, away from their home base, to earn the money to provide for the family.

> Years ago the woman, she was the breadwinner. And she had to see that the children was clothed through selling the pegs and the flowers, or whatever she made, or whatever the men made. And she had to survive. She had to put that bread on the table for the family. And also the clothing. What she couldn't buy she had to beg.[19]

Most travellers' occupations past and present have one over-riding factor in common: in all cases the traveller has to bargain or negotiate prices with the gaujo. Furthermore, travellers pride themselves on being able to strike good deals, highly advantageous to themselves. They are extraordinarily adept at putting themselves in the dominant role in any negotiation with a gaujo. When I once asked a flower-seller in Totnes High Street if she was a Mrs Small as I had heard that a lady of that name was working the area and I knew some of her relations, she evaded my question, read my palm, took £2 for a lucky charm, and disappeared up the road.

Before the war hardly any travellers had houses or bungalows. I have encountered only one who, at the time, owned a permanent building of any kind. Travellers lived in tents and waggons. Many travellers have stressed in interview that their life style was a matter of basic survival. They bought provisions in local shops, were sometimes given food and necessaries, occasionally bartered for useful goods, and when ends didn't meet:

> We had to pinch our 'taties, pinch our swedes whenever we could to get something in the pot to eat. And they days there were more chicken around. We used to have a chicken when we wanted it – provided the farmer didn't catch us. And this is what we called survival. And it was hard times.[20]

The travellers' year consisted of finding somewhere semi-permanent for the winter and travelling during the summer. They often followed a travelling route that was traditional to their particular family. This would include certain fairs at fixed times of the year. At the fairs a lot of hard bargaining, horse-dealing, singing, step dancing, and socializing when on.

The travellers' nomadic or semi-nomadic habits had ultimately an economic basis. One traveller referred to moving on 'when the country was finished'. If the women were selling from door to door there would occur a saturation point at which time necessity forced them to move on and work another patch. This is still the case with semi-nomadic travellers today. Despite this material reason for travellers' wanderings, many who were brought up in the life now feel an urge to move at certain times of the year even when the economic reason has gone:

> ... I'd rather be travelling than in a house. I can't help it. The traveller's blood's in me bones and I just can't help it. When the spring of the year comes – I got to go. It's no good. I can't stay in a house.[21]

Although the families studied do not seem to encounter the scale of discrimination and conflict expereinced by others elsewhere it would be wrong to suppose that their lives are trouble-free in this respect. Even the youngest informants, travellers in their teens and twenties, recall that they had to run the gauntlet of playground taunts:

> When I was at school I can remember being called 'gypsy' and all this here, and you was, sort of, cast out of it a bit. But I mean you fought your own battles and they respected you for that really ... The only hounding I did have was when I

went to school, but if anyone said anything they got a smack in the mouth ... I think possibly in some communities like you get this racial thing, its a similar type of thing really isn't it.[22]

This informant agreed that 'things are not so bad now'. Interviews with travellers only fifteen or twenty years his senior produced a more harsh picture.

You was hounded like a – worse than a dog... You never had no rest from it. You couldn't learn nothing at the school.[23]

There are recent examples of discrimination against adult travellers. One involved a traveller's horse being forced down a well overnight and left there to die, and though this is exceptional, there are plenty of lesser, petty ways in which travellers are reminded that they are, indeed, a subgroup in a host society which is, at times, uncertain as to how to relate to them. During a meeting of Devon Education Committee 'to find a site for gipsies and itinerants in the Plymouth area', a discussion took place at the same time as another committee was considering where to site a new reservoir. Councillor Sidney Williams said:'I have always said that we should put the gipsies in Swincombe and then make it a reservoir' – a jest, perhaps, but a tasteless one revealing deeper attitudes.

It is important to strive for a balance. The Westcountry families have not experienced the horrors of 'the heavy mobs'.[24] For the most part their lives are undramatic, but tales of heavy-handed treatment in the not so distant past continue to be handed down through families, giving the younger generation an idea of what their parents and grandparents experienced:

... where ever we went, you know, (if) we was beside of the road and there was a house and they had children: 'Don't go near the gypos, they'll take you away.' We had that all the time. We was always criticized most everywhere we went.[25]

I've remembered it from a little child. I've seen policemen come in Sussex and kick the kettle right over my brother-in-law's mother. And she was just lucky that she had thick clothes on and it was pulled off her quick 'cause she would have been scalded.[26]

Postwar folklorists have taken particular interest in travellers as carriers and users of songs which conform to a somewhat Sharpian view of the vernacular repertoire. Whereas gaujo singers who remember such songs are only infrequently met and tend to be regarded as exceptional even within their own communities, no traveller sees anything unusual about another traveller who sings. And it is undoubtedly true that many travellers know songs derived from broadsides, classic ballads, standard folk lyrics and old love songs. References for recent work in this field are, most notably, Kennedy,[27] MacColl and Seeger,[28] and various LP records in the Topic catalogue.[29] Such works give a good impression of *some* of the travellers' repertoire, but not *all*. Traveller singers are not as selective as the folklorists. If the intention is to collect and publish certain kinds of texts which conform to criteria established by the folklorist then a selective approach may be appropriate. In the last analysis, however, this tells us more about the folklorist than about the travellers. If the researcher wishes to view song as folklore amongst modern travellers *and by doing so gain valuable insights into their culture as it is lived* the selective approach is of very limited value. The *entire* available repertoire, as far as it can be discovered, is necessary for such a task. Travellers do sing ballads and broadsides, but they also sing Victorian tearjerkers, songs originally learnt from 78 rpm records, music hall items (relatively few of these), early hillbilly and cowboy songs, more recent Country and Western, and some modern pop songs. Such songs are performed in family gatherings either at home or in local pubs, at the various country fairs held in the summer and autumn and at weddings, christenings, birthdays, Christmas, and to visiting folklorists.

There is some contextual differentiation between songs. Certain types of song do not figure in large crowds or more public gatherings. Also, one singer told me how she omitted verses from lengthy songs when singing with a large crowd. The differences between public and private contexts for travellers' singing would repay careful study.

It was stated earlier that I have identified two key songs for Westcountry travellers. The one *not* dealt with here is 'Twentyone Years', a Nashville Country and Western or hillbilly song possibly from the 1930s. It tends to be a 'public' song, although not invariably. 'The Highwayman Outwitted', the subject of this study, tends to be a 'private' song, again not invariably. It is also a short narrative ballad of a type that would readily have been admitted as a folk song by the folk song pioneers, Sharp, Baring-Gould, Kitson, Broadwood, etc. The first task in interpreting its possible meanings is to examine the contexts in which I have heard it performed.

My first contact with travellers and their songs was in 1973. A non-gypsy singer in Ivybridge, South Devon, suggested that I, along with my colleagues who shared my interest,[30] visit a nearby travellers' site because he had heard them sing when he worked with some of them. We went to the site and underwent a series of difficult negotiations in which it was obvious that the man we spoke to was attempting to put us off. We announced from the start that we were interested in meeting singers. Singing, for travellers, is a significant, intimate activity not usually offered to outsiders. It was predictable that we would have to earn the right to gain access to this song culture. We were not so much a threat, as in the case of gaujo authorities, but an intrusion. Our travellers were always "busy", they would see us next week, next Saturday in the pub (and then not turn up), and we were told to go to country fairs or seek out some aged travellers living at the other end of the country.

Doggedly we returned to the site and spoke to our man. One early evening a younger traveller passed us by and was called over with the promise that he knew some songs. He did come to speak with us. Within minutes, as we stood amongst the scrap, trucks, dogs, and trailers he sang to us his version of 'The Highwayman Outwitted'. After that he sang a few more songs, and the other travellers eventually kept an appointment to meet us and sing in a local pub. Dozens of people turned up, although our first singer, Nelson Penfold, was not there. On this and subsequent occasions Sophie Issacs ('Aunt Soph'), an elderly lady clearly regarded as the singer of the group,[31] sang many songs including 'The Highwayman Outwitted' early on in the first session.

Not long after this episode we were referred to another traveller, Bob Small of Abbotskerswell. We spent a frustrating evening just missing him in various pubs. After trying a few we rang the next pub on his round and asked for him. Our long series of failed negotiations with other travellers might have suggested to us the possibility that Bob Small would have moved on by the time we reached the pub. It might also have taught us not to expect much in the way of songs. In fact he remained where he was and met us. He was more immediately open about his songs than our previous informants, his first song being another version of 'The Highwayman Outwitted'.

From here onwards our song research amongst travellers became smoother. We had made our initial contacts and word had got round that we were 'barmy but harmless' as was pointed out years later. 'The Highwayman Outwitted' took great prominence in all these early visits. Nearly every singer knew it.

In 1975 we met Amy Birch of North Devon, a handsome woman with a powerful voice and an active repertoire of varied songs. We arranged to record her in her mobile home one winter evening and did so in the presence of her husband, adolescent sons, and one of her two daughters. Eight years later she told me of her feelings concerning that initial session. Apart from being a salutory note to fieldwork, the following extract from a taped interview is important because it shows the distrust we were held in, pinpoints the private nature of the song tradition amongst travellers, and also hints at a slight feeling of disadvantage that was felt at being asked to sing by people who had not yet earned the right to hear songs. The latter point is important in my subsequent contextual analysis of 'The Highwayman Outwitted', a song which, as we have seen, was invariably performed during our first visit. I give the relevant extract of interview followed by a transcription of Mrs Birch's version of the song.

Q: When we first called ... what was your reaction to that at the time, if you don't mind me asking? Did you think that was fair enough that people should come and ask for songs?

A: No, not at first really, I thought it was a bit of a liberty really. (Laughs) If you saw me in a pub and asked me to sing a song I would have quite willingly done it. I automatically say you don't know who it is coming to the doors. Could be anybody. Unless we know anybody it isn't often we invite anyone in at all, we kind of people. We'll go outside and talk, but not in. I was quite offended to be quite truthful first time you called. I wouldn't be rude and say it, but when you went I were quite annoyed to think such a thing could happen.

Q: Did you think of it as an intrusion?

A: Yes I did. 'Cause I thought when you knew a song it was just something you sang to make yourself happy and just in with the family.

Q: What do you think generally of outsider, gorjies, being interested in travellers?

A: Oh lovely job now. Don't take no notice of it now. The more I knows the better. The more people that join in and know (songs) the better.[32]

Singer's Title: The Old Man In Yorkshire

1. There was an old man live in Yorkshire
   And to market his daughter did go
   She was afraid or a-fear of no danger
   Because she's been on the highway before
2. Well she met with a bold highway robber
   And three chambers he drew from his breast
   Saying: Give my your money or clothing
   Or else you will die in distress
3. Well he stripped that young lady stark naked
   And he gave her the bridle to hold
   There she bade there a-shivering and shaking
   Almost frozen the death with the cold
4. She put her left foot in the stirrup
   And she mounted her horse like a man
   Over hedges and ditches she galloped
   Saying: Catch me bold rogue if you can
5. She rode to the gates of her father
   And she shouted all over the farm
   Saying: Father I've been in quite danger
   But that bold rogue he's done me no harm
6. She put her white horse in the stable
   And she spread a white sheet on the floor
   And from under the flap of her saddle
   She took five thousand pounds or maybe more[33]

   As nearly every singer gave us this song, with little texual variation between versions, although with some variation within the basic melodic shape, it was reasonable to conclude that we had hit upon a song which happened to be exceptionally well-known amongst travellers in Devon. Later investigation showed that the song was well-known with travellers beyond Devon. Some singers subsequently recorded had learnt the song many years previous when they were living in other parts of the south of England. They claimed that the song was popular in Berkshire, Sussex, and Wiltshire. As other fieldworkers had likewise noted the popularity of the song,[34] it seemed important to ask why it was so popular, and why, according to my own experience, was it so frequently offered to researchers early on in the first recording session? With many singers it was the very first song.

We begin with the melody and the way it is sung. It is interesting in that its four lines are sufficiently different from each other to be regarded as A/B/C/D. Few songs of its genre are constructed thus, there nearly always being some formal repetition. Neither is it meter with triple time three main beats to the line and alternating hard and soft cadences[35] a common one in British musical folklore.[36]

This structural type is so uncommon that some standard collections contain not a single song cast in its mould. We may cite, for examples, two collections relevant in different ways to the present study: the Baring-Gould manuscript collection[37] which dealt with a roughly similar geographical area as my own fieldwork, and the MacColl-Seeger collection[38] which also deals with travellers. In the Baring-Gould fair copy out of 202 songs only one can be said to be in the metrical-melodic cast under discussion. That one is 'The Female Highwayman'[39] which belongs to the same family of highwayman biter-bit songs. In MacColl and Seeger, likewise, the type is rare. Out of 72 Scots songs and variants only two can be found: 'My Faither Was Hung For Sheep Stealing'[40] and 'Big Jimmie Drummond'.[41] Of the 86 English songs and variants none are of the type excepting 'The Highwayman Outwitted' itself.[42]

It may be objected that both these collections display areas of selectivity, the Baring-Gould one exceptionally so. My own methods in the field, although undoubtedly not free of criticism, have at least led me to recording every item offered, regardless of its provenance. Other than a few verses of 'My Bonnie Lies Over The Ocean' and a mildly vulgar song called 'Shaving Cream' I have no examples to add to the list.

Does the unusual nature of the tune help to explain its popularity with travellers? Not in isolation, but in combination with other factors it may be seen to have its part to play. It may be accepted that there are, perhaps, other tune types known to travellers some of which are unusual, although, in fact, the number is few. For this one particular unusual tune to exert such a pull on the imaginations of a specific group of singers it must contain possibilities – musical and stylistic – which are strongly in line with their cultural-stylistic outlook. This, of course, begs crucial questions. Given that travellers draw on the same repertoire pool as gaujos, what is different about the way they sing, their preferred vocal *style*, that makes the melody of 'The Highwayman Outwitted' so appropriate to their culture?

In many respects travellers and gaujos sing in similar ways. Travellers have initially absorbed some of the cultural ways and forms of expression of the host culture. With travellers in Britain this definitely extends to songs and aspects of performance style. Yet there are differences, sometimes marked ones. A. L. Lloyd once remarked, in a review of a recorded anthology of Scottish ballads, that 'Good thought they are, the farmer singers seem very formal and matter-of-fact compared with the passionate and inventive 'tinkers''.[43] This is a distinction keenly felt by travellers themselves.

> A traveller's got his own way of singing different to what a gorjie sings. If two men was singing on that (pointing to the televison) and I could not see the picture – if a gorjie was singing and a traveller was singing I think I could pick out the traveller.[44]

> A mile off. If you went to a town and passed a pub you'd say: 'Oh hark, there's travellers singing in there'. You can tell the difference; it's how they talk I think ... You can tell in minute ... Just something in their voice. They can be Scottish, any kind. You can tell they's travellers.[45]

It would be highly problematic to describe gaujo singing style as used in musical folklore in the twentieth century. The unaccompanied singing traditions, exclusively the concern of most folklorists from the early nineteenth century to the present, have to take their place alongside choral and accompanied styles which display a wide range of organizational principles and preferred styles of delivery. To cite random examples, fishermen's choirs, local rock bands, or singing and chanting at a football match could all be studied as folklore. A single monolithic folk style simply does not exist. This, in itself, provides an interesting comparison with travellers' song culture, for an investigation of their singing habits, organizational principles, and repertoire does actually reveal a settled style with clear parameters. The most obvious parameter is that travellers remain doggedly solo. Their ability to sing in groups, with accompaniments, or to accompany is poor. I have recordings of a brother and sister trying to sing the same song together and getting as much as two lines out with each other because they could not compromise their individual speeds. This is not untypical.

The fact that gaujo informal musical culture displays such diversity reflects a range of class, social, economic and productive effort. Gaujo singing, in all its forms, in other words, suggests a range of functions and social meanings.[46] This is, of course, predictable, musical information confirming what we know to be true of our pluralistic society. Travellers, however, despite being resident in this society and adopting many of its conventions, stick to a more singular, albeit adaptable, social and economic organization. This is reflected in their singing style which can be broadly characterized and shown to be less diverse than that of gaujos.

These comparisons are interesting although not, perhaps, very instructive. Further and firmer conclusions can be made by contrasting like against like: the ways travellers and gaujos sing (and sang) *the same type of songs*. Methodologically, cantometrics may be of some assistance here. This method's premise is that song style, analysed through nearly 40 parameters, is an indicator of culture patterns. Alan Lomax claims that 'as people live so do they sing'.[47] It would, of course, be simplistic to list features of song style on the one hand, and socio-cultural factors on the other, mechanically equate the two in what Elborne has called, in this context, a 'mirror hypothesis'.[48] Indeed, this is not Lomax's intention. His findings on song style and culture do point to a structural relationship between the two, but they must be applied pragmatically.

Comparison of traveller and gaujo singing of the same type of songs although in itself not problematic, does leave one question. Why not compare their singing of *any* type of songs? They both, after all, live in the same host culture with the important qualification that gaujo society *is* the host. But, as implied already, a macrocultural cantometric analysis is likely to be inconclusive because in a modern Western society like Britain a vast number of musical styles and possibilities exist. If we included all other ethnic groups (and why not?) we might find nearly all Lomax's possibilities somewhere. Secondly, and implied by the first point, the method applies best to recognizable settled styles. And thirdly, we are attempting an interpretation of a single song which, despite its unusual constructional features, is nevertheless representative of a genre. Our main aim is to establish whether there is anything in the construction and melody of this song which makes it uniquely suited to the way a traveller sings. For this we need only compare it with the way a gaujo would sing it. Even here, of course, there must be considerable leeway. Not all travellers or all gaujos sing the same, but there are broadly defined characteristics in any specific tradition.

A profile of traveller and gaujo singing styles shows many initial points of agreement. They both feature the soloist, although many gaujos enjoy chorus singing. Travellers show less preference here. Texts and musical characteristics agree in both cases although travellers' texts have a much greater tendency to be orally altered, sometimes to the point of jumble. Musical points, constructional and melodic, agree because we are largely dealing with the same repertoire in both cases.

It is when we turn to singing and delivery that differences occur. A small group of parameters cluster together to define the travellers' style as opposed to the gaujo. These parameters are Tempo, Vocal Width, Rubato, and Vocal Effort.[49]

Travellers sing slower. Some sing very slow indeed,[50] particularly women. Men perhaps incline more to the conversational although even here there are some very slow-paced singers.

Vocal Width concerns the use of the vocal apparatus, the cavities, tongue, throat muscles, and glottis. Many travellers, again especially women, appear to sing with narrow width.[51] This is more marked in men when they try to sing very loud, as they often do in pubs during local fairs. Older people seem to adopt a more open-throated delivery.[52]

Travellers' use of Rubato is deceptive. Many sing slowly enough to give the impression of Rubato when little is really being used. However, many travellers use *some* Rubato.

Finally, the Vocal Effort is usually direct, heavy, and sustained, giving a *pressing* effort. This partly accounts for the intense, passionate nature of travellers' singing, and enables those who wish to sing at considerable volume, although by no means all sing loud.

Lomax's researches regarding slow tempi are inconclusive, although he does mention that in some cases it seems to go with poor health. This is true of travellers who still travel or work and live more in the open. Likewise with Rubato the evidence is inconclusive, and Lomax has not tackled the parameter of Vocal Effort.

It is with Vocal Width that we meet correlations which strikingly agree with travellers' culture. A narrow, tense, pinched vocal sound is 'a good indicator of the relative severity of the sexual code of the society, and perhaps of the emotional tensions of the group'.[53] This includes rigid restrictions on premarital sex for women.

> They were very proud. The traveller girls would never have to get married or anything like that you know. They were a virgin when they got married. I remember one which was a long time ago, and she had a baby. I think she got drunk one night, and that was a gorjie was the father of it, and, of course, everybody shunned her. No boys would go with her or anything. In the end she married a (name omitted), but it was a long time before anyone would marry her. This is the type of thing with travellers. And I think same with running around. This is how travellers are. They think if a girl goes out with gorjie perhaps she's going to end up pregnant. Whereas a traveller would respect her more. He would wait, sort of thing.[54]

Later in the same interview we were told that divorces were almost unheard of amongst travellers 'even in bad marriages'.

Lomax mentions the 'emotional tensions of the group' and indeed travellers do seem to be emotionally volatile. Petty quarrels within the family surface quickly and die just as quickly. It is not uncommon at country fairs to see a group of women of the same family weeping together, and, likewise, principally at fairs, fights break out. Traveller's singing style, assertive, declamatory, heroic, passionate, seems to match their emotional and moral outlook. How does this information about song style and culture fit with 'The Highwayman Outwitted'?

All versions begin with a rising martial 4th. This gives the melody a decisive quality ultimately derived from the march.[55] It is commonplace in British traditional song. A random sample of some published collections showed that around 50% of tunes began this way. As examples, in Bob Copper's field collection given in 'Songs And Southern Breezes'[56] 48% begin thus, and in his own family repertoire as selected for 'A Song For Every Season'[57] this rises to 70%. This is not altogether surprising as the Copper Family's tunes display the marked influence of harmonically conceived music – church music, glees, stage songs. The rising 4th as an incipient phrase is a harmonic device which strongly announces the tonality of the tune. Songs tunes collected from travellers, however, do not appear to conform to this pattern. As tunes they are less harmonic, more linear, and consequently they use the rising 4th incipient much less. MacColl and Seeger give only 20% of their tunes beginning thus. Compared to a consistent gaujo figure of c.50% or more this is significant. In my own recordings of travellers the figure drops below MacColl and Seegers 20%.

Travellers are, indeed, melodic/lyrical singers who appear not to feel harmony or harmonic rhythm in a melody. On this basis they can sing slowly and slightly rubato.

The importance of this is that the decisive opening of 'The Highwayman Outwitted' is a gaujo quality. Travellers relish tunes that begin with falling 5th or minor 3rds. The rising 4th implies coming half way to meet the gaujo. It is decisive and therefore appropriate to 'getting on with it' in a recording session with a gaujo folklorist.

As soon as we get into the melody the travellers' values take over in a paradoxical way. Their individual, assertive, passionate, slow, slightly rubato style is better suited to longer melodies, more sustained than 'The Highwayman Outwitted'. Its lines are short, its compass narrow. Even so, travellers contrive to inject much of their typical style into this song. A transcription of the first verse as sung by Phyliss Penfold show what can be done by an inventive singer. She, incidentally, also offered this as a first song.[58]

It sounds impressive when sung, it is utterly within travellers' style, gives a good chance to display all those travellers' singing characteristics which differ from gaujos, and yet it is *easy to sing*. If by singing in a certain style a singer is coding his or her social identity to the listener, a piece of music that makes this task easy will be preferred in a potentially tense or unfamiliar situation, in this case a first recording session with a gaujo folklorist who, at best, is regarded as a curious outsider and at worst an intrusion. This tune has short lines which allow the breathing to be easily controlled, very important if the performer is tense. The arched melody peaks and falls quickly so that some hint of intensity and agility can be given without taxing the voice and the nerves. The narrow compass means that the singer is unlikely to over or under pitch. Singers can therefore 'sing themselves in' before attempting more difficult items. Maximum intensity can be concentrated in these short dynamic phrases with less effort than in other songs. The traveller singer, in short, can announce cultural identity to the fieldworker with confidence, with little fear of going wrong, and does so through a melody which affords an ideal meeting place between traveller and gaujo values.

The nature of a melody can, therefore, be an important factor in determining the song's popularity or key status. However, the suitability of the melody alone should not be expected to explain the great popularity of a key song. The words are equally vital. No matter how ideal a melody may be inappropriate words would never reach key status. And, indeed, the words of 'The Highwayman Outwitted' repay detailed inspection.

Probing the narrative on nonliteral levels of meaning reveals some interesting points of congruence between the symbolic world of the fiction and the acutal world of the travellers' social situation. It is important, for example, that the story takes place during a journey. Travellers can easily identify with a narrative that places the adventure in a travelling context. The heroine of the story is an old man's daughter. This is also important. Travellers have a strong sense of ancestry and family loyalty. The old man/farmer in the song therefore acts as a reference point against which the daughter may be located within a traditional background immediately recognizable to a group which reveres its old. Also, we have seen the women have traditionally been bread winners. The woman in the song in going from home base to *travel* to market (for the family economy) parallels the role of the traveller women.

On another level, a less literal one, it may also be said that a woman who goes out alone on the highway is more vulnerable than a man. This is not a sexist assertion. The first verse of the song itself suggests an impending drama: 'She was afraid or a-fear of no danger'. Were the subsequent events in the narrative those of a normal day there would be no need to mention the fact of her lack of fear. The highway robber in the song, as in most folk and popular literature, is male. The woman would not be assumed to be as physically strong as her male attacker, and she would be in danger of sexual abuse. This latter point is emphasized by the robber stripping her stark naked, not, as in most gaujo versions, only down to her petticoats.

Sexual vulnerability is not the only form of vulnerability suggested by her naked state. She is physically vulnerable in the sense that when naked she has not so much as a heavy boot to defend herself. In any case the robber has guns. At this moment of high drama and danger the woman has no chance of assistance, no friend is nigh, she is stripped of her modesty, of her means of defence, luck and fortune appear to have deserted her. Nakedness therefore suggests two levels of vulnerability: sexual, physical. We should add to this the dramatic impact of nakedness in a social group in which nudity is unheard of, certainly in any public sense. Nakedness is, in any case, an ultimate state. It shows a person as they really are. There are no more secrets. Psychologically speaking nakedness equals aloneness.

The robber is the initiator of the action. The woman merely defends herself, albeit quick-wittedly. Again, this is analogous to the travellers' actual situation. They regard themselves as innocent parties forced to defend themselves, to survive, by whatever means necessary and appropriate against an outside world which tends to be hostile, discriminatory, and powerful. One important form of self-defence developed by travellers is their quick-wittedness, their ability to turn any situation to their advantage. This is clearly the nub of the song. However, it is not *only* the woman's quick-wittedness which saves her. There are two other important factors. Firstly, there is her ability to ride a horse. This is a perfect symbol for travellers. They have been associated with horses for centuries. Even in the more motorized 1970s and 1980s travellers refer with pride to their days as horse-dealers. Some still work with horses, breaking in ponies, or, in one case known to me, running a riding school. Some keep a horse of their own as a pet, and horse-dealing takes place to this day at Bampton Fair in Devon. The fact that the woman in the song saves herself by riding a horse is utterly consistent with travellers' self-image. Furthermore she is a competent rider able to jump over 'hedges and ditches'.

The other important factor is the *slow*–wittedness of the highway robber. Having attained the power of life and death over the woman he is stupid enough to entrust to her the bridle of his horse. This gives her the chance for escape. Travellers have a word in Anglo-Romani for the slow-witted gaujo. The word is 'dinalow'. A dinalow is a slow, stupid, clueless fool and is referred to in a tone of derision. It is clear from their usage of the word that they would not normally apply it to another traveller. When I have asked travellers to give some idea of the way the word would be used I have, on many occasions, been given answers such as the following:

> Ah, get out. Travellers always married travellers, eighty, ninety year ago, before I was born then … If they'd see a girl speaking to a gorjie, they'd say:
> 'Come on you girls. Come away from the *dinalow*'
> Half daft they meant, see.
> 'Come on. Talking to a *dinalow*. Bedtime.'
> Q: Did they think that gorjies were half daft then?
> A: They thought they'd never get in one another's way. (In other words, learn each other's lifestyles.)[59]

This usage of the word forces the conclusion that 'gorjie' (gaujo) and 'dinalow' were synonymous, dinalow being a stronger, more derogatory word. In interviews we have been told that travellers, especially in the past, considered gaujos no match for their offspring because they would not know how to get a living *in the travellers' way*. Gaujos may find employment, but this would be for an employer. One traveller told of the pity he felt for people who had to rely on someone else to give them a job, and how sorry he felt for them when they were made redundant or forced to retire.

> All they know is the journey from home to the factory. That's all well and good until they're made redundant or have to retire. Then they don't know what to do with themselves. *They have no wits to live on.*[60]

This travellers' view of gaujos clearly fits the witless, incompetant highway robber in the song. There is something ignominious about a failed highwayman.

The nub of the tale, the quick-witted reversal of power roles, can be viewed in another revealing way. As we have seen, travellers are notoriously fond of making deals, buying and selling and bargaining to their advantage. On our first visits to sites we have been asked how much we want for our car or, in cases where they know we are musicians, how much for the accordion. Anybody who has stood with a crowd of traveller men in a pub at a local fair knows that a major topic of conversation is deals recently made. One can be forgiven for suspecting some exaggeration.

> I've known my father to go to Brent Fair, not take one horse with him, not bring one back, but he's owned twenty horses in that day.[61]

The tale is typical of travellers' self-image. They have nothing in this world and yet manage to come out on top because they have their wits to live on. The woman in the song was in potential danger, turned the situation round in her favour, and, most crucially, ended up £5000 the richer.

The robber, dinalow that he was, not only missed his chance to rob her, he had a naked young woman at his disposal and failed to take advantage of that. She, as the text carefully points out, 'mounted the horse like a man', in other words with her legs apart, not sidesaddle. This mocks the robber sexually. The horse that is between her legs (significantly white in colour) is in the very place he could have been. He has no more sense than a horse, and any traveller can control a horse. The potentially tragic situation turns comic at this point. The robber cannot press home his unfair advantages.

Finally she rides home and shares her good fortune with her father, taking us back to the importance of the family and kinship. Mention of the family is at the beginning and end of the story, thus, as in many folk narratives, framing the narrative with the home base.

There is, incidentally, no moral qualm about the fact that the £5000 in the robber's saddlebags is doubtless stolen from unfortunates who had fewer wits to live on. Again this echoes many travellers' attitudes. It is up to others to look after themselves. Tom Orchard of North Devon tells a tale about a farmer who was daft enough to buy his own horse from a Gypsy Smith, not recognizing it because Gypsy Smith had painted it white. A friend of the farmer swore it was the same horse and was eventually proved right when the horse recognized its own stable.

> It cost that feller £8 to know when he was well off. Now Gypsy Smith never took him in. He showed him. He taught him when he was well off. He charged him eight golden sovereigns to teach him. Now I don't maintain that the Gypsy Smith was a rogue. Not no way. The farmer was a fool that he couldn't tell his own animal.[62]

To summarize so far: I propose that the narrative of 'The Highwayman Outwitted' has such a hold on the imaginations of travellers because it deals with concepts, values, and situations which are familiar to them in their own lives. In the adventures of the young woman can be seen, in coded form, a typical ideal relationship with gaujos, and a self-image for travellers in the quick-witted heroine. It will be remembered that 'The Highwayman Outwitted' was often the first song offered by singers in field recording sessions. In every case it was offered in the first session.

Many first meetings with travellers consist of a certain amount of fencing. Many travellers' first instinct towards an unknown gaujo is to treat the meeting with caution. Our approach to the group which eventually produced Nelson Penfold and his songs was, it will be recalled, met by a series of rebuffs and unkept promises to meet in various pubs. This 'testing' period is understandable in the light of the harassment, abuse, and suspicion travellers have had to suffer for generations and, is, indeed, a most effective means of self-defence for them. The most important thing for this subgroup to feel is that it comes out on top of any negotiations with the gaujo world. This is not something which, in point of fact, always happens in a wider sense when it comes to claiming and maintaining their human rights. Travellers have no real power base. In interpersonal relationships, however, the case is different

My contention, which perhaps for obvious reasons remains speculative, is that in singing 'The Highwayman Outwitted' as the first, or one of the first, of the songs offered to us, the singers have been sending us a message. We, outsiders, representatives of the gaujo world, like the highwayman in the song, attempt to enter their culture as if by force with the intention of taking for them something valuable. We have already seen how one traveller admitted, in interview, that she thought our intrusion was 'a bit of a liberty'.

> You see ... really and truly when someone strange comes to you and says 'Will you sing?' you don't know who they are. You only take their word for who they are. See, it takes you a little time to adjust. It was a thing I'd never done before and I most probably wouldn't have then if all the children hadn't been there.[63]

The singers, it seems, have picked on a song which shows how the potentially weak and powerless (themselves) are capable of looking after themselves in the face of any intrusion (folklorist). The content of the song, in featuring a fictional character who acts in a way that they admire and are amused by, sorts out, from the very begining, their relationship with the outsider.

It is hard to prove this speculation other than by claiming that the facts, thus analysed, are provocative. On being questioned as to the popularity and use of this particular song most of them have given very little reason. One said that it proved that the girl could look after herself, and another claimed that it was a very 'typical' old song which reminded travellers of the old times. The importance of the horse, the market, and the woman going away from the home base to create the family economy would support this impression. It could hardly be expected that the singers would give analytical reasons for their use of the song. If my contention has foundation it refers to an unconscious response which would not be likely to be verbalized or even realized.

I can offer some support for my contention, however, by reference to other folklore genres used in initial meetings or early on in a relationship and having the same basic structure. Many of our early encounters with travellers have consisted of tricks or jokes of one kind or another. We, the outsiders, were the butt of the jokes. If we could 'take it' we were eventually welcomed. In a structural sense, therefore, A (defined by potential vulnerability) tricks B (defined by potential power but who is attempting to trespass or violate), thus reversing what would appear to be the power roles. The analogy with bargaining, negotiating, and dealing cannot be missed.

After our first meeting with Bob Small we arranged another in a pub in Newton Abbot. For over half an hour Bob played good-natured tricks on us in the form of tests, jokes, riddles, trick questions. Pointing to a little drop of beer in the bottom of my glass Bob said: 'I'll bet you any money that you can't drink that beer up.' After some banter I drank the beer in one swallow. Bob, triumphant, won his bet. You drink *down* not *up*. After many similar tricks our relationship was established. He never used his tricks on us again.

Another traveller made an arrangement with us to record some songs at 6.00 one evening. We were half an hour late. When we arrived she shouted at us:"What kind of time d'you call this?" I was only after many apoligies and explanations that her face cracked and it became obvious that she had set us up for a temporary embarrassment in front of her entire family, all of whom found it highly amusing.

Other travellers have played actual tricks or power games with us, but we must also recall the number of unkept appointments and fool's errands we have been sent on before a relationship becomes friendly. The jokes and tricks effectively create contact, although not yet friendship, at the same time sorting out power relationships. We are thus allowed in on their terms. The song works in a similar way. If we try to take advantage of the situation we will end up humiliated like the robber. It is as if the travellers are reminding us that they are more quick-witted than we might give them credit for.

On the simple premise that if a song (or any other expression) occurs many times within a culture or subculture it must be important we have analysed a key song amongst Westcountry travellers. In doing so we have confirmed the position that 'song can no longer be treated as a wayward, extra, belated, though pleasant afterthought upon the series business of living'.[64] A key song can 'unlock' areas of meaning and understanding of the social group that uses it.

Two constituencies are addressed in the present study: *song research* and *intervention in travellers' culture*. Of course, there is the view that fieldworkers should not intervene or attempt to change things. If this is seriously considered as a point of view it logically leads to the proposition that no research should be undertaken at all, research of any kind being an intervention. In any case, we have seen enough evidence to show that if intervention is not carried out from a sympathetic, balanced point of view, then other forms of intervention in travellers' culture will be and are carried out in inappropriate ways. I suggest that travellers, in Britain at least, need gaujos who wish to genuinely appreciate their culture for what it is, rather than for what it might be imagined to be.

Less urgently, but crucially, in the field of song research (and I regard songwriting and performing both as forms of research, amongst other things) understanding and use is created by intervention – or should we say *engagement*. We are therefore forced back not only to *why* we intervene, as that is an inevitability, but *how* we engage.

Putting these two constituencies together, as in the present study, *via the agent of a third party* (folklorists), logically leads to further questions. One concerns the relationship between observer and observed which is neither a matter of moral neutrality on one part, nor is it peripheral on the other. It is *the* central question upon which others depend. In the case of the present study it involves the social attitudes of gaujos to travellers and travellers to gaujos, centrally, of course, the particular gaujos and travellers involved in the research. It involves the researchers in attempting to understand their own motives for becoming associated with travellers. Are these dispassionate, or are the researchers attempting to solve problems or answer questions about their own culture, and possibly themselves: If so, what are these questions? If any answers are forthcoming are they the answers we want to hear? If not, are we capable of interpreting the answers so that they become acceptable? How do we know if we have done so? As in my case, do our motives change during the course of the research? Has the subject's response to our intervention altered during our acquaintance? How has the subject changed due to our intervention?

Recognition and analysis of key songs cannot supply response to all these areas of questioning, at least not directly. However, they are highly significant items of culture and as such add a tool to our means of understanding.

Notes

1 The distinction between performers and listeners is a notional one in many grass-roots traditions in which many people do both.
2 See Greig 1971: 3; Pickering 1983: 4; Russell 1973:13. For other works relevant to the concept of key songs, although not specifically mentioned as such, see also: Green 1970–1971; Thomas 1972; Cartwright 1981; Bird 1985; Richards 1983.
3 Russell 1973: 13.
4 Dundes 1975: 50–51.
5 The other is 'Twentyone Years', which will be the subject of another study.
6 Yates 1975.
7 Throughout this study I shall use the word 'gaujo', the Anglo-Romani word for anyone who is not a gypsy. G-A-U-J-O is a spelling used by many experts so I use it in my text. However, in quotations from interviews I use G-O-R-J-I-E to phonetically represent the way Westcountry travellers pronounce it.
8 Mr Denis Walsh interviewed on 'Woman's Hour' BBC Radio 4; 8.7.1985.
9 Vesey-Fitzgerald 1944.
10 Vic Legg, Bodmin, Cornwall, 2.7.1983. (Recorded interviews are in the first instance, designated by reference to date and place of interview.)
11 North Devon traveller, anonymous by request, 16.11.1982.
12 MacColl and Seeger 1977: 1
13 Okely 1975: 60.
14 MacColl and Seeger 1977: 2.
15 Acton 1974: 65.
16 Daisy Small, Kingsteignton, Devon, 5.7.1983.
17 Mary Isaacs, Bristol, Avon, 26,7.1983.
18 Mary Isaacs
19 Eddie Holland, Broadclyst, Devon, 18.6.1983.

20 Eddie Holland
21 Vashti Edwards, South Molton, Devon, 24.10.1982.
22 Brian Holland, Halwell, Devon, 16.2.1983.
23 Nelson Penfold, Ivybridge, Devon, 14.2.1983.
24 Hired thugs in Walsall, 1960s. Mentioned and documented in Acton 1974: 177–8. Acton writes that the Walsall events were not unique: 'there is a mass of documentation of similar events elsewhere in the Gypsy Council Papers'.
25 Eddie Holland
26 Daisy Small
27 Kennedy 1975. Kennedy devotes a section of this work to songs collected from travellers.
28 MacColl and Seeger 1977.
29 Yates 1975; Yates 1977.
30 In the early 1970s the informal research team was Paul Wilson, Tish Stubbs, and myself. From 1976 Paul Wilson moved and subsequent research, including most of the recorded interviews here quoted was done by myself or myself with Tish Stubbs.
31 see MacColl and Seeger 1977, on 'Who is a Singer? Who is not?': 19.
32 Amy Birch, near Bampton, Devon, 15.3.1983. The point can hardly be missed in this explicit statement: the folklorist's attentions have altered the tradition.
33 Amy Birch can be heard singing this song on Richards and Stubbs 1981; Nelson Penfold's version is on Richards, Stubbs and Wilson 1979. There are some interesting linguistic features in Amy's text. The use of infinitive for the past participle 'live' (vs. 1 line 1); 'a-fear' (vs. 1 line 3); 'bade' (vs. 3 line 3) as past tense of 'bide'; 'Almost frozen *the* death' seems like a combination of frozen *to* death, and catch *the* death (of cold); 'quite' danger (vs. 5 line 3) seems like a mishearing at some point in the song's life. such features are typical of travellers' texts, some of which may not even add up to strict sense on face value. (The singers and listeners usually know what they *mean*.) This is possibly the result of their learning songs by ear. Even now, with travellers' children in schools and many travellers able to read and write, their outlook and habits are definitely those of a quasi-literate people: books and newspapers are uncommon, they do not write many letters, the letters they do write are as short and functional as possible, they hate and are often baffled by forms and official documents, do not guide themselves by road signs, and so on.
34 For example: see footnote 6 above.
35 Hard and soft cadences. The conventional terminology is masculine and feminine. It is time these were dropped in favour of non-gender terms.
36 See accompanying booklet to Richards and Stubbs 1981, and Simpson 1966: 596.
37 The Baring-Gould MSS is housed at Plymouth City Lilbrary and is available on request.
38 MacColl and Seeger 1977.
39 MS Number 164.
40 MacColl and Seeger 1977: 162.
41 MacColl and Seeger 1977: 295.
42 MacColl and Seeger 1977: 278
43 A. L. Lloyd reviewing 'Scotish Tradition 5: The Muckle Sangs' in *Traditional Music* 2, 1975.
44 Vashti Edwards.
45 Amy Birch.
46 For greater treatment of this equation see Lomax 1968, and Lomax 1976.
47 Lomax 1968: 67.

48 Elbourne 1980: 67.
49 Vocal Effort is not one of Lomax's parameters. I have adapted it from Laban's classification of bodily movement, originally intended for dancers. See Laban 1971, especially 77, for a table of efforts. Ewan MacColl was the first to apply Laban to vocal effort.
50 For example, Phoebe Smith's performance of 'Barbara Allen' on Yates 1975.
51 MacColl and Seeger 1977 consider that the travellers they recorded sang with an 'open-throated, direct delivery' (21). This is not my experience. Westcountry travellers frequently sing slightly nasally, this resulting in a slight (or great) constriction of the throat muscles.
52 Bearing in mind note 51 above, could it be that MacColl and Seeger's informants were predominantly older than mine? If so, what is the implication? That older travellers cannot physically manage the younger style? Or that travellers' style has changed, is changing, in more recent times?
53 Lomax 1976: 125.
54 Dilly Davis, Bratton Fleming, Devon, 16.11.1982.
55 See Marothy 1974: 241.
56 Copper 1973.
57 Copper 1971.
58 This type of singing is notoriously difficult to transcribe. Should the reader wish to get an impression of the style the note values should be regarded as approximate.
59 Jim Hook, Holsworthy, Devon, 5.9.1983.
60 Albert Sykes, passing through Ivybridge, Devon, 17.7.1983, from fieldwork notebook.
61 Nelson Penfold
62 Tom Orchard, Holsworthy, Devon, 20.2.1983.
63 Amy Birch
64 Lomax 1968: 6.

6 The Ethogenics of Music Performance: A Case Study of the Glebe Live Music Club

JOHN L. SMITH

John Smith's concluding case-study contribution to this volume is vital both methodologically and substantively. The tradition of ethnographic field-study, in both its social anthropological and folkloristic versions, has at its heart a relationship of estrangement between fieldworker and informant. Broadly, social anthropology has been conducted by formally educated members of imperialist societies among non-formally educated groups of colonized peoples: the description of 'popular antiquities', which crystallized in the mid-nineteenth century as the study of 'folk-lore', has been undertaken by middle class intellectuals among working class groups both rural and urban, albeit with a heavier concentration on that relatively diminishing class, the agrarian proletariat. There is, of course, one big intellectual advantage in this situation: as a stranger, the fieldworker is less likely than a native might be to take for granted behaviour and values which are proper subjects for description and analysis. The world's libraries are full of the results, and they are valuable. However, the big intellectual disadvantage – quite aside from the possibility of gross misunderstandings, which, we may agree, can occur in any field of study for any number of reasons – is that it is very tricky, both cognitively and morally, to make value-judgments about a culture which is not one's own, and especially when the investigator, whatever his or her personal views on the situation, is in practice a member of a dominant group. Yet value-judgments have to be made, if scholarship in the humanities and social sciences is to be a socially useful activity at all. It is precisely this tension, referred to in the opening essay of this volume, which created the ambiguity to be observed in both the research based on the Victorian idea of 'folk-lore' and the post-war performance practice of the 'folk song revival'; and this which leads Sam Richards to address his observations to the 'two constituencies' of song-research and intervention in traveller-culture.

John Smith picks up where Sam Richards leaves off, by devoting his 'observation' to a situation in which he is naturally a 'participant'; in other words, in which the participation came before the observation and continues alongside it. From inside an organization which, beginning as a conventional folk club, has adapted to recent change in musical taste and audience habits by broadening its area of interest to that of 'live music', while holding onto the folk club's basic interactional model of a low level of separation between 'performer' and 'audience', Smith offers a social psychologist's analysis, drawing on his own intimate experience, of the 'role-rule model' which generates the particular spatial, temporal and functional behaviour of individuals within his special-interest group. Like Russell, he eschews ideal-typical accounts of performance in favour of the close description of an actual, dateable event; and, like Green, posits a correspondence between the individual's performance-career and the contexts and audience-relationships available at a given time. Finally, in a manner reminiscent of Pickering and Green's account of the dialectic of continuity and change within vernacular singing traditions, Smith asserts the importance of the local music club's interactional model, for a society where the performance of popular music is dominated by the different, but equally anti-interactive, models of muzak and heavy amplification, in establishing a critical attitude to songs and singing.

The Glebe Live Music Club provides a weekly venue for the performance of music and song in Sunderland, a town situated in the North East of England.[1] I shall begin by describing Sunderland and the club, before indicating the extent of my involvement with the club as a singer and organiser. Having done this, I shall provide a brief introduction to ethogenic social psychology which will then enable me to move on to an ethogenic analysis of a particular singers night at the club. In conclusion, I shall deal with some broader issues which the club has recently had to confront and I shall discuss these in the context of club's historical development.

Sunderland grew from small settlements along the banks of the River Wear where several shipyards with world-wide reputations were subsequently developed. The population of the town is today approximately 170,000, although the Borough of Sunderland (which includes surrounding districts such as Washington New Town, Hetton-le-Hole and Houghton-le-Spring) has a population of 300,000. The three main industrial occupations in the town have been shipbuilding, coal mining (mines continue to operate extending eastwards under the North Sea) and glass making. These traditional industries have been supplemented by modern light industries in recent years, particularly in the nearby Washington New Town which is also the site of a new Nissan/Datsun car plant.

In the inter-war years, Sunderland declined as a major industrial centre. Throughout the 1960s unemployment was only briefly less than 10% and that was at a time when the national average was 4%. Recently, unemployment has been running at a level of 20% (compared with the national figure of 14%).[2] The fact that Sunderland is an industrial centre (albeit in decline) and that unemployment has been high for some time now may account for the fact that there is plentiful provision of relatively cheap entertainment facilities in the form of social clubs, working men's clubs and ex-service men's clubs.[3] This means that there is plenty of live entertainment in the town which is put on at a relatively low cost by these clubs. This has implications for the Glebe's financial policy, as one of the founder members explains:

> When you're talking about the unemployment and the shortage of money, Sunderland has more working men's clubs than any other town in the country. You're talking about virtually nothing to get into the concert room. You get people now and again come (to the Glebe) asking 'What's the cover charge?' – that's the price to get into the concert room at a Working Men's Club. As soon as you hear that, you think ... and if you say 50p or £1.00, they'll not come in![4]

Generally speaking, the Glebe club is not in direct competition with the working men's clubs, since it does not provide bands or groups whose repertories are dominated by popular chart music. However, these clubs do set a prevailing norm for cheap live entertainment in the town and it is this that has to be born in mind when setting the level of the Glebe club entrance fees.

Comparison with other kinds of club raises the question of how occasioned gatherings at the Glebe can be characterized, and how the club can be located within the broad spectrum of venues for the local performance of live music. Thompson[5] provides a description of the pattern of events at a singing pub in the 1880s (The Wagon & Horses, Juniper Hill, North Oxfordshire): the singing followed a discussion of politics, with the young men starting off, followed by the middle aged men, chorus singing and, finally, a song or two from the old men. Pickering[6] alerts us to the fact that Thomson's account is a generalized one and 'does not present an ethnographic report of a specific evening's activities'. However, setting this aside, the Glebe club evening has a definite structure but it is different from that of Thompson's singing pub. The structure at the Glebe is rendered more explicit by the use of an M/C who divides the evening into periods for song and breaks for talking and the replenishment of glasses. In Thompson's singing pub the order of performance seems to be dictated by age whereas this is not so at the Glebe club where the M/C arranges the order of singing on a more arbitrary basis (although the singers who start or finish sets will normally be relatively well-known at the club). One further difference is that there is seldom a general conversation in which all participate at the Glebe (it therefore follows that there would not be an introductory discussion of politics, or any other topic, for that matter). The people who come to the Glebe club are required to pay an entrance fee and this enables the club to book professional and semi-professional guests; this was not something that happened at the Wagon & Horses. The Glebe repertoire may be compared with Thomson's description of the songs sung at the Wagon & Horses:

> Men and boys still sang the old country ballads and songs, as well as the latest music-hall successes. So, when a few songs were called for at the Wagon & Horses, the programme was apt to be a curious mixture of old and new[7]

The Glebe club repertoire is also a curious mixture of old and new. Of course, what now counts as an old song at the Glebe may well have passed for a new song at the Wagon & Horses in the 1880s! The more contemporary songs at the Glebe are not music-hall successes but are more likely be popular chart successes (although these in no way dominate the Glebe repertoire). The Glebe club has tended to encourage its singers to enlarge the traditional repertoire of local and vernacular songs by drawing on blues idioms, rhythm & blues and the songs of contemporary acoustic guitar singer/songwriters. Indeed, some of the club singers are also songwriters.

It seems to me that the conventional English folk club has normally worked with an idealized model of the repertory of the pub of yesteryear. Thus the latest music-hall successes of the 1880s might be acceptable, but the sort of contemporary material found in the Glebe repertoire would not be regarded as proper folk music. Ironically, then, the Glebe is in fact closer in spirit to the singing pubs of the 1880s than are many of the conventional folk clubs in the 1980s! However, the organization of the evening's singing at a conventional folk club would be fairly similar to that at the Glebe club, involving the use of an M/C and payment of a door fee.

I have never sung in a rural singing pub but I first sang at a folk club when I left school in 1962 (this was a local folk club in Ipswich, my home town). From the start, I knew that I wanted to write songs but did not do so until I had mastered the rudiments of playing the acoustic guitar. I began singing the sort of 'traditional' American and English folk songs one found in the self-instruction guitar books that were available at the time but soon moved on to perform my own material. I left Ipswich in 1968 and did not settle in Sunderland until 1976; in the intervening years I occasionally went to folk clubs in Brentwood, Leicester and Sheffield, although my interest in song-writing and folk music tended to wax and wane somewhat during this period. However, I began to write more songs once I had moved to Sunderland and, at the same time, started to visit the Glebe club. Within a couple of years I was singing there on a regular basis and gradually became more involved with the organization of the club.

In 1982 I published some of my songs in an album[8] which was recorded locally and started to do same 'gigs' in nearby folk clubs on a very limited basis. I also appeared at fund-raising events for local CND and Labour Party groups. In 1984 I started to arrange special events for the Glebe club and played a more active role in the club's administration. In January 1986, I took over the role of principal organizer which means, in effect, that I am responsible for running the club (this involves booking the guests, co-ordinating the activities of other club organizers, acting as a 'floor manager' on club nights, keeping an eye on publicity, arranging the club diary and the rota for M/C's, etc.) At the moment, I am no longer doing any gigs but continue to write songs from time to time.

With regard to my academic background, I am a lecturer in social psychology at Sunderland Polytechnic and it is a social psychological perspective that I have adopted in this study of the Glebe club. To my knowledge, there has been no significant contribution to the study of popular song in vernacular culture by social psychologists.[9] I think that one reason for this is that, over the years, many social psychologists have turned to the methodology of the natural sciences to guide them in their approach to research. In this orthodox approach, investigators typically formulate predictions about social behaviour and then put their hypotheses to the test empirically (this often involves the design of a suitable experiment). One of the consequences of adopting a positivist methodology, such as this, is to place limits on the sort of phenomena that may be investigated. These limits will sometimes arise from practical considerations but also may relate to what the social scientist regards as a legitimate field of enquiry, given his or her adherence to the 'Doctrine of the Objective Experiment'. The social events that take place in a live music club seem, to me, to be particularly ill-suited to investigations rooted in the positivist approach: obviously one could not take a resident singers' night into the psychology laboratory for experimental purposes and I am convinced that the idea of a controlled field experiment in the club's natural environment would be greeted with the utmost derision by its organizers and clientele.

The reason that I feel that it is now possible for social psychologists to offer a contribution to research in this field is that there has, in recent years, been a paradigm shift in academic social psychology[10] and it is largely the perspective of the 'new' paradigm of ethogenic social psychology that I shall be adopting in my analysis of the Glebe club. Harre, Clarke & de Carlo[11] explain how analytical analogies may be applied to vaguely defined phenomena of interest (such as, in the present context, a singers' night at the Glebe club) to highlight certain aspects for study and, drawing on the work of Goffman[12], advocate the comparison of enigmatic social behaviour in everyday life to theatrical performance[13].

If the episode under investigation is treated as a dramatic performance, then the aim will be to reconstruct the script which generates the behaviour contained within the episode. It should be noted that an ethogenic script will not necessarily have the appearance of a conventional play script. The aim will not be to simply provide a transcript of who said what in a given episode. The ethogenic investigator is more likely to provide a higher order description of the episode, containing a specification of the roles occupied by the characters taking part and the social rules which seem to govern the behaviour of the role occupants.[14] This form of script is sometimes referred to as a 'role-rule' model and can be thought of as a template from which the behaviour embedded in a particular kind of episode may be generated. One of the things I shall attempt to do in the course of this chapter is to describe the role-rule model which underpins the Glebe performance environment and to speculate how this model may differ from those relating to other performance environments (such as the singing pub or the conventional folk club).[15]

Just as the action in a play is broken down into a series of constituent parts (the acts and the scenes), so may an episode such as a singers' night at the Glebe club be analysed in terms of the sub-episodes which combine together to form the episode as a whole. Some of these sub-episodes may be related in a hierarchical fashion and this is similar to the way that a series of scenes, when taken together, constitute an act in a play (the act being a unit at a superordinate level to the scene). My first task in developing a dramaturgical analysis of the resident singers' evening which took place on 4 December 1985, therefore, is to delineate the constituent episodes. The main body of the evening is bounded by the arrival and departure of the players. Within these two delimiting episodes occurs a series of performance episodes which possess

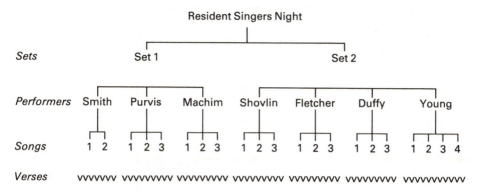

Figure 1   Hierarchical Structure of Resident Singers Night

hierarchical structure. A schematic representation of the performance episodes which indicates their structure is presented in Figure 1.

It may be noted that the fact the the performance episodes possess hierarchical structure[16] poses the methodological problem of where in the hierarchy attention should be focused. It would be possible for me to take the singers night as my superordinate level and then move downwards to provide a detailed analysis of the performance of one particular song by one particular performer. This could well involve the production of a subordinate hierarchical tree containing reference to particular verses in the song, to bars or phrases within the verses, and even to the production of individual notes within the bars or phrases. I would regard this as a perfectly acceptable direction in which to develop the research, although it is not the direction that I have chosen to follow in this chapter. If anything, I shall move upwards in the hierarchy by attempting to relate my detailed analysis of the singers' night to some of the broader episodes (each comprising many such nights) in the club's history.

Before discussing the events which took place on 4 December 1985, I shall deal with some aspects of the drama which are broadly common to all such episodes.

The scene for a club night starts with the furniture arrangement in the bar which is favoured by the pub staff and this has to be reorganized by the club organizers before the start of the night. In addition to this, the P.A. system has to be set up and a rudimentary sound check completed before members of the audience start to arrive at about 8.00 p.m. This preliminary episode may be regarded as setting the stage. The stage may be regarded as the space provided by the physical boundaries of the room, together with 'back-stage' areas provided by the entrance lobby, the male and female toilets and a storeroom behind the bar itself.[17] It should be noted that what I have described as the stage amounts to the stage in terms of my dramaturgical analysis of the episode. However, there is, within this, a rostrum where musical performance takes place. A diagramatic representation of the scene is given in Figure 2.

The scene thus set should not be thought of as being merely an arrangement

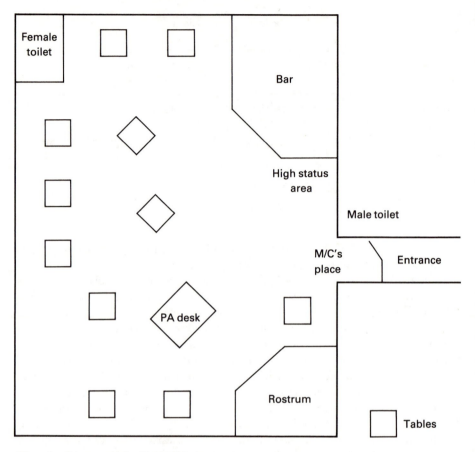

Figure 2   Diagram of the Glebe Clubroom

of physical objects, since norms will already have been developed with regard to how this space is typically used.[18] If the space is thought of as territory, then the setting takes on a socially meaningful texture[19] and the use of space will provide information about the social status or roles of those who may legitimately occupy it, or not, as the case may be.[20]

Perhaps the most obvious space to which territorial rights are attached is the rostrum in the corner of the room. Within the main performance episodes, the rostrum is reserved for the person performing, the M/C or the person working the P.A. Even here, simple rules would obtain: the M/C must not walk onto the stage in the middle of a performance; a performer who has finished his or her quota of songs (normally two to three for floor singers) must vacate the stage unless requested to stay for the performance of a further song by the M/C; no member of the audience may occupy the rostrum.

Other territorial rights may be summarized as follows: the M/C for the night has first claim to stand in the passage way to the exit door; the people who collect the door money always have first claim to the table by the door (partly for practical reasons); the corner of the bar (nearest to the rostrum) is occupied by senior members of the audience, very regular resident singers and senior organizers. In my experience, many conventional folk clubs do have a high status area; the location of this space at the Glebe may have something to do with the fact that it provides easy access to the bar, the men's toilet and the stage (it is the case that most of the occupants of this space at the Glebe are men).

I shall have cause to return to these territorial norms when analysing the events which took place during the singers evening on the 4 December 1985. I have already indicated that ethogenic scripts tend to take the form of the specification of role-rule models, rather than the form of a conventional play script. Marsh *et al*, in their study of life on the soccer terraces, for example, were able to describe a wide range of roles available to fans and this, in part, enabled to them to develop the idea that a new fan (a novice) could progress along a career path in terms of his aspiration to occupy the various role positions available.[21] Following Marsh *et al.*, I shall explore this idea in the context of the Glebe club and shall proceed by describing the range of role positions available to the members. Before doing so, I would like to point out that, whilst the conventional distinction between 'actors' and 'audience' is generally straightforward in theatre, the distinction may become blurred in the dramaturgical analysis of social behaviour. This is particularly true of the situation at the Glebe where a given individual may occupy a position in the performance role set but, excluding the time spent in performance at the rostrum, will also occupy a position in the audience role set. The relation between these two role sets (performance and audience) is asymmetrical since there will be people who occupy audience roles but do not occupy a position in the performance role set.

To some extent commitment to the club cuts across audience, performance and organizational role sets and bestows status on senior members of the club and, to a lesser extent, regular visitors to the club. Individuals falling into these categories may be distinguished from novices and occasional visitors (the issue here is simply whether an individual comes to the club more or less every week and, if so, how many years that person has been supporting the club). Since all club members occupy an audience role while only some occupy performance and organizational roles, I will discuss the audiences roles first.

Regular visitors to the club would be expected to get to know other regulars, at least to the extent of having a chat at the bar during intervals, etc. With the passage of time, regulars may come to be regarded as senior members of the club and thereby gain access to the high status territory at the rostrum-end corner of the bar (see Figure 2). These categories cannot be sharply defined and the position is complicated by the fact that the process of transition from one category to another (novice to regular; regular to senior member) may be accelerated in cases where an individual also takes on an organizational or performance role.

When novices are present in the audience (especially if in large numbers), the M/C will often articulate two of the basic rules of the club: the audience should keep reasonably quiet while the singer performs; people should try to coincide the trips to the bar or toilet with the beer breaks during the evening. Novices may well join in with chorus singing but would not normally be expected to do much else.

One role open to performing and non-performing club members, alike, is that of the heckler. A heckler is someone who directs witticisms at the performer of the moment or to the M/C (it may be noted that some performers respond better than others to heckling). To some extent, a stock of ready made heckles (clichés) exists in the club and regular hecklers would be expected to produce these on cue. These will not necessarily be spoken; some may involve the production of vaguely musical vocal noises at certain points in a well known Glebe song, for example.

Turning now to the performers, a novice will normally be given a special introduction by the M/C stating that this is the first time the person has performed at the club. This cues the members of the audience to be particularly generous should any mistakes occur and indicates that aggressive heckling would be frowned upon. A warm applause is normally given, whether or not the performance merits it. It is widely acknowledged that to perform first time takes a lot of 'bottle'. A novice who begins to come to the club to sing regularly will soon be regarded as a resident singer and I feel that the important factor here is a demonstrable commitment to the club rather than artistic ability (the term 'singer' is used within the club to encompass both vocalists and instrumentalists). Resident singers should be prepared to play whenever they are called upon to do so by the M/C; this means that they must sometimes take the more unpopular early spots, before the audience is fully warmed up, if requested. Normally, a resident singer would not be expected to start or finish the evening's singing. As a particular resident singer gains acceptance (and status), that person may be asked to play during the later part of the evening, rather than early on. Some familiarity and back-chat on stage with other resident singers would be perfectly acceptable and, to some extent, expected.

An experienced resident singer is someone who will have been a resident singer for some time and will have shown themselves to be sufficiently competent to finish the evening's singing. If there are many singers in on a given evening they may sometimes be asked NOT to play by the M/C. The assumption is that the experienced resident singer will not take offence or regard it as a negative comment on his or her ability; if anything, it is an acknowledgement that their status is unquestioned. Experienced resident singers are expected to be able to deal with difficult audiences, they should not be put off by heckling and, preferably, they should give the audience as good as they get in this respect. It is not uncommon for experienced resident singers to have the status of playing outside the club, perhaps doing gigs as the guest artist for other clubs in the region.

The role of M/C is open to experienced resident singers. Excellence in musical performance is not an essential prerequisite for this role. Rather, it will be an advantage if the performer has a flare for dealing with difficult audiences and engaging in witty repartee with the hecklers. The most important functions of the M/C involve time-keeping and the organization of the programme of singers into sets with adequate beer breaks in between, together with the task of keeping reasonable order in the house whilst performance takes place. The interaction between the M/C and good hecklers frequently contributes to the generation of a lively and entertaining atmosphere in the club but, on occasions, the M/C may need to suppress the over-zealous (and possibly drunken) heckler if the heckling threatens to disrupt the proceedings.

The regulars may occupy one (or more) of the organizational roles available in the club. However, since the summer of 1984, these roles have been subject to a continual process of review and renegotiation. As a rough guide, the principal organizer is responsible for booking guests artists, looking after the club diary and acting as floor manager on club nights; the treasurer keeps the accounts, runs the weekly raffle and pays the guests. Apart from this the following jobs are done by a further group of helpers: collecting the door money, doing the publicity and posters, keeping the club records, looking after the P. A., organizing special events and providing food for these events.

The foregoing amounts to a rudimentary description of the role-rule model which underpins the performance environment at the Glebe club and suggests that a reasonably wide range of social career paths are open to its members.[22]

I turn now to a consideration of the resident singers night which took place on 4 December 1985. This was a 'quiet' night by usual standards, in the sense that attendance was low and slow to build up. The night was also atypical in so far as it started rather late and there was even some discussion as to whether the proceedings should go ahead as usual. In other words, the role-rule model which operates almost imperceptibly on most evenings was strained on this occasion. This has the advantage, for the ethogenic investigator, of bringing rules and norms to the surface for explicit negotiation amongst the participants in a way that would not normally happen.

The evening may be broken down into the following sub episodes which, in a dramaturgical analysis, may be regarded as equivalent to the acts or scenes of a play:

> 7.30– 8.50 Assembly
> 8.50– 9.45 First Set of Songs
> 9.45–10.05 Break & Drawing the Raffle
> 10.10–11.00 Second Set of Songs
> 11.00–11.15 Packing up and dispersal

As mentioned above, the assembly episode went on for rather a long time. By 7.45 the furniture had been arranged but the P.A. had not been set up. One experienced resident singer was sitting playing his guitar to one of the regulars, the P.A. person and a publicity organizer were reading the paper, the door person was leaning on the bar, and the bar person was reading a book. The singer started to play snatches from Isaac Guillory numbers (a recent guest artist to the club) and conversation turned to Isaac's playing. By 8.00 those present numbered 8 and anxiety was being expressed concerning the whereabouts of the P.A.

By 8.15 the P.A. had arrived, as had the M/C for the night. The P.A. was assembled by the P.A. person, the M/C and one of the resident singers. There were still only about 15 people in by 8.30. The treasurer and the M/C were engaged in guitar talk at the bar, two of the experienced resident singers were chatting about whether or not to put a Barcus Berry Hot Dot[23] in the new guitar one of them had brought to the club for the first time; their conversation then turned to Martin Carthy who had played at the club the previous week. Two occasional visitors came in, looked round and walked out, presumably on the grounds that it would be a particularly thin event.

At 8.45 the first set had still not started. This is of some methodological interest, since were it not for the fact that I had singled out this evening for taking extensive research notes, I am sure that I would have intervened to get things moving. I commented on this at the time in my field notes and recorded my decision NOT to intervene, for if I had it is most unlikely that the negotiation which I am shortly to describe would have taken place.

At 8.50 an attempt was made to start the second episode of the evening (i.e. the first set of songs). The M/C opened with the humourous remark: 'Is the gas on' (referring to the P.A. power supply).

One of the regulars replied:

'Why? Are you cooking, like?'

This is an example of someone risking a social hazard in order to establish a reputation as a heckler. If the audience laughs (and not many did on this occasion) then the reputation is secured.

The M/C then called for silence, stating that the talkers were spoiling it for the rest of the hundreds of people who were in. This supports the idea that the M/C has the function in the role-rule model of managing audience noise, adroitly done here by the use of irony.

The M/C then took the extremely unusual step of asking the audience what should happen:

'What are we going to do tonight? Do you just want to sit around and have a relaxed sort of sing-song and a drink and a chat? Or shall we try and put something on? Free night and all! 'Cause, if a few more people come in we'll make you pay – it'll be the same old crap, like, but we'll make you pay for it! What d'ya want ta dee?'

This underlines the distinction between a Glebe performance night and an evening of live music in the pub. The alternative suggestion sounds close to the sort of thing one might find in a singing pub and this was clearly thought to be something quite different. The decision not to charge for entry was based on numbers (about 15 present) and suggests that the role-rule model supporting the Glebe performance enviornment demands a quorum of about 20 persons. Beneath the quorum the event could not be brought off.

Again, the M/C asked the audience whether they wanted to just sit around and pretend that they were enjoying themselves. Whereupon the P.A. person retorted: 'After I've set all this bloody P.A. up!'

Clearly, the M/C can solve the problem of how to run what looks like being an exceptionally thin night (and this was primarily his problem) by defining the night as unviable and writing it off, as it were. But to do this would be to upset the P.A. person who, by then, had done half of his job and would have to do the other half (taking it down) anyway. The M/C gets round this by asking the audience for suggestions. It was, perhaps, because there were no novices in the room that these negotiations continued in such an explicit fashion, for some time. Eventually, the M/C took a vote on who the audience wanted to sing and I was nominated to start the evening's singing. This caught me unawares, since the M/C traditionally starts the singing, as he admitted: 'This is a dirty rotten snydy back-stabbing trick that I've done here because whoever does the gobbing (M/C's job) is supposed to do the first song.' Again, one of the rules governing behaviour at the Glebe club is stated explicitly.

The opening of this evening contrasts markedly with the usual procedure for starting the evening. For example, a singers night almost exactly one year previous to the one presently under consideration was also a quiet night but was opened with the following words by a different, yet more experienced, M/C: 'Good evening. Welcome to the Glebe Folk & Blues Club. I was thinking of coming round and thanking you all personally – there's that many in tonight, like!' (Resident Singers Night: 12.12.84) Here, the point that a quorum barely existed was made but, nonetheless, the evening proceeded with minimum fuss.

I list, below, the songs sung during the two performance sets of the evening, under the names of the individual singers.

Set 1
John Smith
'Holocaust on the Home Front' (John Smith)
'Motor Mechanic Fred' (John Smith)

Colin Purvis
'Sally Gee' (Trad)
'The Entertainer' (Scott Joplin: quitar instrumental arranged by Eric McCleod)
'As soon as this pub closes' (Alex Glasgow)

Tony Machim
'Vigilante man' (Woody Guthrie: ar. Ry Cooder)
'That's the way' (Led Zeplin)
'Hurricane' (Bob Dylan)

Set 2

George Shovlin
'I'm a lover not a fighter' (Lazy Lester)
'San Franciso Melody' (Tom Waites)
'Miss Lazy Green' (Trad Blues)

Martin Fletcher
3 Blues Harp Solos

Christine Duffy
'Save me' (Joan Armatrading)
'It must be love' (Ricky-Lee Jones)
'A man you don't meet everyday' (Pogues, Trad)

Tom Young
'The man who lives in bottles' (Kieran Halpin)
'Lady came from Baltimore' (Tim Hardin)
'Everyday' (Buddy Holly) … The Finale
'Peggy Sue' (Buddy Holly) … The Encore

Two of the songs played were requested from the floor: Colin Purvis asked me to play my own song about the horrific effects of a nuclear holocaust and Christine Duffy asked Colin to do 'The Entertainer.'[24] Because I hadn't played the CND song for some time, I made several mistakes. I also felt more nervous on stage than usual because I was aware of the fact that I was recording the proceedings for research purposes. I think this also inhibited me in terms of my stage banter with the audience. This tension between modes of presence is germane to participant observation research.

Over the course of the evening there were several examples, in the talk from the stage, which support the notion that the Glebe club generates its own network of social relations. I made reference to the fact that Tony Machim had built several copies of a guitar pre-amplifier which I had designed to fit in a tobacco tin and that several of the guitarists were now using these to feed their guitar bugs direct into the P.A. amplifier. Tony Machim announced that Tom Young had made him a glass bottleneck and that Tom could do the same for anyone else who wanted one. Martin, the blues harp player, asked if anyone present was interested in playing blues guitar with him.[25] This talk points to a host of satellite episodes (some had already taken place whilst others had the status of episodes which could possibly take place in the future) which involve the action and interaction of individual members outside the spatio-temporal boundaries of a club night. It is, in part, this kind of activity which makes the Glebe club a collective, as opposed to an aggregate of individuals who all happen to like a similar sort of music. In this way, the club builds bridges and connections between individual biographies.

This sort of talk also breaks frame with the stage performance (construed as an artistic product) and has a meta-fictional flavour to it. The performers at the Glebe are speaking openly about some of the backstage activities which contribute to their performance on the rostrum. There were many other ways in which performers drew the audience's attention to the fact that a performance was taking place, thus making the process of the production of the performance transparent. At one point the M/C provided a meta-comment on the style of his own performance by saying: 'Me patter's terrible!' Tony Machim explained that the reason why he was going to play Dylan's song 'Hurricane' was that he'd read in the papers that Reuben Carter, nicknamed the 'Hurricane', had been released from prison. Then, commenting on the song, he said: 'It's 11 verses long and I reckon I'll get at least 9 out of the 11 right.' Again, this is a meta-comment involving a prediction concerning his ability to remember the song. Tom Young explained that he stored his LP's in alphabetical order at home and had selected the songs that he was going to play from albums filed under the letter 'H' (Halpin, Hardin, Holly). Admittedly this was said with some degree of irony, but his statement nonetheless drew attention to a possible decision making process governing his contribution to the Glebe repertoire that night.

The ending of the evening turned out to be as problematic as the opening had been. Normally, the closing ritual is a simple affair: the M/C thanks all the performers and then askes everyone to drink up quickly and go home (often expressed in the phrase 'Sup-off and bugger-off!' This week, Tom Young (who was the last singer but not the M/C) began the closing 'patter' after the finale: 'Next week we've got Fiona Simpson and if everybody comes next week there'll be 20 people here. But there should be more than that because Fiona Simpson's great! I'd like to thank you all for coming tonight. What else do you say?' The M/C then provided the prompt: 'Sup-off and, er ......' Tom Young responded: 'And sup-off and piss off and get your beers back to the bar.' To which was added, from the audience: 'Do your talking outside.' Tom then repeated this but the attempt to close the evening was not successful; in fact it became a lengthy parody of the closing ceremony. Eventually someone suggested that he played another song, which he did.

At the end of this encore, the M/C took the stage and simply said: 'That's it. Thank you for your attendance and your attention. It was great, it turned out canny.'[26]

Returning again to the analysis of spatial behaviour, it was interesting to note that during the uncertainty at the early part of the evening, the M/C sat at a table within the audience. However, when the night picked up and the decision was made to charge an entrance fee of 50 pence after all, the M/C took up his post at the entrance alcove. He signalled to the last singer, Tom Young, to play the last song of the evening and then returned to his seat in the audience. It was at this point that Tom Young tried to say the words which constituted the closing ceremony. When this failed, the M/C returned to his post in the alcove by the door (re-asserting his authority, in my opinion) and signalled for one more song (the encore). As soon as this was finished he moved straight to the stage and ended the night (with the short speech I have given above).

Additional information concerning the role-rule model governing performance at the Glebe may be gained by an examination of some of the broader episodes in the club's history (in other words by shifting attention upwards in terms of the hierarchical structure of Glebe episodes). George Shovlin, a founder member, summarizes the club's development as follows:

I think the main two periods of time are the initial years with Brigante,[27] which coincided with folk music being much more popular ... the very successful years were 73–76 and I think from 76–80 there was a sort of moderately successful period and from '80 onwards, I think there's been, in line with the national situation, I think there's been a decline. And that's why I'm so concerned now, basically. Because I see the problems of the Glebe at the moment – I think, unless something's done, the problems are terminal.[28]

This reading of the situation was shared by many of my interviewees and suggests that the history of the club can be construed in terms of the four stages of establishment and initial success (73–76); of consolidation (76–80); of decline (80–84); and of change, following a recognition of the club's problems (84–86).

From the ethogenic standpoint, it will be of interest to explore the extent to which the problems recognized by the club and the changes introduced during the most recent stage can be related to the role-rule model which served the club so well in the earlier stages in its history. In order to gain a wider perspective on the matter, I shall first comment on the role-rule models of singing pubs and conventional folk clubs before dealing directly with the recent changes at the Glebe.

Dunn,[29] in her analysis of an evening's singing at the Blaxhall Ship, a village pub in Suffolk, states that: 'The performance environment is created by each village community, its blood and marital ties, its common employment sources, and its shared activities.' The performance of song would thus appear to be a natural extension of existing social relations in what is already a close-knit community. However, Dunn's account suggests that, even in the relatively remote and small Suffolk village of Blaxhall, the conditions necessary for such a performance environment may be fast disappearing:

> What Bob [one of her sources] has to say gives an indication of the state of the singing tradition in this part of Suffolk. Because of these American servicemen, and because of the darts club, 'fruit' machine and juke-box, which have been fostered by the landlord to attract young people, there is a possibility that singing in the pub will fall off greatly.[30]

Oscar Newman has drawn attention to the fact that control over the social behaviour that takes place in a given environment may be greatly facilitated by ensuring that the hierarchical organization of space is preserved and clearly defined.[31] Whilst Newman's research was carried out in a completely different context to that of song performance in British pubs (he was concerned with the incidence of crime on large urban housing estates in New York), his notion of defensible space does provide us with another way of looking at the performance environment. Newman suggests that problems may arise when the hierarchical organization of space breaks down and there is no buffer between public space (e.g. the street, in his studies) and private space (e.g. the interiors of individual apartments, in his studies). The buffer can be provided by the creation of a semi-public area (e.g. courtyards) together with semi-private zones (e.g. communal vestibules containing the entrances to a small number of individual appartments). In terms of a closely-knit rural community, it may be possible to regard the street outside the pub as part of the semi-public area, with public space starting at the village boundaries. If this is so, then the space within the pub (i.e. the bars) would be equivalent to a semi-private zone and it is in this zone where cultural tradition dictates that song performance may take place without interference.

However, the spatial sanctity of the Blaxhall village is not something that can, any longer, be taken for granted. Dunn[32] comments on the fact that non-local residents, including American serviceman, now come to its pub whereas in former decades:

> Pub customers were generally village people or their relatives and acquaintainces from neighbouring villages. Traffic through Snape (a nearby village) is now much more common because the Snape road is a quick route to the American air base at Bentwaters and because of concerts at the Maltings, and increased numbers of strangers now stop at the pubs in the village.

She also comments on the fact that whilst walking was once the most common form of transport, there is now 'much greater facility for travel, by bus, train and private car than there was in the younger days of most of the native inhabitants.'[33]

I would suggest, therefore, that the public space which hitherto began at the parish boundaries now intrudes into the village in a way that it did not previously. This will have a knock-on effect in terms of the hierarchical organization of space within the village. The space in the street outside the village pub will no longer be semi-public; it will be a public zone. Therefore, the space within the pub itself will no longer be semi-private; it will need to be construed as semi-public. The pub, as bricks and mortar, still exists as a performance environment for song but the social texture of the space within the pub has changed; it now resides at a different level in the spatial hierarchy. And this may account for the increase in distractions and disruptions to song performance. Among other things, the unprecedented increase in car ownership in post-war Britain has meant that few small rural villages can, any longer regard the territory within their parish boundaries as semi-public, at least, not to the same extent as they may once have done so.

One solution to the problem of providing a good performance environment in a pub where the pervading space is semi-public is to create, within the pub itself, a new semi-private zone and thereby re-establish the spatial hierarchy. I suggest that the spatio-temporal marking off of a particular room on a particular evening as a 'Folk Club' does just that. This enables a separate set of rules governing the social behaviour of those who choose to enter that environment to be developed. In other words, a new role-rule model which suits the performance environment may be created, or may evolve.

The role-rule model adopted by folk clubs serves the purpose of overcoming the problems of distraction and disruption which singing pubs, such as the Blaxhall Ship, are experiencing. In my view, it is very similar to the model I have already described for the Glebe club and I think that the model did serve the Glebe club well during the 1970's. However, some of my interviewees attributed the period of decline at the Glebe, in part, to the adoption of this model and to the fact that the rules were being enforced too strictly.

> Folk clubs have a bad reputation. People see it as a place where people will tolerate anything, no matter how bad or boring. They have to sit quiet; they can't move about; can't talk; only buy beer when allowed to. That's why folk clubs tailed off. Changing the name [of the Glebe] is a good thing.[34]

If such rules are rigidly enforced, and the audience doesn't like it, then the audience may simply vote with their feet, and it was felt that this could account, at least in part, for the dwindling audiences at the Glebe club. A relaxation of such rules might, therefore, be a good thing. But to what extent should that be taken? George Shovlin, one of the founder members, was at least prepared to give serious consideration to a major relaxation of the rules and suggested that the Glebe could model itself on the situation which exists when bands play live music in pubs. In other words, there would be no attempt to inhibit audience conversation during performance and the idea of using an M/C to orchestrate the evening would be abandoned.[35]

In some respects, this proposal sounds as though George Shovlin was advocating a return to the model of the singing pub but I think there are some important reasons why this suggestion should not be construed in this light. If the wheel were merely being re-invented, as it were, then, presumably, the problems of disruption to performance which I have noted in relation to the singing pubs would still be with us. But advances in technology in the form of powerful P.A. systems have provided contemporary performers with a solution to this problem. It is by no means obvious how one might deal with the impact of P.A. systems on the role-rule models underpinning performance environments, from the ethogenic perspective. However, given that the Glebe club did acquire a P.A. system in the summer of 1984 (as part of its general stragegy for recovery) I feel that it is important in the context of the present analysis that I do attempt to do this. It will be useful to begin with a comparison of singing pubs, folk clubs, rock/pop music in pubs and, lastly, pub music/musak provided by tape or juke box.

Singing pubs, such as the Blaxhall Ship, do not make use of a P.A. system. I have already noted that the performance environment may be subject to distraction and interference. The conventional folk club also tends not to make use of a P.A. system but gets over the problem of distractions to performance by implementing a rather strict system of social rules. The pub rock band does not really have to contend with the problem of audience noise, since the amplification is frequently so great that audience conversation becomes almost an impossibility (communication regresses to the non-verbal level with signs, gestures and lip-reading being used as a substitute for talk). Pub musak (on tape) is designed to provide innocuous background music and is not meant to interfere with customers' conversations. Because of the comparatively recent advances in technology and the fact that powerful P.A. systems are now more widely available, it would be possible for performers at the Glebe club to generate the number of decibels necessary to render fluent conversation in the audience difficult, unpleasant or impossible. Another possibility would be for Glebe performers to fulfill the function of simply providing live musak (instead of a tape) at their pub venue. As an organiser and singer, I feel that neither of these possibilities would provide a satisfactory solution to the Glebe club's problems.

It may be helpful to think of the performer as competing for the audience's attention (it is, after all, common to speak of a performer winning or losing the audience). This agonistic facet of live performance may be most pronounced where there is some ambiguity concerning the definition of the social situation qua performance environment. For example, in the old days, anyone going into the singing room of a rural pub would know that singing was the main activity to take place in that room. Most of the people going into a folk club would know that they were letting themselves in for a music performance and not for an ordinary evening of chit-chat in a pub. But if people come into a pub room where live music is playing, they may, understandably, define the situation as if it were an ordinary evening at the pub, drawing on their experience of taped musak as a model for the event. It is in this latter situation that performers and members of the audience may be in competition: the audience may wish to carry on conversation in the ordinary manner, the performers wish to be heard. The solution to the Glebe's problems, voiced by George Shovlin (see above), whereby the performers simply played in a pub setting (i.e. simply happened to provide live music to anyone who was in the pub on that night), would, in my opinion, maximise the agonistic relationship between performer and audience.

The Glebe club opted for a compromise solution to this problem. A P.A. system was purchased in order that a small increase in audience noise might be matched by a modest degree of amplification of the sound produced by the preformers. Thus the club was able to relax the rules governing audience noise but these rules were not dispensed with entirely. Admittedly this is an aesthetic judgement, but I feel that the level of amplification needed before such rules may be dispensed with as irrelevant would not suit much of the music played at the Glebe club.[36] If this is dismissed as merely a matter of personal taste, there still remains the strong possibility that high levels of amplification would destroy the interactional model between performers and audience.

I think that there is another important reason as to why the Glebe club should not attempt to provide live musak in its pub venue. In order to get to this it will help to think about what makes good musak successful.

Musak makes little demands on listeners' attention thus leaving them free to devote most of their concentration to some other activity (which is usually chatting with nearby companions). If a version of the song is present in memory, then it will be easy for them to switch their attention in and out of the song without losing their place, as it were. Clearly, hit songs which have had wide popular success and have received maximum air-play in the past will work best for most people on this count. It follows from this that the Glebe performers whose repertoires contain such material will do best in a live musak situation.

The performers who will find this situation most difficult are the singer/songwriters whose material will not have been heard outside the Glebe club to any appreciable extent. The question arises as to whether this matters a jot. Why shouldn't the performers merely recycle the popular music of the day and, to some extent, the popular standards or 'golden oldies' of yesterday? Why should the performance of some of the more established vernacular songs, the more obscure blues songs or the work of contemporary song-writers be given any kind of performance environment, save perhaps the environment provided for the singer by the walls of his or her home? In order to gain some purchase on this question, I propose to construe song as a form of talk and then to discuss it from the ethogenic perspective.

Songs written down, stored in someone's memory, or recorded on tape or disc may be seen as possible speech acts to be realized in performance (in the case of the Glebe club this would be live performance). Harré argues that the primary human reality is persons in conversation and, in this context, sees persons as the locations of speech acts.[37]. However, whilst people need to be taken as no more than social atoms for an analysis of public conversation, they do have a secondary structure: their mental organization as individuals.[38] Rejecting the conventional Cartesian duality between mind and body, Harré puts forward an alternative duality: a 'duality between person and self'. The self is merely a concept. He states his basic thesis as follows:

> Animate beings are persons if they are in possession of a theory – a theory about themselves. It is a theory in terms of which a being orders, partitions and reflects on its own experience and becomes capable of self-intervention and control.[39]

This theory of self, Harré suggests, derives from the way the concept of person is used in the public-collective talk produced by people belonging to a given linguistic community:

> It (the self) is a theoretical concept whose source analogue is the socially defined and sustained concept of 'person' that is favoured in the society under study and is embodied in the grammatical forms of public speech appropriate to talk about persons. Our personal being is created by our coming to believe a theory of self based on our society's working conception of a person.[40]

It may, however, be more useful to think of our society as sustaining not one, but several, working conceptions of the person based on the important social categories arising from class, ethnic and sexual divisions.[41] It is reasonable to suppose that the differences between the various social groups in terms of wealth, power and status will be reflected in public-collective talk which makes reference to the occupants of these social categories. In the case of gender, for example, it is more likely that masculine, as opposed to feminine, pronouns and proper names will be associated not only with a wider range of occupational roles but also with occupations of a higher status. It may also be the case that there is a tendency for masculine, as opposed to feminine, pronouns and proper names to be linked with more powerful verbs. The self-concept of individual group members may thus be tainted by the prevailing stereotype of the group to which they belong.[42] The effect of this will be to reduce the likelihood that inferior groups will demand social change since they will come to hold the theory that they are, indeed, inferior human beings. The public-collective talk which provides the source analogue for this theory must therefore be regarded as serving an ideological purpose; it helps to conceal domination as domination.[43]

Song does not exempt itself from critical scrutiny merely because it is talk set to music. Thus the repertoires of particular performance environments may be examined for the extent to which they support or challenge prevailing stereotypes and, in so doing, support or challenge the status quo. This leads me back to the question I raised earlier, as to whether the Glebe club should do anything other than provide live musak. Since I have already argued that hit songs etc. will do best in a live musak situation, an acceptable answer to this question presents itself providing it could be assumed that the less well-known material in the Glebe repertoire was more radical then the sort of material the singers would draw on when playing live musak; in order to give a voice to radical song, the role-rule model which supports the present performance environment at the Glebe club should not be abandoned in favour of one geared to the production of live musak.

However, in order to avoid the discussion of what, I believe, would amount to a series of excessively wide generalizations about musical styles, I shall return to a consideration of the context in which song is produced. I wish to suggest that the role-rule model which supports the Glebe performance environment is conducive to the development of a critical attitude to song amongst the members of the club, although I can see no reason why this should, of necessity, happen. I have previously said that the singing of a song may be regarded as equivalent to the production of a speech act. Other things being equal, speakers are normally held responsible for the things they say. Harré draws attention to this facet of talk when he suggests that an act of commitment goes along with a claim to knowledge: 'to claim to know something is actively to engage one's moral standing on the matter'.[44] Whilst there may, or may not, be knowledge claims embedded in a particular song, to sing a song is, I suggest, to activley engage one's moral standing on thé matter and the fact that singers may be called to account for the songs they sing provides a basis for distinguishing between performance environments in terms of the extent to which those environments facilitate the accounting process.

A singer performing from the Glebe rostrum enjoys little spatio-temporal segregation from the audience: apart from the duration of the song, the singer sits or stands with the audience; singers buy their beer from the same bar as the audience; singers use the same toilets as the audience; and even when singers are separated from the audience by virtue of the fact that they are occupying the rostrum, there is scant protection from the hecklers. Glebe singers, then, are maximally available to be called to account for their performances by other members of the club. This is not the case in the large scale pop/rock live venues where singers are typically spirited away to back-stage areas, such as dressing rooms, when not occupying the stage. It would be possible for accounting episodes to take place at small scale live musak events but the singer is only required to provide background music on such occasions; it would seem inappropriate to take the singer to task on any other grounds in that situation. The extent to which the singer of a song which is mechanically reproduced (i.e. disc, tape, and, in this context, even live performances on radio or television) can be drawn into an accounting episode with the listeners is minimal, since the singer will not normally share the same spatio-temporal location with the listeners. One reason why Glebe singers may be particularly sensitive to the accounting process is that they are embedded in a network of social relations generated by the club and on which the performance environment itself depends; a resident singer cannot be a resident singer and not be part of the moral order resulting from these social relations.

I have tried to show that, whilst there is no guarantee that performance environments. supported by role-rule models similar to the Glebe's will necessarily result in the production of radical song (or, through the accounting process, the critique of reactionary song), such environments do provide singers and audiences with the opportunity to work towards this.

NOTES

1   The club meets in the upstairs bar of the 'Royalty' public house, Chester Road, Sunderland.
2   Information based on the Sunderland 'Borough Guide', n.d.
3   There are about 65 social clubs listed in local directories as having a Sunderland telephone number. This compares with 95 pubs and bars and confirms that the ratio of clubs to pubs is high.
4   Interview: Bruce Storey: 3.10.84.
5   Thompson 1971: ch 4.
6   Pickering 1984.
7   Thompson 1971: 62.
8   John Lewis Smith 1982.
9   There is, for example, no mention of such studies in the major undergraduate social psychology textbooks, such as: Tedeschi, Lindskold & Rosenfeld 1985; Baron & Byrne 1984; Worchel & Cooper 1983; nor, to my knowledge, in the major social psychological journals.
10 A critique of the traditional paradigm together with proposals for a 'new' paradigm to take its place may be found in Harré & Secord 1972.
11 Harré, Clarke & De Carlo 1985: 41.
12 Goffman 1959.
13 See also Harré & Secord 1972: ch 10 and Harré 1979: ch 10 for a fuller account of the way in which the dramaturgical standpoint is adopted for use in ethogenic analysis.
14 Harré & Secord 1972: ch 13 define role as "that part of the act-action structure produced by the subset of rules followed by a particular category of individual."
15 In this study I worked as a participant observer and recorded my observations in the form of field notes. In addtion to this, I have drawn on a stock of 40 C90 cassettes containing interviews with club members, proceedings of business meetings, and recordings of several resident singers evenings at the club, which I have been collecting since summer, 1984. As the organiser of the club, I also have full access to all club records, including the accounts and a list of the guests booked by the club.
16 Harré, Clarke & De Carlo 1985: 21–22, contrast 'constitutive hierarchies' where the parts of one level become the wholes of the next, with 'regulative hierarchies' in which the choice of highest-level goals determines subordinate goals, right down to the steps taken to bring off some intermediate task.

17 Goffman 1959 alerts us to the possibility that different behaviours may be appropriate in different performance regions such as back and front stage.

18 Argyle 1975: 316, points to the way corners of pubs and clubs are used by certain groups of regulars as an illustration of human territorial behaviour.

19 See Harré 1979: 198, for a discussion of the social texture of space and time.

20 Sommer 1969: 20, provides a discussion of leadership and status in terms of spatial behaviour, for example.

21 Marsh *et al.* 1978: ch 3.

22 The position here is not dissimilar to that described by Marsh *et al.* 1978: 66, in their study of life on the English soccer terraces: 'Two distinct aspects of the career process are to be distinguished. The first of these, the between-group graduation process, is concerned with movement from one group to another and with the fact that membership of a particular group affords a certain status in relation to members of other groups. The second, the within-group development process, is concerned with the establishment of certain well-defined status positions within each group and with the acquisition of the appropriate social knowledge to equip a member to 'carry off' the performances required by such roles.'

23 The 'Hot Dot' is a piezo pickup manufactured by Barcus Berry. It is an encased crystal in the shape of a cylinder smaller than one eighth of an inch in diameter and is connected with a wire lead. This pickup is generally inserted in a hole drilled in the bridge of the guitar. (See Brosnac 1983: 10.)

24 Christine had already told me in an interview that she was working on her guitar playing and was interested in ragtime. Interview: 12.10.84.

25 Martin eventually performed with a guitarist and a base player on a resident singers' night several weeks later (19 February 1986).

26 Michael Pickering, the editor of this volume, recorded the following conversation at 11.00 p.m. on the night in question, whilst in the Gents toilet at the Glebe club: 'Funny how these evenings turn out. It looked drastic at first, but look how it's turned out!' 'That's it. You have to give it to those who turn up regular. They're the backbone.' 'Well, that's what pulled it all up, the quality of the residents. If it wasn't for them, the club would die.' 'That's right. In fact, they're sometimes better than the guests!'

27 Brigante was the club's resident folk group during this period.

28 Interview: George Shovlin 24.9.84.

29 Dunn 1980: 47.

30 Dunn 1980: 101.

31 Newman 1974.

32 Dunn 1980: 21–23.

33 Dunn 1980: 21–23.

34 Interview: Kev Philipson 11.4.85

35 Interview: George Shovelin 24.9.84

36 Anderson 1986: 26, in a discussion of the technical aspects of providing P.A. for folk music makes the point that a rock band P.A. operator can 'make a real dog's breakfast of it with incredible ease!'

37 Harré 1983: 58.

38 Harré 1983: 75.

39 Harré 1983: 93.

40 Harré 1983: 26.

41 See Giddens 1979: 115 for a discussion of the interplay of the modes of domination based on these divisions.

42   An individual's self-concept is linked to group membership in Tajfel's definition of social identity: 'that part of an individual's self-concept which derives from his knowledge of his membership of a social group (or groups) together with the value and emotional significance attached to that membership.' Tajfel 1981: 255.

43   See Giddens 1979: 193–196 for a discussion of the principal ideological forms.

44   Harré 1983: 49.

7 Conclusion: Studying the Everyday Arts

MICHAEL PICKERING and TONY GREEN

The forms and modality of the cultural life treated in this volume are part of the process of group self-making occurring within the contexts of everyday situations. What 'culture' amounts to here is an aggregate of symbolic ways and means by which individuals and groups wield the phenomena of mundane social and material existence, how they make meanings and evaluations in relation to that existence. The central problem for us has been how to understand both theoretically and in definite, concrete situations and milieux the aesthetics of such everyday culture, in this case as manifest through the medium of popular song. Song as cultural product and practice cannot be studied in isolation from other social and cultural processes: it has to be understood in its complex relations with those other processes and in terms of the manner of their organization. Popular songs outside of the mass market of their production and distribution become, in ways both strikingly obvious and teasingly subtle, manifestations of the pattern of particular ways of life, and have perforce to be studied as such. This means for us that the specific art-form of song and singing within vernacular milieux is regarded axiomatically as animating certain intersubjectively realized feelings and conceptions of life as lived from day to day, and from cradle to grave. The study of popular song as created and/or adopted by groups and communities is but one means among many of understanding what it is that makes people (including ourselves) culturally tick.

It would be wrong to assume that song and singing as vernacular cultural forms and activities, particularly historically, can be presented exactly in their own terms. We reject the idea that other periods and other cultures as studied have an existence utterly independent from us, and are able to speak to us, in our own time and culture, directly for themselves. Yet at the same time the cultural phenomena of our analyses indubitably exist or have existed, and in seeking to conceptualize our object of study precisely because our relationship to it is complex and mediated – by, among other things, our own interpretations – we have been concerned not to embark on a mission of theoretical colonialism, but rather to explore territories outside the ambits of our own known, everyday cultures with whatever conceptual and methodological tools seem to us useful. In the project of cultural cartography we start from a position of respect for people's experience and knowledge, but we believe that we can neither expect their inner workings to be directly amenable to our gaze nor hope that they contain unchanging essences that will be delivered to us on intoning some philosophical nostrum. We cannot feel or understand the content and contours of popular experience and knowledge outside of our cultural groupings as if they were our own, but that is not equivalent to claiming that we cannot apprehend them at all: we are realists enough to reject that idea as well. Analytical mediations and experiential knowledge of cultural life apart from our own are of course quite distinct, but the former are the only way we can ever connect with the latter, in any sustained fashion, and in this sense it is impossible to escape from what all differentiated social groups do in the process of their interaction, which is to engage in a cultural and ideological translation of each other. As Geertz has it: 'We are all natives now, and everybody else not immediately one of us is an exotic'.[1]

We do not deny that the problems and puzzles which open up from this fact are inordinately difficult. Paradoxes, enigmas and unruly data abound, theories for handling the raw material proliferate, and as we celebrate and attend to cultural diversity, here and the world over, it may seem at times that we are coming to know less and less about more and more. It is better to face that perturbation squarely than opt for the delusion of some master key to the riddles of culture. We must all of course work out our position on the grand questions of cultural and historical studies, however hazardous the exercise, and we should do so with as much critical acumen, humanity and good humour as we can muster. Idealism, determinism and a dozen and one other ever-present intellectual pitfalls await us along the way. Yet it is because there are serious difficulties and dangers attendant on the study of everyday culture that we feel it is vital to stress the need for reflexivity and adequate contextualisation in this field, as in any other of the humanities and social sciences. It is with that need in view that we have edited this volume and written our own contributions.

Social contextualization and self-reflexive interpretation seem to us, in relation to the present transitional nature of the field of study in which we are engaged in this volume, to be the intellectual disciplines most needed if we are to move forward. Putting it most simply, contextualization in cultural analysis involves the apprehension of modes and frames of meaning understood as elements of the everyday practice of particular forms of social life conducted by historically located subjects, while reflexivity involves concern with how this apprehension is accomplished, and is 'the inevitable accompaniment of any method which demands scrutiny of its own terms and procedures'.[2] We insist upon these intellectual disciplines in vernacular cultural analysis because as general methodological orientations they challenge the prescriptivism that has marked the study of 'folk' song and other 'folkloric' genres since their 'discovery' during the upsurge of European Romanticism in the late eighteenth and early nineteenth centuries. The old 'folk' paradigm seems to many today to be quite unsatisfactory, but as yet there seems to be no alternative of any considerable scope. We are in any case suspicious both of the quest for such an alternative and of its desirability. That is the reason we prefer to advance the case for attention to cultural life from the participants' point of view, and for the effort to understand cultural forms and processes relationally, rather than to seek the enthronement of some new 'universally applicable' paradigm. Adopting and applying a reflexive and contextualist attitude to the object of our study will not ensure the advent of some definitive guide to the puzzles of the culture/society nexus. All it will do is guard us against interpretative sophism by helping us question our questions.

We cannot of course proceed without conceptual questions or particular aims of analysis, and as editors ours have been posed and pursued within a general framework of cultural materialism. Moreover, as we have stressed, it is impossible to relativize fully: we cannot move outside of our cultural and historical skins at will, and we cannot pretend to be neutral on such issues as capital and class. Our point is simply this: that it is only possible to make sense of how others make sense if we allow theory to relativize evidence and evidence to relativize theory; and that studying the everyday arts requires various conceptual tools, not some multi-purpose one. We refuse obeisance to any Imperial Highness of Meaning.

Many of the problems involved in attempting to contextualize the everyday arts socially and historically remain unsolved. Though we feel that there is much to be learnt from how they have been tackled and discussed in such critical practices as the sociology of art and literature, communication and cultural studies, anthropology and social history, all we can suggest here, by way of our conclusion, are certain ways we feel future research into vernacular popular song should be conducted.

We take it as given that the shift from a narrow concentration on the work of art as either text or tune (or both), to a wider focus on the everyday arts as communicative events, has now been accomplished. Within this shift, however, there is an imbalance of attention which, though understandable, requires urgent redress. Namely, that while closely contextualized interpretations of the texts of vernacular popular songs in performance are now numerous, the same is not true of their tunes. This is only partly an accident of institutional development (there are more scholars with literary than with musical experience at a level commensurate with the undertaking); more centrally, it is the product of a limitation in the methodology itself. Words are a good medium for the analysis of verbal acts; the careful reading of texts in context, supplemented where possible by the critical glosses of their singers, provides the foundation for, at least, a plausible provisional account of their literary content, in a particular place and time. It has yet to be shown that a singer's comments on melodies are useful or likely to be useful, even as a starting point; and, more generally, the relationship between words and music in popular song remains enigmatic. It seems that some other methodology is needed, ideally one which would embody the laudable determination of Lomax and his collaborators to explore the relationships between words, tunes, performances styles and social structures, while avoiding the less laudable determinism and grossness of generalization which vitiates their work. Until a sociological and historical aesthetics of music properly develops, the study of vernacular song as a musico-literary entity will remain heavily biased towards its verbal dimension of signification.

We can at least proceed by studying this latter dimension relationally. The point of conceiving popular song as existing within particular socio-historical cultural contexts is not so much that the text will inform us about its lived contexts nor that its contexts will inform us about the lived text, but rather that, as well as this, a song text, its immediate situational contexts of performance and transmission, and more broadly the social structural and historical contexts in which it happens, and to which (however indirectly or opaquely) it necessarily relates, all interconnect in the sense that they occur processually as a series of mediations of each other. Therefore, no matter what our primary focus of attention in respect of vernacular song (e.g., single text, repertory, genre), we need to be prepared to keep in view this ordering of text-context frames and relationships in order to grasp the complex movements occurring between them.

We should note a rather tricky problem here. Detailed evidence of such phenomena as modes of song performance, the specific milieux in which performances occur, and the social interaction of which song performance is usually a part, is relatively easily acquired through participant observation techniques in situations to which the researcher has access, and is by contrast difficult to come by (at times exceedingly so) in historical research. The different essays here reflect this problem, and the almost total lack of interest among the early folk song collectors in the ethnography of song performance has not helped. Conversely, the interconnectedness of vernacular songs and their immediate milieux of performance with broader institutional and structural configurations is more commonly the preoccupation of historical research in the vernacular cultural field; distance in time as well as distance through time seems to conduce treatment of the questions involved in this complex interconnectedness to a relativeley greater degree than through the more present-focused ethnographic orientation to the study of vernacular song. This is a problem to which serious attention will have to be paid, for in researching song and singing traditions in both time present and time past we have to attend to the social and material realities textually drawn upon and drawn into song texts by way of experiential assimilation, and by affective and intellectual apprehension. We should perhaps first clear the ground of certain misconceptions regarding the study of song cultures of the past.

History is not simply the historian's values in narrative disguise. Historical reconstruction is always made from within a particular position, but the whole point of a methodological emphasis upon the need for contextual and reflexive interpretative strategies is that affiliation in whatever direction has to work with and through the historical evidence – the range of available mediations of the past – and this is (and must be) always susceptible to criticism and challenge. If it is to have any value, historical cultural analysis cannot be *reduced* to a particular political or ideological stance. Song texts and the other historical evidence to which they stand in complex relation are not *materia* that can be moulded and manipulated at will, and are not open to an infinite number of voluntaristic ascriptions of meanings and values. They are without doubt – particularly in terms of their complex relation – sites of conflict between different readings, but such readings have to relate to what is there, however problematic the constitution of such phenomena. What follows from this is firstly that the historical evidence of and circumambient to particular song cultures is material to be interrogated not for some absolute truth, but rather for the varying accounts provided of the real historical process to which it stands in testimony; and secondly, that the reconstruction of meanings and values in relation to song texts 'inherited from the past' occurs in determinate historical conditions: it is a process which is itself historically conditioned. These considerations take us into a tangle of epistemological as well as historiographical issues, and in the present concluding discussion to this book we are not at liberty to unravel their implications much further. We would like simply to note that while those who attended in the Victorian and Edwardian periods to what was then referred to as Folk-Lore can justly be indicted for their evolutionism and social Darwinism, these were formations of thought deeply characteristic of English intellectual culture during these periods, and the fact that we have to a great extent progressed beyond them should not induce complacency in us. Historiographical reflexivity is a difficult practice. Such errors as the importation of alien values into historical cultural analysis; reification, or the elision of critical apparatus and object of analysis; the exercise of normative bias in the face of contradictory historical evidence or text/context disjunctures; and the application of a crude historical realism, which dismisses particular song texts because history can be shown to be quite different – all these are easy traps to fall into, and it behoves us to exercise modesty and discretion as well as learn respect when we engage in the study of popular song cultures of the past.

Posing the task of vernacular song analysis in the ways we have during the course of these concluding remarks is not to suggest that all aspects of the matter will thus be covered. Our call to seriousness could for example easily allow the *jouissance* of the text/tune to be overlooked. Nevertheless, we do believe that if we are to gain some sense of what songs contribute to particular structures of feeling and thinking, and of how they inform the experience and understanding of specific groups in lived cultures, then that will only be accomplished by moving through and between the orders of text-context frames and relations as we have roughly outlined them. There remains a good deal of work to be done. Holistic studies of particular vernacular song cultures are too few in comparison to studies of individuals and their repertories, and there are massive financial and institutional constraints against the full presentation even of the latter. Women's singing needs much more attention, as do the song traditions of special interest groups such as hunts and rugby clubs. Religious, jingoistic and patriotic songs in lived cultures have been far too much ignored; singing in domestic contexts has not received sufficient attention, at least in contrast to singing in social institutional contexts; and regionalist formations and affiliations in connection with the vernacular arts require more than touristic celebration. But everyone can supply their own shopping list of empirical research needs. That is why we have concentrated in this conclusion on questions of perspective and approach.

Such questions are not solely academic. They involve us in the politics of culture. This is important most of all because of the way the cultures we are studying are socially placed. Vernacular popular cultures are by definition subordinate to both 'high' culture, and to the imperatives of the culture and leisure industries. They are cut across by antagonisms of interests and conflicts of forces. Because of this vernacular cultures cannot be considered as (or part of) coherent value and meaning systems; such a notion is quite fallacious, though of course attempts at coherence are continually made within them. Vernacular cultures exist in the interstices of broader cultural institutions, in negotiated space. This existence is ever fraught: 'them' as we have seen can so easily seep into 'us'. What this entails in relation to hierarchical orderings of domination and subordination – and to the stratifications and forces animated by this relationship as integral features of an inegalitarian social order – is ideological process. As Richard Johnson has put it: 'Ideologies always work upon a *ground*: that ground is *culture*'.[3] In its moments of self-making a vernacular culture exists in tension between the creative effort to make meaning, and the fixed ideological structures which exist to shape that effort. That is one reason (among others) why vernacular cultures cannot simply be 'read' as if they were a direct or unproblematic realization of group or class experience. What is politically critical for working class and social minority groups is the extent to which, and the ways in which, their specific lived cultures are alternative in experience and resistant in stance to that which seeks to subsume or subdue them, in the process of their making and remaking. It is this process of cultural self-making to which song in vernacular milieux contributes, though of course song is also at the same time one way in which 'them' can seep into 'us'. Vernacular cultures count because they are one of the crucial ways identity and consciousness are attained and maintained, formed and reformed, but always in terms of this dialectical movement of containment and resistance. That is what makes the study of them, and of the significances of popular song within them, finally of any worth.

Notes

1   Geertz 1983: 151.
2   Natanson 1974: 243.
3   Johnson 1979: 234.

Bibliography

Abrahams, R. 1963, *Deep Down in the Jungle: Negro Narrative Folklore from the Streets of Philadelphia*, Chicago.

   1968, 'Introductory Remarks to a Rhetorical Theory of Folklore', *Journal of American Folklore*, 81.

   1970a, *A Singer and her Songs: Almeda Riddle's Book of Ballads*, Baton Rouge, La.

   1970b, 'Creativity, Individuality and the Traditional Singer', *Studies in the Literary Imagination*, 3.

   1972, 'Personal Power and Social Restraint in the Definition of Folklore', in Paredes, A. and Bauman, R. 1972.

Abrahams, R. and Foss, G. 1968, *Anglo-American Folksong Style*, Englewood Cliffs, N.J.

Acton, T. 1974, *Gypsy Politics and Social Change*, London.

Adam, J. and White, B. 1912, *Parodies and Imitations, Old and New*, London.

Adorno, T. and Horkheimer, M. 1979, *Dialectic of Enlightenment*, London.

Amis, K. 1978, *New Oxford Book of Light Verse*, London.

Anderson, I. 1986, 'Tricks of the Trade: Hints on Painless P.A. for Folk Gigs', *Folk Roots*, 31.

Anderson, W. 1923, *Kaiser und Abt*, Helsinki *(Folklore Fellows Communications 42)*.

Argyle, M. 1975, *Bodily Communication*, London.

Ashby, A. 1917, *Allotments and Smallholdings in Oxfordshire*, Oxford.

Ashby, M. 1974, *Joseph Ashby of Tysoe, 1859–1919*, London.

Ashton, J. 1977, 'Truth in Folksong: Some Developments and Applications', *Canadian Folk Music Journal*, 5.

Babcock, B. 1977, 'The Story in the Story: Metanarration in Folk Narrative', in Bauman, R. 1977.

Bailey, P. 1986, *Music Hall: The Business of Pleasure*, Milton Keynes and Philadelphia.

Baker, A. 1854, *Notes from a Glossary of Northamptonshire Words and Phrases*, London.

Bakhtin, M. 1981, *The Dialogic Imagination*, Austin.

Ballard, A. 1908, 'Notes on the Open Fields of Oxfordshire', *Report for the North Oxfordshire Archaeological Society*.

Baron, R. and Byrne, D. 1984, *Social Psychology: Understanding Human Interaction*, Boston.

Barrand, T. 1978–9, 'Nothing is Sacred: Parody in Folk Song', *Come for to Sing*, 5, 1.

Barrett, W. 1891, *English Folk Songs*, London.

Barron, F. 1986, 'Monologues and Comic Songs', *This England*, 19.

Bauman R. 1977, *Verbal Art as Performance*, Prospect Heights.

Bean, W. 1921, *Trees and Shrubs Hardy in the British Isles*, London.

Beesley, A. 1841, *History of Banbury*, London.

Bell, C. and Newby, H. 1974, *The Sociology of Community*, London.

   1975, *Community Studies*, London.

Bell, J. 1971, *Rhymes of Northern Bards*, Newcastle (originally 1812).

Belsey, C. 1983, 'Literature, History, Politics', *Literature and History*, 9, 1.

Ben-Amos, D. 1972, 'Toward a Definition of Folklore in Context', in Paredes, A. and Bauman, R. 1972.

   1976a, *Folklore Genres*, Austin.

   1976b, 'Analytical Categories and Ethnic Genres', in Ben-Amos, D. 1976a.

Berman, M. 1983, *All That is Solid Melts Into Air*, London.

Bethke, R. 1976, 'Verse Recitation as Barroom Theatre', *Southern Folklore Quarterly*, 40, 1–2.

Bird, E. 1985, 'Lord Randal in Kent: The Meaning and Context of a Ballad Variant', *Folklore*, 96, 2.

Blacking, J. 1971, 'The Social Value of Venda Riddles', *African Studies*, 20, 1.

Blagden, C. 1954, 'Notes on the Ballad Market in the Second Half of the Seventeenth Century', *Studies in Bibliography*, VI.

Booth, M. 1981, *The Experience of Songs*, New Haven, Conn.

Bott, E. 1957, *Family and Social Network*, London.

Bourdieu, P. and Passeron, J. 1977, *Reproduction in Education, Society and Culture*, London.

Bowley, A. 1900, *Wages in the United Kingdom in the Nineteenth Cetury*, Cambridge.

Brăiloiu, C. 1960, *Vie Musicale d'un Village*, Paris.

Bratton, J. S. 1986, *Music Hall: Performance and Style*, Milton Keynes and Philadelphia.

Braverman, H. 1974, *Labour and Monopoly Capital*, New York.

Bringemeier, M. 1931, *Gemeinschaft und Volkslied*, Münster in Westfalen.

Bronson, B. 1959–72, *The Traditional Tunes of the Child Ballads*, Princeton.

Brosnac, D. 1983, *Guitar Electronics for Musicians*, London.

Buchan, D. 1968, 'History and Harlaw', *Journal of the Folklore Institute*, 5.

   1984, *Scottish Tradition: A Collection of Scottish Folk Literature*, London.

Burrow, J. 1978, 'The Sense of the Past', in Lerner, L. *The Victorians*, London.

Cartwright, C. 1981, 'Black Jack Davy: Cultural Values and Change in Scots and American Balladry', *Lore and Language*, 3, 4/5.

Chamberlain, M. 1986, 'Community Romance', *New Statesman*, 9th May.

Chambers, E. 1925, *The Mediaeval Stage*, Oxford.

Chambers, J. and Mingay, G., 1966, *The Agricultural Revolution, 1750–1880*, London.

Chaney, D. and Pickering, M. 1986, 'Authorship in Documentary: Sociology as an Art Form in Mass Observation' in Corner, J., *Documentary and the Mass Media*, London.

Chaplin, S. 1972, *A Tree with Rosy Apples*, Newcastle upon Tyne.

Chappell, W. 1965, *Popular Music of the Olden Time*, New York (originally 1856–9).

Chappell, W. and Ebsworth, J., 1871–93, *The Roxburghe Ballads*, London.

Child, F. 1965, *The English and Scottish Popular Ballads*, New York (originally 1882–98).

Clarke, J. et. al., 1979, *Working Class Culture*, London.

Clarke, R. 1974, *The Longshoremen*, London.

Cobbett, W. 1973, *Rural Rides*, Harmondsworth (originally 1830).

Cohen, A. 1982, *Belonging*, Manchester.

   1985, *The Symbolic Construction of Community*, Chichester.

Cohen, S. 1985, *Visions of Social Control*, Oxford.

Copper, B. 1971 and 1975, *A Song for Every Season*, London and St. Albans.

1973, *Songs and Southern Breezes*, London.

Corr, G. 1973, 'Private McCaffery's Revenge', *Lancashire Evening Post*, December 17th.

Cray, E. 1978, *Bawdy Ballads*, London.

Creighton, H. 1932, *Songs and Ballads from Nova Scotia*, Toronto.

Curry, J. 1981, *The Bever Book of School Verse*, London.

'Daily Express' Community Song Book, 1927, London.

Davison, P. 1971, *Songs of the British Music Hall*, New York.

Dawney, M. 1974, *The Iron Man*, London.

Dean-Smith, M. 1954, *A Guide to English Folk Song Collections, 1822–1952*, Liverpool.

Dellheim, C. 1985, 'Notes on Industrialism and Culture in Nineteenth-Century Britain', in Cantor, N. and King N. *Notebooks in Cultural Analysis*, 2.

de Witt, H. 1970, *Bawdy Barrack-room Ballads*, London.

Dixon, J. 1846, *Ancient Poems, Ballads and Songs of the Peasantry of England*, London.

Dobrowolski, K. 1975, 'Peasant Traditional Culture', in Shanin, T. *Peasants and Peasant Society*, Harmondsworth.

Dorson, R. 1972, *Folklore and Folklife*, Chicago.

Dundes, A. 1965, *The Study of Folklore*, Englewood Cliffs, N.J.

1966 and 1965, 'Metafolklore and Oral Literary Criticism', *The Monist*, 1. (Reprinted in his *Analytic Essays in Folklore*, The Hague.)

1969, 'The Devolutionary Premise in Folklore Theory', *Journal of the Folklore Institute*, 6.

Dunkin, J. 1823, *The History and Antiquities of the Hundreds of Billington and Ploughley*, London.

Dunn, G. 1980, *The Fellowship of Song*, London.

D'Urfey, T. 1719–20, *Wit and Mirth, or, Pills to Purge Melancholy*, London.

Eagleton, T. 1976, *Marxism and Literary Criticism*, London.

Easthope, A. 1977, 'Marx, Machery and Greek Art', *Red Letters*, 6.

Eco, U. 1984, 'The Frames of Comic "Freedom"', in Sebeok, T. 1984.

Edwards, C. and Manley, K. 1985, *Narrative Folksong: New Directions*, Boulder, Co.

Elbourne, R. 1975, 'The Question of Definition', *Yearbook of the International Folk Music Council*, 7.

1980, *Music and Tradition in Early Industrial Lancashire, 1780–1840*, Woodbridge.

Elias, N. 1974, 'Towards a Theory of Communities', in Bell, C. and Newby, H. 1974.

Fahey, W. 1984, *Eureka: the Songs that Made Australia*, Sydney.

Falassi, A 1980, *Folklore by the Fireside: Text and Context of the Tuscan Veglia*, Austin.

Ferris, W. 1970, *Blues from the Delta*, London.

Finnegan, R. 1977, *Oral Poetry*, Cambridge.

Fischer, E. 1981, *The Necessity of Art*, Harmondsworth.

Folk Music Journal, 1965, in progress.

Foster, G. 1965, 'Peasant Society and the Image of Limited Good', *American Anthropologist*, 67.

Fox, R. and Jackson Lears, T. 1983, *The Culture of Consumption*, New York.

Frankenberg, R. 1973, *Communities in Britain*, Harmondsworth.

Fuller, T. 1840, *The History of the Worthies of England*, London (originally 1662).

Fussell, G. 1949, *The English Rural Labourer*, London.

Gammon, V. 1982, 'Song, Sex and Society in England, 1600–1850', *Folk Music Journal*, 4, 3.

1985, 'Popular Music in Rural Society: Sussex 1815–1914', Unpublished Ph.D. thesis, University of Sussex.

Gardham, S. 1982, *An East Riding Songster*, Lincoln.

Geertz, C. 1975, *The Interpretation of Cultures*, London.

1983, *Local knowledge: Further Essays in Interpretive Anthropology*, New York.

Georges, R. 1969, 'Toward an Understanding of Storytelling Events', *Journal of American Folklore*, 82.

Gepp, H. 1924, *Adderbury*, Banbury.

Giddens, A. 1979, *Central Problems in Social Theory*, London.

Gilchrist, A. 1938, 'Sacred Parodies of Secular Folk Song', *Journal of the English Folk Dance and Song Society*, 8, 3.

Gilman, S. 1974, *The Parodic Sermon in European Perspective*, Wiesbaden.

Glassie, H. 1971, *Pattern in the Material Folk Culture of the Eastern United States*, Philadelphia (originally 1968).

n.d., '"Take that Night Train to Selma": An Excursion to the outskirts of Scholarship', in Glassie, H., Ives, E. and Szwed, J.

Glassie, H. Ives, E. and Szwed, J. n.d., *Folksongs and their Makers*, Bowling Green, Ohio.

Goffman, E. 1959 and 1978, *The Presentation of Self in Everyday Life*, Harmondsworth.

1961, *Encounters*, Indianapolis.

Goldstein, K. 1972, 'On the Application of the Concepts of Active and Inactive Traditions to the Study of Repertory', in Paredes, A. and Bauman, R., 1972.

Goldstein, K. and Ben-Amos, D., 1975, *Folklore, Performance and Communication*, The Hague.

Gramsci, A. 1985, *Selections from Cultural Writings*, London.

Graves, A. 1847, *The Irish Song Book with Original Irish Airs,*, Dublin.

Gray, H. 1909–10, 'Yeoman Farming in Oxfordshire', *Quarterly Journal of Economics*, XXIV.

1959, *English Field Systems*, London.

Green, A. 1970–1, 'McCaffery: A Study in the Variation and Function of a Ballad', *Lore and Language*, 3, 4, 5.

1972a, review of Harker, D., 1971, *English Dance and Song*, 34.

1972b, 'Dialect and Traditional Song', *Transactions of the Yorkshire Dialect Society*, LXXII, (xiii).

1976, 'Walter Wheeler and Dangerous Dan: a West Riding Collier Poet and his Monologue', *Souther Folklore Quarterly*, 40, 1–2.

1978a, 'Only Kidding: Joking among Coal-Miners', in Green, A. and Widdowson, J., 1978.

1978b 'Stereotypes and Ecotypes: Three Books on English Working Class Culture', *Scottish Journal of Sociology*, 3, 1.

Green, A. and Wales, T., 1974, 'Foreword' to *Reminiscences of Horsham: the Recollections of Henry Burstow*, Norwood, Pa.

Green, A. and Widdowson, J., 1978, *Language, Culture and Tradition*, Sheffield.

Green, F. 1820, *A History of theEnglish Agricultural Labourer, 1870–1920*, London.

Greene, R. 1871, *A Quip for an Upstart Courtier*, (ed. C. Hindley), London.

Greene, R. 1962, *A Selection of English Carols*, Oxford.

Greene, T. 1982, *The Light in Troy: Imitation and Discovery in Renaissance Poetry*, New Haven, Conn.

Greenway, J. 1953, *American Folk Songs of Protest*, Philadelphia.

Greig, R. 1971, 'The Social Context of Traditional Song', *Lore and Language*, 5.

Grosart, A. 1879, *The Works of Nicholas Breton*, Edinburgh.

Habermas, J. 1971, *Towards a Rational Society*, London.

Haggard, L. 1979, *I Walked by Night*, Bungay.

Halliwell-Phillips, J. 1850, *The Loyal Garland*, London.

Halpert, H. 1939, 'Truth in Folk-Songs: Some Observations on the Folk-Singer's Attitude', in Halpert, H. and Herzog, G. 1939.

    1951, 'Vitality of Tradition and Local Songs', *Journal of the International Folk Music Council*, 3.

Halpert, H. and Herzog, G., 1939, *Traditional Ballads from West Virginia*, New York.

Hamer, F. 1967, *Garners Gay: English Folk Songs Collected by Fred Hamer*, London.

Hamilton, W. 1884–9, *Parodies of the Works of English and American Authors*, London.

Hammond, J. and B., 1966, *The Village Labourer*, London.

Harding, M. 1980, *The Mike Harding Collection: Folk Songs of Lancashire*, Manchester.

Harker, D. 1971, 'John Bell the Great Collecter', in Bell J., 1971.

    1981, 'The Making of the Tyneside Concert Hall', Popular Music 1.

    1985a, 'The Original Bob Cranky?', *Folk Music Journal*, 5, 1.

    1985b, *Fakesong*, Milton Keynes and Philadelphia

Harré, R. 1979, *Social Being*, Oxford.

    1983, *Personal Being*, Oxford.

Harré, R. Clarke, D. and De Carlo, N., 1985, *Motives and Mechanisms: An Introduction to the Psychology of Action*, London.

Harré, R. and Secord, P., 1972, *The Explanation of Social Behaviour*, Oxford.

Hasbach, W. 1920, *A History of the English Agricultural Labourer*, London.

Havinden, M. 1968, 'Agricultural Progress in Open-Field Oxfordshire', in Minchington, W. *Essays in Agrarian History*, Newton Abbot.

Hawthorn, J. 1973, *Identity and Relationship*, London.

Hearn, F. 1978, *Domination, Legitimation and Resistance*, Westport, Conn.

Heilfurth, G. 1954, *Das Bergmannslied*, Kassel.

Heller, A. 1984, *Everyday Life*, London.

Henderson, W. 1937, *Victorian Street Ballads*, London.

Heyck, T. 1982, *The Transformation of Intellectual Life in Victorian England*, London.

Hillery, G. 1955, 'Definitions of Community: areas of agreement', *Rural Sociology*, 20.

Hobsbawm, E. and Ranger, T. 1983, *The Invention of Tradition*, Cambridge.

Hobsbawm, E. and Rudé, G., 1969, *Captain Swing*, London.

Hoggart, R. 1969, *The Uses of Literacy*, Harmondsworth.

Holloway, J. 1972, *The Euing collection of English Broadside Ballads*, London.

Holme Valley Beagles Hunt, 1948, *Hunters' Songs*, private publication.

Hone, W. 1818, *The Three Trials of William Hone*, London.

Hoskins, W. 1977, *The Making of the English Landscape*, London.

Howes, F. 1969, *Folk Music of Britain and Beyond*, London.

Hutcheon, L. 1985, *A Theory of Parody: The Teachings of Twentieth Century Art Forms*, New York.

Hymes, D. 1962, 'The Ethnography of Speaking', in Gladwin, T. and Sturtevant, W., 1962, *Anthropology and Human Behaviour*, Washington, D.C.

Ives, E. 1964, *Larry Gorman: The Man who Made the Songs*, Bloomington.

    1971, *Lawrence Doyle, the Farmer Poet of Prince Edward Island: a Study in Local Songmaking*, Orono, Maine.

Jackson Bate, W. 1971, *The Burden of the Past and the English Poet*, London.

Jackson Lears, T. 1985, 'The Concept of Cultural Hegemony', *American Historical Review*, 90, 3.

Jauss, H.R. 1975, 'The Idealist Embarrassment: Observations on Marxist Aesthetics', *New Literary History*, 7, 1.

Jenkins, J. 1972, *The English Farm Wagon*, Netwon Abbot.

Jerrold, W. 1913, *A Century of Parody and Imitation*, London.

Johnson, R. 1979, 'Three problematics: elements of a theory of working class culture' in Clarke, J. et. al.

Journal of American Folklore, 1888, in progress.

Journal of the Folk Song Society, 1899–1931, 1–35.

Joyner, C. 1975, 'A Model for the Analysis of Folklore Performance in Historical Context', *Journal of American Folklore*, 88.

Keating, P. 1971, *The Working Classes in Victorian Fiction*, London.

Kennedy, P. 1975, *Folksongs of Britain and Ireland*, London.

Kerr, B. 1941–3, 'Irish Seasonal Migration to Great Britain, 1800–38', *Irish Historical Studies*, 3, 12.

Kitchin, G. 1931, *A Survey of Burlesque and Parody in English*, Edinburgh.

Korson, G. 1938, *Minstrels of the Mine Patch*, Philadelphia.

    1943, *Coal Dust on the Fiddle*, Philadelphia.

Laban, R. 1971, *The Mastery of Movement*, London.

Ladurie, E. 1981, 'Carnivals in History', *Thesis Eleven*, 3.

Laing, D. 1985, *One Chord Wonders*, Milton Keynes and Philadelphia.

Lasch, C. 1981, 'Mass Culture Reconsidered', *Democracy*, October.

Laslett, P. 1965, *The World We Have Lost*, London.

La Trobe, J. 1831, *The Music of the Church*, Thames Ditton.

Legman, G. 1970, *The Horn Book*, London.

Lentricchia, F. 1983, *Criticism and Social Change*, Chicago.

Lévi-Strauss, C. 1965, 'The Structural Study of Myth', in Sebeok, T. 1965, *Myth, a Symposium*, Bloomington.

Lightwood, J. 1905, *Hymn-Tunes and their Story*, London.

Limón, J. 1983, 'Western Marxism and Folklore', *Journal of American Folklore*, 96.

Lloyd, A. 1952, *Come All Ye Bold Miners*, London.

    1967, *Folk Song in England*, London.

Lobel, M. And Crossley, A. 1969, *The Victoria County History of Oxfordshire*, IX, Oxford.

Lomax, A. 1959, 'Folk Song Style', *American Anthropologist*, 61.

    1967, 'The Good and the Beautiful in Folksong', *Journal of American Folklore*, 80.

    1968 and 1978, *Folk Song Style and Culture*, New Brunswick, N.J.

    1976, *Cantometrics: audiocasettes and handbook*, Berkeley.

Lord, A. 1960, *The Singer of Tales*, Cambridge, Mass.

Lowenthal, L. and Lawson, I. 1963, 'The Debate on Cultural Standards in Nineteenth Century England', *Social Research*, 30, 4.

Lyle, E. 1976, *Ballad Studies*, Cambridge.

MacColl, E. 1954, *The Shuttle and Cage: Industrial Folk Ballads*, London.

MacColl, E. and Seeger, P. n.d., *The Singing Island*, London.

    1977, *Travellers' Songs from England and Scotland*, London.

MacDonald, D. 1960, *Parodies: An Anthology from Chaucer to Beerbohm – and After*, New York.

MacIntyre, A. 1982, *After Virtue*, London.

Malraux, A. 1951, 'Art, Popular Art, and the Illusion of the Folk', *Partisan Review*, 18.

Markiewicz, H. 1967, 'On the Definitions of Literary Parody', in *To Honour Roman Jakobson*, II, The Hague.

Marothy, J. 1974, *Music and the Bourgeois: Music and the Proletarian*, Budapest.

Marsh, P. Rosser, E. and Harré, R., 1978, *The Rules of Disorder*, London.

Marshall, M. 1981, *The Book of Comic and Dramatic Monologues*, London.

Marx, K. 1977, *Grundrisse*, Harmondsworth.

McCormack, T. 1969, 'Folk Culture and the Mass Media', *Archives Européenes de Sociologie*, 10, 2.

McQuail, D. 1983, *Mass Communication Theory*, London.

Mierge, B. 1979, 'The Cultural Commodity', *Media, Culture and Society*, 1.

Merriam, A. 1969, review of Lomax, A., 1968, *Journal of American Folklore*, 82.

Mingay, G. 1968, *Enclosure and the Small Farmer in the Age of the Industrial Revolution*, London.

Montague, M. 1893, *The Letters and Works of Lady Mary Wortley Montague*, London.

Motherwell, W. 1827, *Minstrelsy, Ancient and Modern*, Glasgow.

Namier, L. 1959, *Charles Townshend, His Character and Career*, Cambridge.

Namier, L. and Brooke, J. 1964, *Charles Townshend*, London.

Natanson, M. 1974, 'Solipsism and Sociality', *New Literary History*, 5, 2.

Narvaez, P. 1977, 'The Folk Parodist', *Canadian Folk Music Journal*, 5.

Nash, W. 1985, *The Language of Humour*, London.

Nettl, B. 1970, review of Lomax, A. 1968, *American Anthropologist*, 72.

Newman, O. 1974, *Defensible Space*, London.

'News Chronicle' Song Book, n.d. (post 1922) London.

Okley, J. 1975, 'Gypsies Travelling in Southern England' in Rehfisch (ed.), *Gypsies, Tinkers, and Other Travellers*, London.

    1983, *The Traveller-Gypsies: Changing Cultures*, Cambridge.

Oliver, P. 1984, *Songsters and Saints: Vocal Traditions on Race Records*, Cambridge.

Opie, I. and P. 1959, *The Lore and Language of Schoolchildren*, London.

    1985, *The Singing Game*, Oxford.

Ong, W. 1982, *Orality and Literacy*, London.

Ostendorf, B. 1982, *Black Literature in White America*, Sussex.

Pahl, R. 1968a, 'Newcomers in Town and Country', in Munby, L. *East Anglian Studies*, Cambridge, 174–199.

Pahl, R. 1968b, *Readings in Urban Sociology*, Oxford.

Palmer, R. 1973, *The Painful Plough*, Cambridge.

Paredes, A. and Bauman, R. 1972, *Toward New Perspectives in Folklore*, Austin.

Parker, A. 1876, *A Glossary of Words Used in Oxfordshire*, London.

Pegg. B. 1976, *Folk: A Portrait of English Traditional Music, Musicians and Customs*, London.

Pegg, C. 1985, 'Music and Society in East Suffolk', Unpublished Ph.D. thesis, University of Cambridge.

Perkin, H. 1978, *The Origins of Modern English Society, 1780–1880,* London

Pickering, M. 1981, 'The Four Angels of the Earth: Popular Cosmology in a Victorian Village', *Southern Folklore Quarterly*, 45.

    1982, *Village Song and Culture*, London.

    1983, 'The Farmworker and "The Farmer's Boy"', *Lore and Language*, 3, 9.

    1984, 'Popular Song at Juniper Hill', *Folk Music Journal*, 4, 5.

    1986a, 'Bartholomew Callow – Village Musician', *Musical Traditions*, 6.

    1986b, 'Black Masks, White Faces: "Nigger" Minstrelsy in Victorian England', in Bratton, J.S. *Music Hall: Performance and Style*, Milton Keynes and Philadelphia.

    1986c, 'The Dogma of Authenticity in the Experience of Popular Music', in McGregor, G. and White, R. S. *The Art of Listening*, London.

    1986d, 'Song and Social Context', in Russell, I. *Singer, Song and Scholar*, Sheffield.

Plant, R. 1974, *Community and Ideology*, London.

Porter, J. 1985, 'Parody and Satire as Mediators of Change in the Traditional Songs of Belle Stewart', in Edwards, C. and Manley, K. 1985.

Prawer, S. 1978, *Karl Marx and World Literature*, Oxford.

Propp, V. 1968, *Morphology of the Folktale*, Austin (originally 1928).

Prothero, R. 1912, *English Farming Past and Present*, London.

Pulling, C. 1952, *They Were Singing*, London.

Purslow, F. 1965, *Marrow Bones: English Folk Songs from the Hammond and Gardiner Mss.*, London.

Rawlinson, R. 1979, ' "Coat of Arms" Mugs', *English Dance and Song*, 41, 3.

Reaney, B. 1970, *The Class Struggle in Nineteenth Century Oxfordshire*, Oxford (History Workshop Pamphlet 3).

Reed, M. 1984, 'The Peasantry of Nineteenth Century England: a Neglected Class?', *History Workshop*, 18.

Reeves, J. 1958, *The Idiom of the People*, London.
   1960, *The Everlasting Circle*, London.

Richards, S. 1983, 'Joe Hill: A Labour Legend in Song', *Folk Music Journal*, 4, 4.

Richards, S. and Stubbs, T., 1979, *The English Folksinger*, Glasgow.

Richardson, C. 1968, 'Irish Settlement in mid-nineteenth Century Bradford', *Yorkshire Bulletin of Economic and Social Research*, 20, 1.

Robbins, R. 1952, *Secular Lyrics of the XIVth and XVth Centuries*, Oxford.

Roberts, L. 1959, *Up Cutshin and down Greasy*, Lexington, Ky.

Robinson, J. 1978, 'Regency Radicalism and Antiquarianism: William Hone's *Ancient Mysteries Described* (1823)', Leeds Studies in English, N.S., 10.

Rollins, H. 1967, *An Analytical Index to the Ballad – Entries (1557–1709) in the Register of the Company of Stationers of London*, Hatboro, Penn. (originally 1924).

Rose, M. 1979, *Parody/Metafiction: An Analysis of Parody as a Critical Mirror to Writing and Reception of Fiction*, London.

Rosselson, L. 1979, 'Pop Music: Mobiliser or Opiate?', in Gardner C., *Media, Politics and Culture*, London.

Roud, S. and Smith, P. 1985, *A Catalogue of Songs and Songbooks Printed and Published by James Catnach 1832*, West Stockwith.

Rowntree, B. and Kendall, M. 1913, *How the Labourer Lives*, London.

Russell, I. 1970, 'Carol-singing in the Sheffield Area', *Lore and Language*, 1, 3.
   1973, 'A Survey of the Christmas Singing Tradition in South Yorkshire 1970', *Lore and Language*, 1, 8.
   1977, 'Traditional Singing in West Sheffield, 1970–72', Unpublished Ph.D. Thesis, University of Leeds.
   1986, *Singer, Song and Scholar*, Sheffield.

Scott, H. 1946, *The Early Doors: Origins of the Music Hall*, London.

Scottish Students' Song Book, 1897, London.

Sebeok, T. 1984, Umberto Eco, V. V. Ivanov, Monica Rector, *Carnival!*, Berlin.

Sennett, R. 1977, *The Fall of Public Man*, Cambridge.

Sennett, R. and Cobb, J. 1977, *The Hidden Injuries of Class*, Cambridge.

Sharp, C. 1972, *English Folk Song: Some Conclusions*, Wakefield (originally 1907).

Sider, G. 1976, 'Christmas Mumming and the New Year in Outport Newfoundland', *Past and Present*, 71.

Sifakis, C. and M–L. 1978, *Beginner's Guide to Antique Watches*, New York.

Simpson, C. 1966, *The British Broadside Ballad and Its Music*, New Brunswick, N.J.

Smith, M. 1892, *The Autobiography of Mary Smith*, London.

Sommer, R. 1969, *Personal Space*, Englewood Cliffs, N.J.

Stacey, M. 1974, 'The Myth of Community Studies', in Bell, C. and Newby, H., 1974.

Stearns, P. 1980, 'The Effort at Continuity in Working Class Culture', *Journal of Modern History*, 52, 4.

Steblin-Kamenskij, M., 1973, *The Saga Mind*, Odense.

Stephens, W.B., 1986, *Education, Literacy and Society, 1830–1870*, Manchester.

Stewart, S. 1978, *Nonsense: Aspects of Intertextuality in Folklore and Literature*, Baltimore.

Stone, C. 1914, *Parody*, London.

Stone, L. 1969, 'Literacy and Education in England 1640–1900', *Past and Present*, 42.

Sturt, G. 1966, *Change in the Village*, London.

Stroud, D. 1975, *Capability Brown*, London.

Sturge Gretton, M., 1914, *A Corner of the Cotswolds*, London.

Sturge Henderson, M. 1902, *Three Centuries in North Oxfordshire*, Oxford.

Tate, W. 1967, *The English Village Community and the Enclosure Movements*, London.

Tedeschi, J. Lindskold, S. and Rosenfeld, P., 1985, *Introduction to Social Psychology*, New York.

Temperley, N. 1979, *The Music of the English Parish Church*, Cambridge.

Thomas, G. 1972, 'McCaffery: A Soldier's Song of Protest', *Lore and Language*, 7.

Thomas, M. 1981, 'Sheep of the Peaks', *Livestock Heritage*, 1, 1.

Thompson, E. 1963 and 1968, *The Making of the English Working Class*, London and Harmondsworth.

Thompson, F. 1971, *Lark Rise to Candleford*, London.

Thompson, J. 1908, *Complete Poetical Works*, (ed. Logie Robertson, J.), Oxford.

Thomson, R. 1975, 'The Development of the Broadside Ballad Trade and its Influence upon the Transmission of English Folksongs', unpublished Ph.D. thesis, University of Cambridge.

Tiddy, R. 1923, *The Mummer's Play*, Oxford.

Tribe, K. 1981, *Genealogies of Capitalism*, London.

Trilling, L. 1976, 'Why We Read Jane Austen', *Times Literary Supplement*, 5 March.

Turner, M. 1972, *The Parlour Song Book: A Casquet of Vocal Gems*, London.

Tyler, E. 1975, *Clocks and Watches*, Maidenhead, N.Y.

Utley, R. 1963, *The Last Days of the Sioux Nation*, New Haven, Conn.

Vesey-Fitzgerald, B. 1944, *Gypsies of Britain*, London.

Walton's New Treasury of Irish Songs and Ballads, 1968, Dublin.

Watson, I. 1983, *Song and Democratic Culture in Britain*, London.

Watson, W. 1964, *Closed Systems and Open Minds*, Edinburgh.

Wedderburn, J. and R. 1848, *A Compendious Book of Psalms and Spiritual Songs commonly known as 'The Gude and Godlie Ballates'*, Edinburgh (originally 1578).

Wells, E. 1950, *The Ballad Tree*, New York.

Weiner, M. 1981, *English Culture and the Decline of the Industrial Spirit 1850–1980*, Cambridge.

Whitten, N. and Szwed, J., 1970, *Afro-American Anthropology*, New York.

Wilgus, D. 1959, *Anglo-American Folksong Scholarship since 1898*, New Brunswick, N.J.
1968, 'The Hillbilly Movement', in Coffin, T. *Our Living Traditions*, New York.

Widdowson, J. 1976, 'The Language of the Child Culture: Pattern and Tradition in Language Acquisition and Socialization', in Roger, S. *They Don't Speak our Language*, London.
1978, 'Language, Tradition and Regional Identity: Blason Populaire and Social Control', in Green, A. and Widdowson, J., 1978.

Williams, A. 1923, *Folk-Songs of the Upper Thames*, London.

Williams, R. 1961, *Culture and Society*, Harmondsworth.
1975a, *The Country and the City*, St. Albans.
1975b, 'On High and Popular Culture', *Cambridge Review*, May.
1976, *Keywords*, Glasgow.
1977, *Marxism and Literature*, Oxford.

Willis, P. 1979, *Learning to Labour*, Farnborough.

Wilson, M. 1972, 'The Wedding Cakes: a Study of Ritual Change', in La Fontaine, J., *The Interpretation of Ritual*, London.

Woodham-Smith, C. 1962, *The Great Hunger*, London.

Woods, F. 1979, *Folk Revival*, Poole.

Worschel, S. and Cooper, J. 1983, *Understanding Social Psychology*, Homewood, Ill.

Wright, P. 1985, *On Living in an Old Country*, London.

Wright, T. 1860, *Songs and Ballads, with other short Poems*, London.

Wuthnow, R. *et al.* 1984, *Cultural Analysis*, London.

Young, A. 1813, *General View of the Agriculture of Oxfordshire*, London.

Zimmerman, G. 1967, *Songs of Irish Rebellion*, Dublin.

Discography

Bland, D. and Leader, B. 1975, *A Fine Hunting Day*, Greetland (Leader LEE4056).
Engle, T., Greig, A., Greig, R. and Yates, M. 1977, *Frank Hinchcliffe: In Sheffield Park*, London (Topic 12TS308).
Engle, T. and Lloyd, A. 1973, *Bob Hart: Songs from Suffolk*, London (Topic 12TS225).
Engle, T., Summers, K. and Yates, M. 1975, *Jumbo Brightwell: Songs from the Eel's Foot*, London (Topic 12T196).
Engle, T. and Yates, M. 1974, *Flash Company*, London (Topic 12TS243).
MacColl, E. and Seeger, P. 1961, *The Elliotts of Birtley*, London (Xtra 1091).
Richards, S. and Stubbs, T. 1981, *An English Folk Music Anthology*, New York (Folkways FE38553).
Richards, S., Stubbs, T. and Wilson, P. 1979, *Devon Tradition*, London (Topic 12TS349).
Russell, I. 1981, *Merry Mountain Child: Arthur Howard*, Penistone (Hill and Dale HD006).
Smith, J. 1982, *Just for the Record*, Sunderland (Lewis Music).
Yates, M. 1975, *Songs of the Open Road*, London (Topic 12T253).
Yates, M. 1977, *The Travelling Songster*, London (Topic 12TS304).

Index